The Chinese Stock Market

ADVANCES IN CHINESE ECONOMIC STUDIES

Series Editor: Yanrui Wu, *Associate Professor in Economics, University of Western Australia, Australia*

The Chinese economy has been transformed dramatically in recent years. With its rapid economic growth and accession to the World Trade Organisation, China is emerging as an economic superpower. China's development experience provides valuable lessons to many countries in transition.

Advances in Chinese Economic Studies aims, as a series, to publish the best work on the Chinese economy by economists and other researchers throughout the world. It is intended to serve a wide readership including academics, students, business economists and other practitioners.

Titles in the series include:

The Evolution of the Stock Market in China's Transitional Economy
Chien-Hsun Chen and Hui-Tzu Shih

Financial Reform and Economic Development in China
James Laurenceson and Joseph C.H. Chai

China's Telecommunications Market
Entering a New Competitive Age
Ding Lu and Chee Kong Wong

Banking and Insurance in the New China
Competition and the Challenge of Accession to the WTO
Chien-Hsun Chen and Hui-Tzu Shih

The Chinese Stock Market
Efficiency, Predictability and Profitability
Nicolaas Groenewold, Yanrui Wu, Sam Hak Kan Tang and Xiang Mei Fan

The Chinese Stock Market

Efficiency, Predictability and Profitability

Nicolaas Groenewold
University of Western Australia, Australia

Yanrui Wu
University of Western Australia, Australia

Sam Hak Kan Tang
Chinese University of Hong Kong, Hong Kong

Xiang Mei Fan
Hunan Normal University, China and University of Western Australia, Australia

ADVANCES IN CHINESE ECONOMIC STUDIES

Edward Elgar
Cheltenham, UK • Northampton, MA, USA

Published by
Edward Elgar Publishing Limited
Glensanda House
Montpellier Parade
Cheltenham
Glos GL50 1UA
UK

Edward Elgar Publishing, Inc.
136 West Street
Suite 202
Northampton
Massachusetts 01060
USA

A catalogue record for this book
is available from the British Library

ISBN 1 84376 622 1

Printed and bound in Great Britain by MPG Books Ltd, Bodmin, Cornwall

Contents

Figures

Tables

Acronyms

ADF	augmented Dickey-Fuller
ADR	American depository receipt
ANN	artificial-neural-network
ARCH	autoregressive-conditional-heteroskasticity
ARIMA	autoregressive-integrated-moving-average
BLL	Brock, Lakonishok and LeBaron
CAPM	capital asset-pricing model
CNY	Chinese New Year
CPI	consumer price index
CSRC	China Securities Regulatory Commission
DD B&H	demand deposit buy-and-hold
DoW	day-of-the-week
E B&H	equity buy-and-hold
EGARCH	exponential GARCH
EMH	efficient markets hypothesis
FEVD	forecast-error-variance decomposition
GARCH	generalized-autoregressive-conditional-heteroskasticity
GDP	gross domestic product
GF	goodness-of-fit
GJR	Glosten, Jagannathan and Runkle
GMM	generalized methods of moments
IPO	initial public offering
IRF	impulse-response function
OLS	ordinary least squares
OTC	over-the counter
PBOC	People's Bank of China
PP	Phillips-Perron
PRC	People's Republic of China
QDII	Qualified Domestic Institutional Investor
QFII	Qualified Foreign Institutional Investor
RMB	*renminbi* (Chinese currency unit, equivalent to *yuan*)
SASAC	State-owned Assets Supervision and Administration Commission
SCSC	State Council Securities Committee
SD	standard deviation
SOE	state-owned enterprise
SSB	State Statistics Bureau

SSE	Shanghai stock exchange
SZSE	Shenzhen stock exchange
TD B&H	term deposit buy-and-hold
TEJ	Taiwan Economic Journal
TVE	township and village enterprise
VAR	vector-autoregressive
VECM	vector error-correction model
VMA	vector moving-average
WEMH	weak form of the efficient markets hypothesis
WTO	World Trade Organization

Preface

The Chinese stock market is an exciting but also bewildering topic to research. The two stock exchanges (in Shanghai and Shenzhen) which constitute the Chinese market were instituted only in the early 1990s following the opening of the Chinese economy to greater market activity and to the rest of the world since the late 1970s. Since then there has been a rapid but controlled development of the market, as the government attempts to reap the benefits of well-functioning financial markets but without loss of control of the broad parameters of economic activity and decision-making.

Despite the rapid and continuing developments over the past decade, our research shows that the Chinese stock market is still relatively isolated from world financial markets, suggesting that there is still some considerable way to go in the development of a regulatory framework before the market is efficient and fully integrated in the global market. Therefore, not only is there still much to be learned about the way the Chinese market works, but this learning must take place against the background of a constantly-changing regulatory environment – both exciting and bewildering.

The short history of the market means that long-period data such as is common for the US market in particular are not available. Neither is there a long history of research on the behaviour of the Chinese market. Nevertheless, given the growing availability of detailed data on the market, there is now sufficient information to enable researchers to address the basic questions regarding, particularly, the efficiency of the market and there has recently been a correspondingly rapid increase in the number and scope of empirical studies in the area. We add to this research by focussing on the use of time-series data to examine a number of empirical issues. We devote a chapter (Chapter 2) to a critical descriptive analysis of the development of the market since its inception and a further chapter (Chapter 3) to a broad-ranging survey of empirical work on the Chinese market which is relevant to our own subsequent research. We then launch into the core of the book (Chapters 4-8) by reporting the results of extensive empirical work on topics such as market efficiency, profitability and trading rules, the return-turnover relation, interrelationships between greater China share markets and the effect of regulatory changes on the return-turnover relation in the energy sector.

The material in this volume was prepared for a wide audience ranging from academia and research students to business economists and trade advisers. It will be of particular interest to researchers and practitioners who are involved in the Chinese stock market. Lecturers may also find this volume a valuable reference for units focusing on business and finance in China.

The completion of this book would have not been possible without the help of many individuals and institutions. In particular, we would like to acknowledge Chris Branston, Miriam Groenewold, Annisa Lau, Patricia Wang, Chee Kong Wong, Gina Yoon and Hui Yu for their excellent research assistance. Work on this book also benefited from a Departmental Research Grant (Economics, UWA), a School Research Grant (Economics and Commerce, UWA), a UWA Research Grant and a Chinese University of Hong Kong grant.

N. Groenewold
Y. Wu
S Tang
X. Fan

1. Introduction

1.1 CHINESE ECONOMIC GROWTH AND MARKET REFORMS

The Chinese economy has been growing rapidly for the past 25 years since its opening in 1979. Its per capita GDP growth rate increased from an average of 0.4 per cent per annum in the 1960s to an average of 8.4 per cent per annum in the 1990s. As a result, Chinese citizens in 2000 enjoy an average per capita income close to US$900, which has lifted millions of Chinese above the absolute poverty benchmark of US$2 per day. If China is able to maintain its rate of growth at the current 8 per cent per annum level, its per capita income will double in less than 9 years, and by 2030 it will reach approximately US$7200, which is higher than the per capita income of any African or Latin American country today.[1] Such a growth rate, moving China from a condition of extreme poverty to the status of an upper-middle-income country within a time span of less than 50 years, will be a remarkable achievement.

The impressive growth experience of China so far results from a fundamental shift of ideology away from a centrally-planned economy to a market-oriented economy under a communist regime. Economic reforms allow ordinary Chinese citizens to respond to market incentives that were non-existent in a centrally-planned economy. In pursuing their own material well-being, a new class of Chinese entrepreneurs quickly emerged to take advantage of the newly available economic freedom, which has become the main engine of growth for the country. The spontaneous surge of township and village enterprises (TVEs) in the early 1980s is a good example of the tremendous increase in productivity when people are given the chance to respond to market incentives.

Despite successes in market restructuring which have taken place so far in China, the Chinese economy still faces a difficult hurdle: namely, how to reform the huge, inefficient, loss-making state sector. Since the state sector remains a major player in the Chinese economy, how to increase the efficiency of these uncompetitive state-owned enterprises (SOEs) has become a pressing issue for the government. Measures such as freeing prices and shareholding to contractual incentives aimed at introducing market incentives have been tried by the government to reduce inefficiency. However, there is still no consensus among Chinese economists as to which policy reform is the most effective one. As McMillan (2003) argues, the successful restructuring of farms and rural industries which has taken place in China so far was initiated by people from the bottom up rather than from the top down and was based on trial and error rather than a clear theoretical framework. Given the past successes of this approach, what is clear is that the Chinese government will likely adopt a similar approach in reforming the inefficient state sector.

An important platform for restructuring the Chinese SOEs is the local stock market. If the SOEs are allowed to be privatized through shareholding so that they are subject to financial disciplines and hard constraints, managers will be more likely to act in the interests of stockholders, rather than those of the state and themselves. In other words, corporate governance can be enhanced through privatization because the main sources of inefficiency in Chinese SOEs are poor management, lack of accountability and transparency, and corruption. However, such a move causes uncertainties for the existing stock holders and has to be implemented with great care. For instance, when in July 2001, the China Securities Regulatory Commission (CSRC) announced a scheme in which state shares would be sold off and listed, it met with plunging share prices, angry investors and criticism from intra-government bodies. The plan had to be withdrawn. Nevertheless, privatization went ahead subsequently and there is now an increasing number of SOEs with their ownership transferred from the state to private investors.[2]

It is against this backdrop of rapid growth and restructuring of the Chinese economy that the chapters of this book are written. As China is undertaking a historic experiment to transform its economy to a market based one, we set the goal of examining specifically the stock market performance (efficiency, predictability and profitability) as a result of continuing reforms. The urgency of further reforming Chinese SOEs is highlighted by a recent announcement from the head of the State-owned Assets Supervision and Administration Commission (SASAC), Li Rongrong, that: "SOEs must be run as corporations and not government agencies. That means shareholders must exercise their supervisory powers and that these corporations must abide by board supervision" (*South China Morning Post* [*SCMP*], 8 October 2003, A6). The implications of such reforms are that managers of SOEs will no longer get promotions based on political connection or ideology, but on their ability to earn a profit. If they do not earn a profit, they will be demoted or removed. How does the market performance (efficiency, predictability and profitability) of SOEs change in response to both past and anticipated future reforms? The book contributes to an assessment of the effectiveness of restructuring in areas of corporate governance, industrial policy and financial deregulation and there is no better place to begin this assessment than looking directly at the performance of the stock market where most of the listed firms are SOEs.

Thus, China's spectacular growth over the last 25 years is linked to its market-oriented reforms. Despite the success of these reforms, the Chinese government faces continuing challenges in its efforts to sustain the current high level of growth. It is against this background that we further our investigation of China's stock market efficiency in subsequent chapters.

1.2 THE LINK BETWEEN SOE REFORM, FINANCIAL DEVELOPMENT AND ECONOMIC GROWTH

What are the implications for its financial markets and its long-run growth prospects if China fails to reform its SOEs? Can China maintain its current high rate of growth? These are serious questions that have important long-run implications. It is clear that failing to reform uncompetitive, loss-making SOEs will hinder the development of Chinese financial markets, which in turn would have a serious adverse effect on long-run economic growth. In the following paragraphs, we examine evidence that links SOE reforms to financial development and to long-run economic growth.

An important reason for China to accelerate SOE reform is its increasing economic ties with the rest of the world. Since 2001, China has formally joined the World Trade Organization (WTO), which calls for allowing foreign investment into almost all industries except for sensitive defence-related ones. Numerous foreign institutions target the Chinese stock market as a means of participating in China's economic growth. For instance, UBS has become the first foreign bank to buy into mainland Chinese shares via the Qualified Foreign Institutional Investor (QFII) Scheme. For China, foreign institutional investment represents an invaluable source of capital for Chinese enterprises. In addition, the participation of foreign institutional investment in the Chinese stock market will increase stock market liquidity, reduce volatility and improve the standard of corporate governance.

Encouraging foreign companies to buy into SOEs is an attractive option for the Chinese government. However, foreign institutional investors will be reluctant to put their money into Chinese SOEs when these enterprises are plagued by poor management, corruption, and lack of accountability and transparency. Foreign investors are also reluctant to enter the market when Chinese financial market regulations are slack and unenforceable. A 2003 survey conducted by the American Chamber of Commerce has found that four in five US companies in Shanghai are dissatisfied with the rules and regulations governing their investments in China. (*SCMP*, 15 September, A2)

In general, empirical literature confirms that financial development is not simply a byproduct of economic development, but is itself a driving force that promotes and sustains economic growth. The empirical literature on the relationship between financial development and economic growth is summed up by Levine (1997, p.688) as "The preponderance of theoretical reasoning and empirical evidence suggests a positive, first-order relationship between financial development and economic growth. The body of work would push even most skeptics toward the belief that the development of financial markets and institutions is a critical and inextricable part of the growth process and away from the view that the financial system is an inconsequential sideshow, responding passively to economic growth".

Empirical evidence shows that the proper functioning of banks and stock markets are especially important for long-run economic growth. For example, Levine and Zervos (1998) find that both stock market liquidity (measured by the value of domestic shares traded) and banking development (measured by the value of loans made by commercial banks) positively predict growth, capital accumulation, and productivity improvements, even after controlling for economic and political factors. This result reflects the fact that financial markets serve the important roles of evaluating prospective entrepreneurs, mobilizing savings for investment in productivity-enhancing, innovative products and diversifying investors' risk. All these functions facilitate resource allocation, physical capital accumulation and faster economic growth.

In sum, there is a growing consensus that a well-functioning financial system enhances long-run economic growth. There are serious doubts, however, about the ability of the Chinese financial system, in its current state, to play its required role. Financial markets in China are not performing as they should in a healthy economy mainly because they are policy-based rather than market-based. Privatizing SOEs and state banks as well as attracting foreign institutional investors are essential instruments in improving the functioning of the Chinese financial system.[3] Failing to do so will result in a poorly performing financial system, which leads to misallocation of precious resources and spells disaster for millions of Chinese who have yet to experience the material well-being of economic development trickling down to them.

1.3   PRINCIPAL PROBLEMS CONFRONTING THE CHINESE STOCK MARKET

The principal problem facing the Chinese financial sector or, particularly, its stock market is the holding of a large amount of non-tradable shares by the state and SOEs. Recent statistics show that 72 per cent of the total market capitalization of Shanghai-listed enterprises consists of non-tradable state shares of SOEs (*SCMP*, 3 October 2003, B2). Since most SOEs are run by poorly trained managers appointed by corrupt officials and are not subject to the usual financial market disciplines, they have little incentive to innovate and compete, leading to inefficiency and wastage. The failure of the stock market in China to contribute meaningfully to help China build world-beating companies or foster innovation suggests that there are profound limitations to the model, and China has now run up against them (*SCMP*, 3 October 2003, B1). Thus, China's inefficient, uncompetitive SOEs have become a hindrance to its long-run growth prospects. Getting rid of state shares or privatizing state enterprises has become a high priority for the government.

In essence, the problems facing the Chinese stock market are not so different from those faced by other emerging markets. Cheng Siwei, the Vice-Chairman of the National Congress of the People's Representative, summed up the following problems facing the Chinese stock market:[4]

- Policy-based market;
- The majority of stocks are non-tradable or illiquid;
- The stock market accounts for only a small share of the financial sector;
- Lack of long-term institutional investors;
- Excessive speculation;
- Excessive volatility and bubble markets;
- Incomplete laws and regulations; and
- Rampant insider manipulations.

The source of all the above problems can be ultimately traced to the initial intention underlying the development of the Chinese stock market, which was to raise funds for the SOEs. From the beginning, market forces have played only a small role in directing the allocation of resources in the Chinese stock market. Rather than well-managed enterprises with good prospects receiving funds, inefficient, poorly-managed SOEs become the winners. When the stock market was first established, a quota system was used under which the provincial governments were given the responsibility of selecting their favourite SOEs for listing. This system had to be abandoned later due to its tendency to cause corrupt practices. An observation which attests to the policy-based Chinese stock market is that almost all SOEs have good performance prior to their IPO, but their performance takes a turn for the worse immediately after listing. Another peculiar observation attesting to the policy-based Chinese stock market is that people flock to buy stocks of those SOEs which have been black-listed as poorly performed, knowing well that such enterprises will be bailed out by the government. In sum, a policy-based market distorts incentives with the result that the allocation of resources will be suboptimal.

1.4 EFFICIENCY, PREDICTABILITY AND PROFITABILITY

Financial markets provide the main channels through which private saving finances potentially profitable investments. When allocating limited funds to competing ends, financial markets specialize in evaluating the risk and profitability of investment projects and the credit worthiness of investors. On the one hand, both savers and investors benefit from reduced transaction costs and, on the other hand, scarce social resources are channelled to their most productive uses as a result of the operation of an efficient financial system. Given the important implications of an efficient financial system, this book embarks on a detailed investigation of the efficiency of the Chinese stock market, which has been rapidly developing and taking up an increasingly important role in the Chinese financial system. In essence, the book provides an assessment of the performance of the Chinese stock market, which emerged only a decade ago amid rapid economic growth and restructuring of the Chinese economy.

Efficiency has taken on a specific meaning in financial economics. Specifically, an efficient market is one in which at any point in time the current asset price reflects all relevant information, so arbitrage opportunities do not exist. This is referred to as the efficient market hypothesis (EMH). When asset prices fully reflect all relevant information, market players cannot systematically predict future price movements, so it is impossible for anyone to profit from buying and selling across different times or places. Thus, according to the EMH, unpredictability of price movement or returns is an essential characteristic of an efficient financial market. A major part of this book tests the Chinese stock market's efficiency by using the predictability implication of the EMH.

In using the unpredictability criterion of the EMH for testing efficiency in the Chinese stock market, we ignore transactions costs incurred in buying and selling stocks. Specifically, efficiency tests in the literature generally calculate autocorrelations or estimate regressions of current returns on their own past values. Significant autocorrelations or regression coefficients are then taken as evidence against the EMH. However the arbitrage argument underlying the EMH does not necessarily require returns to be unpredictable but rather that any predictability is unprofitable. That is, a market can be efficient even if its returns are predictable but unprofitable after accounting for transactions costs. Using the arbitrage argument of the EMH, efficiency can be tested by examining the profitability of trading rules rather than the predictability of returns. In Chapter 5, we will look at the profitability of different trading rules in the Chinese stock market.

The Chinese stock market has been subject to continuous changes in government policy and regulation since its establishment in the last decade. The focal point of this book is then to examine the interplay between efficiency of the Chinese stock market and changes in government policy and regulation under China's market-oriented reforms.

1.5   A LOOK AHEAD

We will discuss the development history of Chinese primary and secondary share markets in Chapter 2. This chapter aims to give a thorough background of development of the Chinese stock market. In particular, we identify four stages: the early stage of stock market development (1983-1991), the transition of the regulatory system (1992-1996), the Red Chips craze and deflation (1997-1999), and WTO entry and state share reduction (2000-present). The features of the two Chinese exchanges (Shanghai and Shenzhen) are described and the current problems they face and prospects for future development will be discussed.

Chapter 3 reviews the existing empirical literature on the efficiency and profitability of the Chinese stock market. This chapter surveys the empirical literature on the Chinese stock market, focusing on that dealing with the EMH, the relationship between prices of A and B shares and the relationship of Chinese stock prices to those in other markets.

Chapter 4 begins to investigate the main subject matter of this book, which is to test the EMH form of efficiency in the Chinese stock market. We use daily observations from 1992 to 2001. The results of the tests will shed light on the impact of financial deregulation, especially that of the banking sector, on the efficiency of the Chinese stock market.

The question of profitability of trading rules is addressed in Chapter 5. As discussed earlier, profitability of trading rules is a more stringent condition of market efficiency since it also accounts for transactions costs. In addition to daily observations, we also use weekly and monthly data for the analysis and see whether the results generated by using the daily data are any different from those of the weekly or monthly data.

In Chapter 6, our focus is on the dynamic causal relationship between returns and trading volume for individual Chinese stock exchanges and for spillovers across the two Chinese stock exchanges. We ask the question whether information contained in trading volume has predictive power for stock returns. If yes, the knowledge of the return-volume relationship can assist us in the analysis of efficiency since the information about trading volume in one market can improve significantly the forecasts of returns of the same market or the other markets, resulting in a violation of the EMH.

Chapter 7 examines the dynamic interrelationships between the Shanghai and Shenzhen exchanges and between them and the two closely related exchanges in Taiwan and Hong Kong. Both foreign and domestic investors would want to know whether arbitrage opportunities exist between the two Chinese stock exchanges and between the Chinese stock market as a whole and the neighbouring stock markets in Hong Kong and Taiwan. If one can predict returns in one market based on the information available in another market, we would have a violation of the EMH since the EMH states that in an informationally-efficient market returns cannot be predicted on the basis of any publicly available information, including returns in other markets.

The last substantial chapter of the book, Chapter 8, examines the relation between trading volume and stock returns for Chinese A shares and ten individual stocks in the energy sector. Also, it investigates the effects of exogenous policy changes, both energy-specific and general, on the stock return-volume relation. Rather than looking at the aggregate return-volume relation as in Chapter 6, Chapter 8 examines the relationship between trading volume and stock return at both aggregate and company levels in China.

Finally, in the concluding chapter of the book, we will summarize the important findings and discuss the implications of these findings for the future development of the Chinese stock market.

NOTES

1. It applies to all except Argentina, which has a per capita income of US$7933 in 2000 (*World Development Table 2000, CD-ROM*).
2. In 2002, 15.1 per cent of the 729 firms listed in the Shanghai stock exchange were owned privately, up from 12.0 per cent in the previous year (*SCMP*, 3 October 2003, B2).
3. The Chinese banking sector is effectively bankrupt by Western standards. China needs to spend 3.5 trillion yuan, or 31 per cent of its GDP to fully bail out its big four state banks (*SCMP*, 24 October 2003, B2).
4. "Cheng Siwei: Chinese Stock Market is Subject to Serious Manipulation", *Ming Pao Daily,* 17 September 2003, p. B2.

2. An overview of Chinese stock market development

Since the Shanghai stock exchange (SSE) was established in December 1990, the Chinese stock market has developed rapidly and in a manner significantly different from the stock markets in the West. In many aspects, the development of the Chinese stock market has been very successful. Although initially the equity markets were used largely as a tool for enterprise reform, today they are no longer experimental and have become a vital part of the national economy. Nevertheless, the Chinese share markets have been and continue to be prone to distortion and it is therefore not surprising that the markets still face substantial and varied challenges and problems.

Recently researchers have shown increasing interest in the Chinese stock market and they have reported the results of work on a limited number of specific problems.[1] This chapter reviews relevant events and their impact on the stock market with the purpose of enabling the readers to understand the history, the present state and the future prospects for the development of the Chinese stock market.

In the next four sections we review the development history of Chinese share markets, both the primary and secondary markets, describing in each section one of the four stages we identify in the development of the market. These are the early stage of stock market development (1983-1991), the transition of the regulatory system (1992-1996), the Red Chips craze and deflation (1997-1999), and WTO entry and state share reduction (2000-present). We then go on in Section 2.5 to analyse the current features of the two exchanges and the problems they now face. Finally, conclusions are set out in Section 2.6.

2.1   THE CHINESE STOCK MARKET

The Chinese stock market can be traced back over 130 years to the late Qing Dynasty when the Shanghai Stock Exchange was first set up in 1869 by foreign firms. Then in 1918 the Beijing Securities Exchange, the first Chinese-operated stock exchange, was established. Since the stock market was basically oriented towards agriculture and family operations, it never played an important role in the economy. After the establishment of the

People's Republic of China in 1949 the two stock exchanges were closed as they were regarded as places for speculation, a capitalist phenomenon inconsistent with the communist ideology of the new government. Hence, the stock market disappeared in China for about 30 years (Liu, 1992). In 1978 the Chinese government began a process of economic reform which included, importantly, the opening up of the economy to the rest of the world. As reform and opening progressed, concomitant changes have also taken place in China's financial system. In this section, we describe the initial stage of the development of the market and distinguish three episodes which led up to the formal establishment of the Chinese stock market – the spontaneous development of share-like securities in the 1980s, the share fever of the late 1980s and the formal setting-up of the two Chinese securities exchanges.

2.1.1   Spontaneous Development of Share-like Securities (1983-1988)

The resurrection of the share market in China began in the township and village enterprises (TVEs) of the southern coastal provinces in the early 1980s. Under the influence of the openness and reform policies, villages began establishing TVEs. Since capital requirements for these new enterprises were more than a single family or even a village could meet, experimentation began with a "co-operative shareholding" structure.[2] Such experiments proved successful in raising capital and soon were quite common, becoming known as the "shareholding co-operative" system.[3]

In 1983 a Shenzhen TVE named the Baoan County Joint Investment Company became the first Chinese enterprise to issue share certificates to the public after the establishment of the People's Republic of China (PRC). In July 1984 the Beijing Tianqiao Department Store was the first state-owned enterprise (SOE) restructured as a company limited by shares, and in November of the same year the Shanghai Feile Acoustics Company issued irredeemable shares to the public. These early transactions were unregulated and represented the tip of a development that was gathering momentum. The enactment of "the decision on the reform of the economic system" in October 1984 greatly promoted the broad development of shareholding co-operative and individual (private) enterprises (Gao and Ye, 1991). The Shenzhen government in 1986 was the first to standardize procedures relating to the restructuring of enterprises into shareholding companies.[4] From 1984 to 1989, lots of shareholding companies were set up all over the country and issued 3.8 billion yuan worth of shares. Of these, 70-80 per cent of the shares came from conversion of existing state assets, and relatively little new capital was raised by issuance of stocks. Moreover, most of the stocks were issued to related companies or employees in the companies and less than 2 per cent were public issues to general investors. In Shanghai, for example, by 1990 there were 1250 non-public offerings compared to only 11 public offerings (Lan, 1997).

The late 1980s was obviously a period of spontaneous fundraising through the issuance of a wide variety of non-standardized shares. At first, individual investors were not interested. They did not understand that shares could appreciate (or depreciate) in line with the given issuer's economic performance or even simply as a result of supply and demand (Walter and Howie, 2001). To entice individual investors, the companies had to pay dividends at fixed rates in excess of the bank deposit rate, and some companies even promised to refund shareholders on demand. So initially shares bore a strong resemblance to debt securities. Investors tended to hold rather than trade securities. However, from the mid-1980s equity issuance became increasingly frequent and shares began to change hands through non-market channels. In August 1986 Shenyang became the first city to initiate formal over-the-counter (OTC) trading followed by Shanghai in September of the same year. Then the Shenzhen government in October approved the formal establishment of OTC trading at various financial institutions. By the end of 1988 there were nine financial institutions conducting OTC trading, eleven business services across the city of Shenzhen, and one institution providing share registry services. In Shanghai some Trust and Investment companies were allowed to establish OTC trading operations with a primary focus on treasury bonds in April 1988. In the following twelve months eight trading counters were established with central government supervision. Yet only eight Shanghai companies' shares were traded on the Shanghai OTC market. So, almost from the outset, Shanghai took on the nature of a central government sponsored market for debt securities, while Shenzhen was the more informal and undisciplined equity market (Walter and Howie, 2001).

2.1.2 Share Fever (1989-1990)

"Share fever" came from the Shenzhen Development Bank, China's first financial institution limited by shares, which announced a dividend based on its 1988 results in March 1989. This announcement marked a major turning point in the Chinese share markets. The bank was exceptionally generous to its investors awarding them a cash dividend of 7 yuan per share (amounting to a 35 per cent cash dividend ratio), a two-for-one stock dividend, and one-for-one stock split. Investors who bought the bank's shares in 1988 for about 20 yuan per share now enjoyed a profit several times their original investment. Just before 4 June 1989 the price of the bank's shares soared in OTC trading from a year-end price of 40 yuan to 120 yuan and ended the year at 90 yuan.[5] Throughout the summer of 1990 prices for the publicly traded Shenzhen companies continued to rise rapidly and the ensuing "share fever" saw funds pouring in from all across China. While the "share fever" was centred on Shenzhen, it gradually extended to Shanghai.

Since only a very limited number of shares were available on the market, prices rose very quickly at this early stage and the share market became wild and speculative. Historical data show that by the end of 1990 total securities were valued at over 200 billion yuan. Of these, stocks only accounted for a very small share. Lan (1997) reported that during this period some shares traded at 10 times, 20 times, 50 times, and even 106 times their face value.

"Share Fever", as the period was characterized, produced a strong reaction from the State Council (Walter and Howie, 2001). Many measures were taken to cool the markets, including daily price movement limits, increased transaction taxes, and ownership-transfer stamp duties. In May 1990 the State Council announced restrictions on the share market experiment, including its limitation to the state sector (SOEs) and the designation of Shenzhen and Shanghai as the only officially recognized OTC markets. These measures led to a market collapse in late 1990.

2.1.3 Establishment of Two Stock Exchanges (1990-1991)

The introduction of OTC trading in Shenzhen and Shanghai was followed by a formal decision to proceed with the establishment of the Shanghai and Shenzhen security exchanges. The intention was to provide a formal venue for security trading in two administrative areas well under the control of the central government. Eventually the Shanghai stock exchange (SSE) was opened in December 1990 and the Shenzhen stock exchange (SZSE) shortly after in February 1991.[6] Both exchanges were heavily promoted by their local municipal governments and had the approval of the nominal regulator, the People's Bank of China (PBOC). Elsewhere in the country OTC trading continued, particularly in Shengyang, Wuhan and Tianjin, each of which sought to establish a recognized exchange but was not successful. With their establishment both exchanges shared an organizational structure similar to a non-profit organization run by members (securities firms and securities agencies) through a general meeting that elects a standing executive committee or council. The council is headed by a director with a separate general manager appointed by the executive council to act as the legal representative for the exchange. In addition, a supervisory committee responsible to the members' general meeting was also established. Both exchanges were subject to the supervision of their respective local PBOC branches.[7]

The opening of the Shanghai and Shenzhen stock exchanges were extremely important historical events. They marked the official foundation of the Chinese stock market even though the scale of the market was quite small (11 listed companies with a total value of 500 million yuan in Shanghai and 5 listed companies with a total face value of 270 million yuan in Shenzhen) (Lan, 1997).

From the early stages of the establishment of China's two exchanges two main types of shares have been traded: A shares and B shares. In this dual market, A shares are common stock issued by mainland Chinese companies, priced and traded in Chinese Renminbi (RMB), listed in either of the two exchanges, and bought and sold by domestic investors only. The A share market was launched in 1990. On the other hand, B shares are issued by mainland Chinese companies, listed in either of the two exchanges, carry a face value denominated in RMB but are traded in foreign currencies (US dollars in Shanghai and HK dollars in Shenzhen) and bought and sold exclusively by foreigners. The B share market was launched in 1992. However, due to the continuously thin trading and small capitalization of the B stock market, B shares have been made available for trading by domestic investors since February 2001. Besides the A and B shares, there are several other types: H shares have been issued by Chinese companies since 1993 and traded on the Hong Kong stock exchange (in terms of HK dollars); N shares are American depository receipts (ADRs) and are issued by Chinese companies and traded on the New York stock exchange in terms of US dollars; and S shares are floated by Chinese companies and traded on the Singapore stock exchange in terms of Singapore dollars. The relative importance of the final two types of shares is small in terms of their capitalization and turnover.

2.2 TRANSITION OF THE REGULATORY SYSTEM (1992-1996)

The exchanges having been formally established, the time now arrived for the development of a regulatory structure within which the stock market could operate efficiently and in a manner consistent with the overall economic policy of the Chinese government. The process of development during 1992-1996 can be divided into two overlapping episodes: the first culminating in the establishment of the State Council Securities Committee (SCSC) and the Chinese Securities Regulatory Commission (CSRC) with the eventual domination of the latter, and the second concerned with the role of the banks in stock trading.

2.2.1 Establishment of the SCSC and CSRC (1992-1994)

In early 1992 Deng Xiaoping undertook a historical trip to the southern province of Guangdong where his support for the shareholding system triggered an explosion of share-trading activity both domestically and internationally. In the meantime, the Chinese economy recorded a rate of growth in real GDP of 12.8 per cent in 1992, 13.4 per cent in 1993 and 11.8 per cent in 1994. However, this fast growth was accompanied by high rates of inflation, which peaked at 21.7 per cent at the end of 1994 (SSB, various issues).[8] Those positive developments dramatically boosted trading in the two stock exchanges. The SSE composite index peaked at 1558.98 on 16 February 1993 compared to its base value of 100 in December 1990;

Table 2.1 Historical data for the SSE index (19 December, 1990 – 31 December, 2002) and the SZSE index (3 April, 1991 – 31 December, 2002) (SSE Base = 100 on 19 December 1990; SZSE Base = 100 on 3 April, 1991)

Year	Open SSE	Open SZSE	High SSE	High SZSE	Date SSE	Date SZSE	Low SSE	Low SZSE	Date SSE	Date SZSE	Close SSE	Close SZSE
1990	96.05	n.a.	127.61	n.a.	12/31	n.a.	95.7	n.a.	12/19	n.a.	127.61	n.a.
1991	127.61	100	292.75	110.37	12/31	12/31	104.96	45.98	05/17	09/20	292.75	110.37
1992	293.74	110.53	1429.01	312.21	05/26	05/26	292.76	107.08	01/02	01/16	780.39	241.21
1993	773.89	251.63	1558.98	359.44	02/16	02/22	750.46	236.52	12/20	12/29	833.8	238.27
1994	837.7	233.13	1052.94	242.65	09/13	07/29	325.89	96.56	07/29	07/29	647.87	140.63
1995	737.72	139.88	926.41	169.66	05/22	05/22	524.43	112.63	02/07	12/28	555.29	113.25
1996	550.26	110.15	1258.69	473.02	12/11	12/11	512.83	105.34	01/19	01/22	917.02	327.46
1997	914.06	334.13	1510.18	518.13	05/12	05/12	870.8	305.81	02/20	01/06	1194.1	381.29
1998	1200.95	389.7	1422.95	439.28	06/04	06/01	1043.02	317.1	08/18	08/18	1146.7	343.85

Year	Open		High		Date		Low		Date		Close	
	SSE	SZSE	SSE	SZSE	SSE	SZSE	SSE	SZSE	SSE	SZSE	SSE	SZSE
1999	1144.89	336.56	1756.18	525.14	06/30	06/29	1047.83	310.65	05/17	05/18	1366.58	402.18
2000	1368.69	414.69	2125.72	654.37	11/23	11/23	1361.21	414.69	01/04	01/04	2073.48	635.73
2001	2077.08	644.66	2245.44	664.85	06/14	06/13	1514.86	439.36	10/22	10/22	1645.97	475.94
2002	1643.49	470.76	1789.89	512.38	06/25	06/24	1357.76	371.79	12/31	01/22	1357.65	388.76

Note: n.a.- not available.

Source: Datastream.

the SZSE composite index was 359.44 on 22 February 1993 compared to its base value of 100 in April 1991 (Table 2.1).[9]

Prior to 1992 the market was quite small, and relatively unregulated. Though extensive regulations were drafted in 1989, they were never implemented.[10] However, after Deng's positive comments in early 1992, all provisional measures and other regulations were brought forward, including the Standard Opinion and the Corporate Law.[11] These imposed a standard framework on shareholding companies and the shares offered to investors. Yet, and not surprisingly given the nature of the Chinese political system, the regulations were imbued with the spirit of state planning, state control and state interest. For example, the Standard Opinion permits a company to issue both common and preferred shares. Meanwhile it also defines a number of different types of shares such as state shares, legal person shares, individual shares and foreign capital shares. These different classes of shares reflect the ownership characteristics of the assets contributed by the promoters of or investors in the new company. According to the Standard Opinion and the Corporate Law, state shares refer to shares held by governmental agencies or authorized institutions on behalf of the state. They include: (a) the shares converted from the net assets of SOEs which have been transformed into joint shareholding companies; (b) the shares initially issued by companies and purchased by government departments; and (c) the shares initially issued by companies and purchased by the investment companies, assets management companies, and economic entity companies authorized to invest on behalf of the state. State shares are not allowed to trade on an open market. Legal person shares refer to shares of a joint stock company owned by another company or institution with a legal person status. There are four types of owners for legal person shares, namely, state-owned, collective enterprises, private enterprises, foreign invested enterprises and institutional legal person shares. The transfer and trading of legal person shares are also restricted. Individual shares, with an officially recognized nickname of A shares, refer to shares that may only be owned by Chinese citizens. A shares have the full function borne by classic stock, and they can be freely traded and transferred in domestic markets. Foreign capital shares include B shares and overseas-listed shares (H shares, N shares, S shares and so on).[12]

The many different classes of shares have their origin in the doctrine of Chinese ownership of productive assets. Prior to economic reform, the ownership structure of an enterprise either took the form of state ownership or collective ownership (collective assets owned by employees). The state had discretionary power to set the price of all products produced by state-owned enterprises regardless of the size of supply and demand, as well as the allocation and transfer of assets among state-owned enterprises. The collectively owned firms could set prices based on the market mechanism. The state could not interfere in their financial affairs such as profit allocation and employment of workers. Under the system of the public ownership, all assets belong to the state on behalf of the people. Following the emergence of the shareholding system, however, policy makers were concerned about the trading of state shares and legal person shares which may erode the state's position of majority shareholding in state-owned enterprises. They were afraid that the trading of state shares and legal person shares would undermine the state's holding of its assets with the result of the loss of their dominant position in the national economy. So the Provisional Measures on the Regulation of State-owned Shares Issued by Companies Limited by Shares was enacted in 1994. According to this law the predominance of the socialist public ownership system would be preserved in the shareholding system by maintaining the controlling position of the state-owned share rights. Here the state-owned shares include state shares and state-owned legal person shares. During the period of the conversion of enterprises into shareholding companies, this policy resulted in the necessary dominant position of state shares and the secondary position of state-owned legal personal shares, with individual shares occupying a third, non-controlling, and minority position. Having thus created a hierarchy in the primary market for shares of the state, legal person, and individuals respectively, the government designed a peculiar secondary market aimed at maintaining in the secondary market the same hierarchy of classes of shares created in the primary market. As a result, the trading of state shares is banned, the trading of state-owned legal person shares is confined within the scope of state-owned enterprises, and members of the Chinese public may trade individual shares among themselves.[13]

As can be expected, such an artificially segmented capital market has resulted in poor liquidity and produced artificial, differentiated prices for various types of shares of the same issuer. With the rapid growth of stock markets, restrictions on trading state and legal person shares have had various adverse effects. For instance, the value of state assets cannot be increased; the enterprise's assets cannot be optimized and restructured and the advantages of a shareholding economy cannot be realized to its full extent. The enormous amount of non-tradable shares limits the function of stock markets as a mechanism to evaluate the management performance of listed companies and poses a serious threat to the secondary market. The problems of state shares have been recognized as a continuing headache for the Chinese government and will be further discussed in Section 2.5.

Another issue that has become a serious concern to the Chinese government relates to the role of the People's Bank of China (PBOC) in the securities market. Before October 1992 the PBOC was not a real central bank and was responsible for all aspects of the regulation and administration of China's financial system. The evolution of the PBOC is as follows: (1) During 1949-1979 the PBOC was the only financial institution whose branches were located in every province and municipality of the country and provided all kinds of financial services including deposits, loans, foreign exchange, insurance and so on. (2) From 1980 to 1985 the PBOC was gradually transformed to play the role of a central bank and several state-owned commercial banks were set up such as the Bank of China, the Agricultural Bank of China, the China Construction Bank and the Industrial and Commercial Bank of China.[14] But they were owned by the State and PBOC was their actual owner and regulator. (3) During 1986-1992 the PBOC exercised comprehensive regulatory as well as administrative control over the financial sector, broadly defined to include the traditional financial sector, insurance sector, and securities.[15] The PBOC further delegated certain regulatory and legislative powers to its provincial and municipal PBOC branches for the regulation of the securities market. As a result, the PBOC, other state-owned banks, the Ministry of Finance and local finance departments were permitted to establish their securities agencies and indirectly participate in the securities market. Figure 2.1 shows that the SSE members increased from 101 to 577 while SZSE members increased from 177 to 532 during 1992-1995.

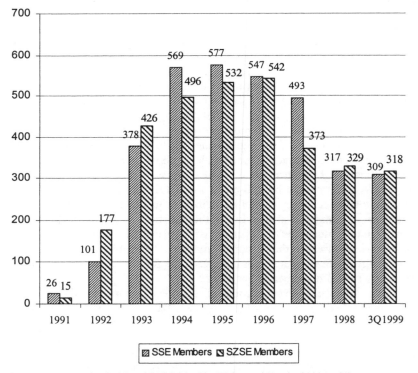

Source: Fact Book of SSE and SZSE (cited by Walter and Howie, 2001, p. 81).

Figure 2.1   Historical data on members of SSE and SZSE (1991-3Q1999)

Thus, the PBOC was both the regulator of and an active participant in (and beneficiary of) the securities market. Not surprisingly by the early 1990s speculation and violation of regulations were rife because of the PBOC official corruption. Policy makers realized that the PBOC as an institution was unsuitable as market regulator. As a result, the Chinese Securities Regulatory Commission (CSRC) and the State Council Securities Committee (SCSC) were set up in October 1992. The SCSC, similar to the Equity Market Office, was a ministry-level government organization and was authorized by the State Council to enforce securities laws. It was the immediate superior of the CSRC during the period October 1992 – mid-1998. The CSRC was a quasi-government, vice-ministry entity and was designed to be the implementing apparatus for the SCSC. The CSRC was responsible for drafting various regulatory measures, overseeing and supervising entities involved in the securities business, compiling the requisite statistics and market analysis to advise the SCSC on policy matters. It eventually became the dominant regulatory body. Its accretion of power has gone through three stages: (1) the establishment and consolidation of authority over the securities and futures markets during 1992-1993, (2) the CSRC's full control over the two exchanges in 1996, and (3) in mid-1998 the SCSC was dissolved and the CSRC became a full ministry-level organization empowered by the 1999 Securities Law.

2.2.2 The Role of the Banks (1994-1996)

The securities firms, the principal players in the Chinese share market, initially originated from the major banks, local government finance departments and Trust and Investment Corporations.[16] Before the establishment of both exchanges, the securities firms mainly engaged in the trading of various kinds of bonds. Since 1991, with the development of the stock market, securities firms developed very quickly and focused their business on stock underwriting and trading. The number of securities firms increased from 44 at the end of 1990 to 87 by October 1992. Naturally, the competition among the securities firms became fiercer and fiercer due to the limited number of listed shares and excessive numbers of securities trading agencies. Some securities firms began to be involved in speculation or trading of futures on the markets in order to survive. The over speculation and high risk in the Chinese share market forced the government to adjust and regulate securities firms. In December 1993, the State Council made a decision to separate the banks from the securities industry and industrial enterprises. Although the State Council permitted banks and industrial enterprises to invest in financial institutions including securities firms, it prohibited securities firms from investing in any sector but the securities industry. The government's effort has been to create a Glass-Steagall-like segregation between securities industries and banking (Wheelock, 1994).

The first step in this process was the separation of the PBOC branches from all economic entities including securities firms. Then in 1994 the PBOC prohibited the Ministry of Finance and local government finance departments from involvement in the ownership of securities firms. The State Council also prohibited the major commercial banks from owning Trust and Investment Corporations which, in turn, usually either owned a securities firm or had their own internal securities department. The Laws of PBOC and the Laws of Commercial Banks enacted in mid-1995 confirmed this segregation, as did the Securities Law enacted on 1 July 1999. The resulting disappearance of bank members from both securities exchanges and the consequent withdrawal of enormous sums of funds from the share market led directly to the share market stagnation between early 1994 and April 1996 (Figures 2.2 and 2.3). This market downturn was exacerbated by the anti-inflation measures which were put into place in mid-1994. It is interesting to note that one of the anti-inflation measures was a virtual halt to the approval of new equity listings both domestically and internationally. The policy to control inflation was successful since by the end of 1995 the inflation rate clearly fell and in early 1996 it declined to below 5 per cent while GDP growth maintained a rate about 10 per cent. The effect on stock prices was even more dramatic – the stock price indices bottomed with the SSE composite index down to 325.89 on 29 July 1994 from 1558.98 eighteen months ago and the SZSE composite Index falling to 96.56 from a previous high of 359.44. Thereafter the Chinese stock market experienced more than two years of stagnation (Table 2.1 and Figures 2.2 and 2.3).

2.3   RED CHIPS CRAZE AND DEFLATION (1997-1999)

With the regulatory framework in place, the Chinese market experienced fluctuations which are not uncommon to stock markets. In this section we look at the brief "Red Chips Craze" associated with the handover of Hong Kong in mid-1997 and the subsequent deflation and stable market until the end of the century.

2.3.1   "Black Monday" and the Red Chips Craze (Late 1996-1997)

In April 1996 the stock market began to recover and prices rose strongly so that by mid-December of that year the average stock price had risen by 120 per cent in Shanghai and by over 300 per cent in Shenzhen. On 11 December 1996 the Shanghai index reached a high of 1258.69 and the Shenzhen index was up to 473.02, the highest in three years with a daily turnover of 37.4 billion yuan (Table 2.1). But 16 December 1996 was "Black Monday" for the Chinese stock market due to the disclosure of illicit speculation by the Shenzhen Development Bank. The government took strict measures to punish the offenders as well as to ease the overheating of the market. Consequently prices fell dramatically in the exchanges – both A share indexes fell by approximately 40 per cent in a little more than a week, after which the market was subdued for some time, with the Shanghai index at around 1000 and Shenzhen index 350 (Figures 2.2 and 2.3).

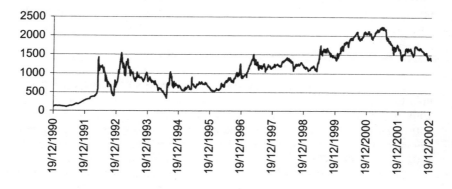

Source: Datastream.

Figure 2.2 The Shanghai Composite Index (1990 - 2002)

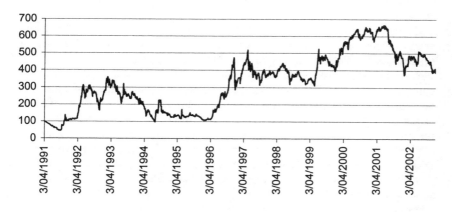

Source: Datastream.

Figure 2.3 The Shenzhen Composite Index (1991 - 2002)

The lull was short-lived, however, since the "Red Chips Craze" in the Hong Kong market terminated the stagnation. Red chips are stocks listed on the Hong Kong Stock Exchange for companies with significant interests in mainland China.[17] As the Hong Kong handover of July 1997 approached, trading in the Red Chip stocks became increasingly frenzied. In 1997 alone there were 16 initial public offerings (IPOs) of such companies including the largest Chinese IPO, China Telecom. This clearly spilled over into the Shanghai and Shenzhen exchanges both of which experienced a sustained upturn in prices for about a year, although there was some downward correction in the weeks leading up to the handover on 1 July 1997.

2.3.2 Deflation and Quiet Markets (1998-1999)

At about the time of the Hong Kong handover, however, the market fell and then lapsed into quiet trading. This was a function of two factors. First, in 1998 it became apparent that China was drifting into a deflationary period with continual decline of the CPI and a rising unemployment rate. Second, China was not wholly immune from the Asian financial crisis after its outbreak in 1997. China's export growth shrank drastically and growth in committed foreign direct investment turned negative for the first time since the early 1990s. This uncertain economic environment also affected Chinese domestic and international new equity issues. In 1998 there was a total of 106 issues (only three of which were B share issues) domestically and two internationally, compared to approximately 200 in the previous two years (323 listed companies in 1995, 530 in 1996 and 745 in 1997). The first half of 1999 saw only 39 A share issues, no B share issues and one issue of H shares.

Despite this, a rally began on 19 May 1999 which pushed share prices up nearly 40 per cent in a little over a month. This recovery followed a number of stimulatory measures initiated one after another. They included allowing state-owned enterprises and up to 5 per cent of the assets of 25 insurance companies to enter the securities market, the implementation of a tax on interest earnings from savings accounts and an expansion of brokerage capitalization. On 15 June the government joined the party by writing the famous *People's Daily* editorial proclaiming, in preparation for the 50th anniversary of the PRC, that the upturn reflected a fundamental improvement in the overall economy. Besides, the Securities Law also took effect on 1 July 1999, which pushed up market sentiment.[18] The Shanghai market promptly shot upward by 600 points (from the 1999 opening index of 1144.89 to a 1999 high of 1756.18 on 30 June) before falling back once again. Activity in the Shenzhen market exhibited similar characteristics over the same period (Table 2.1).

2.4 WTO ENTRY AND STATE SHARE REDUCTION (2000- PRESENT)

From 2000 onwards, the Chinese stock market has experienced a continuing rectification and standardization. The major episodes include China's WTO entry and the debate about state share ownership.

2.4.1 WTO Entry and Bull Markets (2000-mid-2001)

The late 1990s appeared to be a turning point for the Chinese economy. Exports increased and deflationary pressures were reduced. Most large and medium-sized state enterprises were showing signs of recovery, and retail prices were beginning to pick up. Most of all, China and the US reached their trade agreement on China's WTO entry on 16 November 1999. All these developments created a sound basis for a medium- to long-term rally in the stock market, especially for the shares that are likely to benefit from China's WTO entry such as textiles, clothing, and high-tech industries. In fact, in early 2000 the stock market rebounded strongly and maintained bullish trading on expectations of more market-boosting policies and sound economic growth in 2000. The price of A shares soared by more than 50 per cent on the Shanghai exchange and by more than 60 per cent on the Shenzhen exchange in the first eight months of 2000. Later in 2000 several stimulatory measures, such as the establishment of a venture capital market in both stock exchanges and the entry of pension funds into the stock market, were taken by the government and caused further surges in China's stock market. In brief, during 2000 the securities market expanded rapidly with market capitalization increasing from 2647.117 to 4809.094 billion yuan and both exchanges' indices rising strongly (the SSE composite index from 1366.58 to 2073.48 and the SZSE composite index from 402.18 to 635.73) (Table 2.1).

At the start of the new millennium the upturn continued in China's stock market due to investor confidence even though international securities markets fell. On 19 February 2001, the government allowed domestic investors into the B-share market. Thus up to US$75 billion of household savings (deposited in foreign currencies) was made available for stock investment.[19] Since then, greatly increased liquidity has sent B share prices surging. By April 2001 the SSE B share index was up by 130 per cent and the SZSE B index soared 205 per cent. B shares trading and investor sentiment pushed the whole market steadily upward to reach its highest point of 2245.43 in Shanghai on 14 June 2001 and 664.85 in Shenzhen on 13 June (Table 2.1).

2.4.2   State Shares Reduction and the Market Recession (July 2001-Present)

This strong share-price growth was reversed, however, when the government announced its intention to solve the non-tradable share problem by means of state share reduction from 2001. According to the statistical report of the Shenzhen Securities Information Company, by the end of 30 June 2001 there were 1121 listed companies with total non-tradable shares of 259.324 billion, which represents 67.76 per cent of total issued shares. Of these, state-owned shares accounted for 178.606 billion, or 42.23 per cent of the total (Table 2.2). The government planned to complete the sale of state shares over a five-year period with a total of 251.51 billion yuan to be unloaded (Li, 2002). But the state share reduction is considered by investors to be a force driving the market toward a further decline. Most investors felt that the state shares should not be sold at market prices since they generally far exceed net asset values. Following the start of the reduction in July 2001, prices on the Shanghai stock market plummeted to about 1645 points in December 2001 from its peak of 2245.43 in June. The index hit a low of 1514.86 points on 22 October. Over the same period the Shenzhen composite index sank to 439.36 points on 22 October from a high of 664.85 on 13 June (Table 2.1). Influenced by the collapse of the A share market, the B share market also witnessed a sharp downward adjustment after an extraordinary month-long rally, dropping from its peak of 220 points in mid-year to 160 points by the end of 2001 in Shanghai.

Besides the implementation of state share reduction, other measures introduced in 2001, including the introduction of rigid supervision measures and tougher rules to delist debt-ridden firms, also sparked market fears, which reinforced the bearish performance in the second half of the year. The market bounced back slightly, however, as the state share reduction programme was suspended on 23 October 2001. In order to further shore up investor confidence in the market, the Minister of Finance announced a stamp duty cut from 0.4 per cent to 0.2 per cent on 16 November. The upward trend continued in the following months. Expecting the market to remain firm in 2002, on 12 May, the CSRC announced that the state share reduction scheme would be resumed in a new form, designed to replenish China's under-funded social welfare system. As a result, investor confidence collapsed again and the market price fell quickly.

However, the central government soon moved to suspend once again the controversial state share reduction scheme – it was argued that the complicated plan would require lengthy study before regulators could devise a comprehensive plan widely accepted by the markets and that it had other ways to raise money for the social welfare system. This announcement not surprisingly boosted the market, and the indices increased by more than their daily limit. The Shenzhen index peaked at 512.38 points on 24 June and the Shanghai index at 1789.89 on the second day (Table 2.1). A record volume of trade (4851.8061 million yuan) and daily turnover (49.48 billion yuan) for the year were also reported on 24 June 2002. However, the market reversed and the indices moved downward in the second half of 2002. In July the stock price indices still remained at around 1700 in Shanghai and around 500 in Shenzhen. Yet, from the beginning of August, the SSE composite index fell steeply to the 2002 low of 1357.65 points on 31 December and the SZSE composite index lost 123.62 points (from the peak 512.375 in June to 388.755 at the end of the year) (Table 2.1). Moreover the combined turnover of the two exchanges fell 27 per cent to 2.8 trillion yuan. This is because of poor corporate results, frequent initial public offerings and especially a lack of policy incentives. At present the market sentiment is weak. Some investors are nervous and trying to pull out of the market by selling their stocks while waiting for market-boosting steps by the government.

Table 2.2   State shares in SSE and SZSE (30 June 2001)

Items	SSE	SZSE	Total
No. of listed companies (1000)	507	621	1121
Total capital (billions of shares)	164.004	230.359	394.363
Non-tradable capital (billions of shares)	102.761	156.563	259.324 (67.76%)
State-owned capital (billions of shares	70.438	108.168	178.606 (42.23%)
Domestic legal person shares (billions)	18.949	32.563	51.512 (13.06%)
Other legal person shares (billions)	9.807	11.597	21.404 (5.43%)
Total market capitalization (billion yuan)	2199.288	3163.77	5363.058
Tradable market capitalization (billion yuan)	835.475	1053.315	1888.79

Notes: Here state-owned shares include state shares and state-owned legal person shares. Yuan is the Chinese currency unit. In 2002, US$1=8.27 yuan approximately.

Source: Shenzhen Securities Information Company, http://www.cninfo.com.cn.

2.5   ACHIEVEMENTS AND PROBLEMS

2.5.1   Market Scale: Expanding Rapidly

The Chinese stock market has achieved impressive progress over the last 12 years. Since their establishment the two exchanges have expanded rapidly in terms of market capitalization, turnover, funds raised and numbers of firms listed. By the end of 2002 China had 1224 listed domestic companies with a total market capitalization of 3832.9 billion yuan, or about 30 per cent of current GDP. The number of stock account holders reached 68.8408 million (Table 2.3). From 1991 to 2002 total raised capital through share offerings amounted to 872.236 billion yuan of which A shares accounted for 670.677 billion yuan. International investors contributed the remainder with US$4.959 billion for B shares, US$20.425 for H shares and other markets contributing 8.85 billion yuan.[20] This clearly underscores the relative importance of China's domestic markets to corporatization.

A prominent feature of the market is that the B share market has not expanded as rapidly as the A share market. As Table 2.4 illustrates, the market for A shares has grown dramatically since 1990. By the end of 2002, there were 361.6 billion A shares issued on the Shanghai exchange with a market capitalization of 2492.142 billion yuan and more than 33.269 million investor accounts opened for A shares. In contrast, the B share market has been considerably smaller ever since B shares were first issued in 1992. By the end of 2000, there were 8507 million B shares issued on the Shanghai exchange with a market capitalization of 33.454 billion yuan and 0.202 million overseas investor accounts. From 19 February 2001, trading in B shares became permissible for Chinese individuals and legal persons with foreign currency accounts. B share market capitalization increased sharply from 33.454 to 65.606 billion yuan in a year as B shares became the investors' favourites and by the end of 2001, the number of B share accounts had increased to 0.9297 million, 4.6 times the number of a year earlier.

To sum up, over the last decade, China's stock market has achieved substantial growth. China now ranks among the top 10 countries in terms of market capitalization. Within Asia, China is ranked second after Japan. China's stock market will continue to grow with market capitalization being expected to double by the end of 2005.[21] However, future development will be affected by several problems which are addressed in the following sections.

2.5.2   Dominance of Manufacturing Sector in the Share Market

By the end of 2002, 1224 Chinese companies had completed initial public offerings with four broad categories: A shares, B shares, H shares and Red

Table 2.3 Trading summary for Shanghai and Shenzhen exchanges, 1990–
          2002

Years	Listed Companies (A or B)	Market Capitalization[a] (billion yuan)	Stock Turnover (billion yuan)	Total Investors[b] (10,000)	Market Capital/ GDP (%)
1990	8	1.2	n.a.	n.a.	0.06
1991	14	10.9	4.6[c]	11.0	0.56
1992	53	104.8	32.4[c]	111.2	4.38
1993	183	352.2	362.7	423.5	11.22
1994	291	369.1	818.2	574.9	8.43
1995	323	347.4	403.6	685.2	6.02
1996	530	984.2	2133.2	1207.9	14.52
1997	745	1752.9	3072.2	3387.2	23.44
1998	851	1950.6	2354.4	3910.7	24.52
1999	949	2647.1	3132.0	4482.0	32.26
2000	1088	4809.1	6082.7	5801.1	53.79
2001	1160	4352.2	3830.5	6650.4	45.38
2002	1224	3832.9	2799.0	6884.1	n.a

Notes: [a] Market Capitalization is computed as the total number of shares on issue multiplied by their market price; [b] Only for SSE for 1991-1996; [c] Only for SSE.

Sources: *SSE and SZSE Fact Books*, http://sse.com.cn, http://www.cninfo.com.cn and http://www.csrc.gov.cn.

Table 2.4 Comparative statistical data for Shanghai A and B share markets

Years	Issued volume of B share (billion)	Issued volume of A share (billion)	Market capitalization of B shares (billion yuan)	Market capitalization of A shares (billion yuan)	B share investor accounts (10,000)	A share investor accounts (10,000)
1993	1.8	18.9	12.8	206.8	1.02	422.49
1994	3.1	38.8	11.7	248.4	1.91	573.00
1995	3.5	46.4	9.2	243.4	2.89	682.50
1996	4.5	62.6	16.2	531.6	4.93	1203.03
1997	6.8	90.8	18.6	903.2	13.93	1706.77
1998	7.4	120.6	10.1	1052.5	16.79	1991.61
1999	8.1	149.9	14.0	1444.1	18.43	2272.33
2000	8.5	194.7	33.5	2659.6	20.21	2943.32
2001	9.1	307.4	65.6	2693.5	92.27	3326.93
2002	9.3	361.6	44.2	2492.1	n.a.	n.a.

Source: SSE fact books in 2001 and market data in the web page, http://www.sse.com.cn.

Chips (Table 2.5).[22] The A share companies have tended to be small and unfocused with a wide variety of businesses. Typical A share IPOs have been of the order of $US50 million representing a 25 per cent ownership interest. Disclosure tends to be extremely poor. While the B share companies are larger and subject to listing requirements similar to overseas listing transactions, ongoing transparency is only marginally better than A share companies. The IPOs tend to be somewhat larger with the largest about $US250 million. The H share companies are Chinese state-owned enterprises that have gone through major restructuring designed to satisfy the requirements for an international issuance, one leg of which is almost always in Hong Kong. H share IPOs generally have ranged from $US100 to 600 million. In comparison with the A share companies, H share companies represent focused businesses having a strong position in China's domestic economy. These companies have been selected by the government to be listed as part of the overall state enterprise reform effort. The intention is not only to raise foreign funds but also to transform them into modern enterprises that follow international management practices and are allowed to cope with market challenges. The Red Chip companies are Hong Kong registered companies into which Chinese assets have been injected, usually in shares for asset swap. The asset injection comes both prior to and as part of the listing, and might continue thereafter with minority shareholder approval. In general, Red Chip companies are holding companies with typically little specialization in any one industry and, for the most part, are rather poor in terms of management and earnings. Many of them are the result of so-called "back door" listing in which a non-listed Chinese company acquires a relatively dormant listed company in Hong Kong and then injects mainland assets. They tend to be conglomerates in which the Hong Kong entity is used as a funding vehicle for its Chinese operations or for the further acquisition of Chinese assets.[23]

Table 2.5   *Summary of listed companies by shares categories (except Red Chips)*

Year	A or B	B total	H total	A only	B only	H only	A & B	A & H
1998	851	106	43	727	26	25	80	18
1999	949	108	46	822	26	27	82	19
2000	1088	114	52	955	28	33	86	19
2001	1160	112	60	1023	24	35	88	25
2002	1224	111	75	1085	24	46	87	29

Source: http://www.csrc.gov.cn.

In the early days Chinese share markets were created to assist SOE reform. As a result, most of the listed companies, both international and domestic, are transformed SOEs. At first, these SOEs listed their stocks on the domestic stock market. But China's stock market is not effective in regulating listed firms and protecting investors' interests with the result that many transformed SOEs regarded the market as a mere financing tool and have failed to carry out anticipated reforms. In order to overcome their inefficiency and inability to operate at a profit, selected Chinese companies have been permitted to list on overseas exchanges with the selection partly based on the importance of certain sectors to the state plan. So it is not surprising that the largest number of candidates for international listing comes from the infrastructure industry (largely highways and ports) and then power (and power equipment), followed by transportation, petrochemicals and chemicals, and steel.

Figure 2.4 demonstrates the distribution of listed companies in China for 2001 and shows that listed Chinese companies are largely dominated by manufacturing ones. However, since mid-1999 there has been a change in the composition of new listings following a shift in government policy. Until 1998, the government's industrial policy emphasized the development of basic industries, energy and agriculture. Since mid-1999 China's policy has gradually changed to foster the development of knowledge-based high-tech industry. Therefore, it has been easier for high-tech companies than for others to secure government permission to list on the exchanges. As a result, hi-tech industry listing has increased and the restriction on financial institutions to go public has been gradually relaxed. There are now more than five shareholding banks. These changes will be helpful in improving industry structure and enhancing international competitiveness as listing decisions become increasingly driven by economic rather than political considerations.

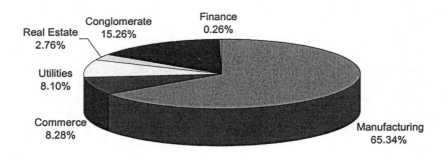

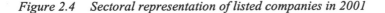

Source: http://www.csrc.gov.cn.

Figure 2.4   Sectoral representation of listed companies in 2001

If we also consider the geographic distribution of listed companies, we see a large gap between the representation of companies from coastal and interior regions. As Table 2.6 indicates, 13 of China's 32 provinces occupy the top ten spots in the two stock exchanges and they account for roughly 65 per cent of all listings. Moreover, eight of these are coastal provinces and cities which have contributed 42.41 per cent of the total in SSE and 44.98 per cent in SZSE, while these eight provinces represent less than one third of the total provincial-level regions and about 25 per cent of the population. This type of geographic distribution is also found for H shares and reflects the unbalanced development of the Chinese regions despite the long-term policy to narrow the gap between the coastal and interior regions.[24]

In summary, China has permitted more than 1224 enterprises to enter the share market, domestic or international. The selection of these companies for listing reflects a policy of screening for favoured sectors and an economic screening for being allowed to raise capital internationally. Since the number of successful international issuers has been few, the original sector policy grip has been relaxed so that enterprises from nearly all but the most sensitive industries can now seek an international listing.[25] Domestically there is an almost endless supply of potential issuers from the state-owned sector. Recently the non-state or private sector has been permitted to issue shares. At the National People's Congress held in March 1999, China's Constitution was revised to give the non-state sectors the same legal recognition as the state sector by providing some bank financing as well as opening capital markets to the non-state sector. Perhaps the addition of such companies is the only way that domestic exchanges can offer a fully diversified equity product to their investors as the mature equity markets do.

2.5.3 Equity Structure: Poor Liquidity and the Problem of State Shares

As mentioned previously, China is renowned for its extravagant variety of shares, e.g., A, B, H, N shares and Red Chips. Other ones include state shares, legal person shares, overseas legal person shares, social legal person shares, internal person (employee) shares and so on.[26] According to market principles, a stock market should be "open, fair, and just" while the stock should be characterized by the "same rights, same interests, and same obligations for the same stock". But, in Chinese share markets, differentiated types of shares were conferred with different sets of rights, interests, and obligations. For example, state shares and legal person shares cannot be traded. Only individual shares, which make up one third of all shares issued, can be freely sold. At present approximately 70 per cent of domestically issued stock is frozen in the form of state and legal person shares, which results in an unreasonable equity structure and severe non-liquidity. This point is illustrated well by Table 2.7, which shows the composition of shares listed on the Shanghai exchange in October 2002.

Table 2.6 Top provinces of incorporation of Shanghai and Shenzhen A & B companies (December 2001)

Provinces	Shanghai		Provinces	Shenzhen	
	No. of companies	% total		No. of companies	% total
Shanghai	130	20.12	Guangdong	118	23.18
Zhejiang	43	6.35	Sichuan	30	5.89
Jiangsu	41	6.35	Liaoling	28	5.50
Beijing	41	6.65	Hubei	28	5.50
Shandong	34	5.26	Shandong	27	5.30
Liaoning	31	4.80	Hunan	25	4.91
Hubei	30	4.64	Beijing	23	4.52
Sichuan	28	4.33	Jiangsu	22	4.32
Fujian	24	3.72	Fujian	18	3.54
Heilongjiang	22	3.41	Hainan	16	3.14
Sub-total	424	65.63	Sub-total	335	65.82
Others	222	34.37	Others	174	34.18
Total	646	100.00	Total	509	100.00

Sources: SSE Fact Book, 2001 and the web pages http://www.sse.com.cn and http://www.szse.com.cn.

This equity structure, which is overwhelmingly concentrated in state shares and legal person shares, arguably has some adverse consequences. On the one hand, the agents of state enterprises (the managers) actually control the listed companies due to the lack of real ownership (nominal state ownership) and have become the big shareholders due to the large proportion of state shares. This coincidence of ownership and management not only leads to internal control and the invalidity of corporate governance mechanisms, but also infringes on the interest of small and medium shareholders. Big shareholders can easily misappropriate the funds of a listed company and subvert the interests of small-medium shareholders. The Shanjiu Medicine incident, where big shareholders withdrew 95 per cent of the net assets of the firm, shocked the whole securities market.[27] On the other hand, relatively few tradable shares on the market have stimulated speculation on the secondary markets. China adopted administrative pricing from the start in contrast to market pricing in mature markets. A-share pricing, for all intents and purposes, was based on a formula which applied a 15 times P/E ratio to the average of the company's past three years' profits, that is, the offer price equals the taxed profits multiplied by 15.

Table 2.7   Shanghai stock exchange capitalization structure (31 October 2000)

Shares	Total Issued Value (10 000 yuan)	%	Total Market Capitalization [a] (10 000 yuan)	%
1. Promoter shares	10 649 127.26	55.923	137 997 205.30	59.437
State shares	7 733 724.85	40.613	99 020 791.51	42.650
Domestic legal person shares	2 710 784.94	14.236	35 762 037.29	15.403
Overseas legal person shares	204 617.47	1.075	3 214 376.45	1.384
2. Social legal person shares	1 107 367.45	5.815	16 061 679.64	6.918
3. Internal shares	117 950.13	0.619	1 798 103.00	0.774
4. Preferred shares or other	112 581.33	0.591	1 684 174.69	0.725
5. Pay fund	66 772.61	0.351	1 245 948.39	0.537
Total non-tradable	**12 053 798.78**	**63.300**	**158 787 111.00**	**68.392**
1. A shares	5 182 799.48	27.217	70 787 684.36	30.489
2. B shares	850 713.77	4.467	2 598 540.36	1.119
3. H shares	955 112.80	5.016	0	0
Total tradable	**6 988 626.05**	**36.70**	**73 386 224.72**	**31.608**
Total	19 042 424.83	100.00	232 173 335.72	100.00

Note: [a] Market capitalization is the total number of shares including a value for non-tradable shares on issue multiplied by their market price.

Source: SSE Fact Book, 2001, http://www.sse.com.cn.

Recently Chinese practice has changed significantly.[28] This has been driven by a problem with the P/E approach. Firstly, reliance on past performance is obviously no guarantee of future performance. For example, earnings may have declined from a high to a low level during the three-year period, assuming that the company was encountering difficulties. Secondly, a common multiplier of 15 treats all companies equally, but companies are not equal. In comparison with the average P/Es and turnover rates in the United States and other share markets, A share markets have higher P/E ratios and higher turnover rates. Table 2.8 shows that A shares are traded at a P/E ratio of 40-50 times and turnover ratios of 300-500. Whereas New York shares generally have a P/E ratio of 15-22 times; most B shares, H shares and Red Chips are traded at a P/E ratio of 10-30. In Hong Kong and New York exchanges the turnover ratios are below 100. This provides evidence of the highly speculative nature of the Chinese stock market. With the distorted equity market, stock prices are easily manipulated by the market makers and the P/E ratios fluctuated relatively widely and quickly. As a result, financial reports do not reflect a company's fundamentals and prospects. Although China's secondary markets are quite active and constantly expanding, they have not yet been used as an instrument to value companies efficiently. On the contrary, the government has often manipulated the share price and the market trend by floating new policy ideas and issuing new regulations.

Recently, the government appears to have decided to solve the problem of non-tradable shares by reducing state shares in a bid to optimize equity structure, eliminate the system deficiency of state ownership and further develop the share market. According to the original design in the early 1990s, the non-tradable shares were to be temporarily withheld from circulation. Thus they would be released for trading at some point in the future. Actually in late 1999, state share reduction was proceeding in two minority state-controlled companies: Beijing Zhongguancun Science-Tech and Guangdong Kelon. The process ran into two problems: how to price the non-tradable shares and when to open for trading. In August 1999 Zhongguancun announced a one-for-one rights offer for A share holders priced at the original IPO level of 5.78 yuan. Obviously given the secondary market price at the time of 30 yuan, the rights issue was a guaranteed money winner for any current A share investors. Not unexpectedly, the closing price of the share prior to ex-rights rose to 33.80 yuan. The next morning the Shenzhen exchange announced the new price, a weighted averaged price of 26.02 yuan per share, reflecting the dilution caused by the rights issue.[29] Unfortunately, the market that morning opened at 23.42 for the Zhongguancun shares, down by the 10 per cent mandated daily trading limit, and the next day the shares traded down again by the 10 per cent limit to 21.08 yuan. By the third day the shares closed at 19.01 yuan, down almost 44 per cent from the pre-rights share price. The market reaction reflects investor expectations of much lower pricing. Some thought the post-rights price should reflect only the tradable A shares in the company's capital base and not the non-tradable legal person shares. So the price per share should be 19.79 yuan.[30] Apparently retail investors do not attribute any value to non-tradable shares. The case of Zhongguancun suggests that successfully reducing the proportion of state shares will come at the cost of a significant decrease in secondary market values and the overall market capitalization of the companies involved (Walter and Howie, 2001).

When state shares became tradable and at what price are still serious unresolved issues. Such uncertainty has increased investors' pessimistic mood about the future of China's stock market. Recently, at a Chinese business conference, a senior government figure suggested that the value of

Table 2.8 Comparison of turnover ratios and P/E ratios among Shanghai, Shenzhen, Hong Kong, and New York markets

Years	Shanghai				Shenzhen			Hong Kong			New York	
	Turnover Ratio (%)	P/E Ratio (%)		Turnover Ratio (%)	P/E Ratio (%)		Turnover Ratio (%)	P/E Ratio (%)			Turnover Ratio (%)	P/E (S&P) Ratio (%)
		A shares	B shares		A shares	B shares		HSI	H shares	Red Chips		
1992	--	72.65	17.4	--	57.52	35.56	53	--	--	--	44	22.7
1993	341	42.48	--	213	44.21	20.11	61	--	--	--	53	23.4
1994	787	29.67	9.94	472	10.67	7.02	55	--	11.61	--	53	18.2
1995	396	16.32	8	180	9.8	6.01	38	--	10.05	--	59	18.5
1996	591	32.65	14.04	902	38.88	14.07	41	--	10.85	--	62	20.6
1997	326	43.43	11.99	466	42.66	10.67	90.92	12.29	14.84	--	65.71	23.9
1998	297	34.38	6.04	283	32.31	5.71	61.95	12.36	7.11	10.44	69.88	27.2
1999	315.6	38.13	10.05	299	37.56	10.38	50.6	27.89	--	--	74.62	31.3
2000	360.4	59.14	25.23	509	58.75	13.06	62.99	12.74	--	--	82.4	25.2

Years	Shanghai			Shenzhen			Hong Kong				New York	
	Turnover Ratio (%)	P/E Ratio (%)		Turnover Ratio (%)	P/E Ratio (%)		Turnover Ratio (%)	P/E Ratio (%)			Turnover Ratio (%)	P/E (S&P) Ratio (%)
		A shares	B shares		A shares	B shares		HSI	H shares	Red Chips		
2001	449.1	37.59	43.39	483	40.76	25.3	--	15.06	6.26	18.57	--	31.1
2002	--	34.5	30.16	--	38.22	17.51	--	--	--	--	--	--

Notes: The method of calculating for the share turnover ratio for Shanghai and Shenzhen was as follows: turnover ratio = total number of shares traded in the year/total number of shares in circulation at the end of the year. The P/E ratio is calculated by taking the market price of a share and dividing it by the company's earning per share at the end of year.
--Not available.

Sources: Turnover ratios for 1992-2000 from Chen and Shih (2002, p.39); Shanghai and Shenzhen P/E ratios for 1992-1998 from Walter and Howie (2001, p.68) and Almanac of China's Finance and Banking in 2002; New York P/E ratios from http://nyse.com and HIS P/E ratios from http://www.hkex.com.hk/.

state and legal personal shares is approximately 20-25 per cent of the market price of A shares trading on the secondary markets.[31] So it is important for any state share reduction scheme to consider the element of investor psychology including that of the state itself. To maintain market stability, a good scheme has to involve as a first step a substantial reworking of the current market relationship between the state and investors. If the non-tradable shares were sold at the current market price without any compensation for existing investors, any attempt to resolve the market liquidity problem would incur strong resistance by investors and hence create market instability. However, on 4 November 2002 the circular that allows listed companies to sell non-tradable shares to foreigners by public tender was announced by China's securities regulator, the Finance Ministry and the State Economic Trade Commission.[32] For the government, the sales of these state shares and legal person shares is crucial to improving corporate transparency and raising money for social welfare funding. For the existing investors, once the non-tradable shares flow into the market, the overall price of the shares will most likely be driven down by the enlarged supply, thus making it impossible for them to recover their investment. Such worries explained much of the lackadaisical trading and the falling index in the A-share markets in late 2002.

2.5.4   Few Institutional Investors

Investors are normally categorized as either professional (institutional), or retail. Retail investors are individuals investing their own funds, as opposed to institutional investors, a category representing a variety of entities using institutional, that is, other people's funds to invest. In the past decade, the vast majority of market participants in China were individuals with the securities houses added in to stir the soup. In the 1990s the government sought to build a base of so-called 'institutional investors' who, presumably by holding shares for long-term gains, would bring greater stability to the markets. As a result, market participants have become somewhat more diverse. Yet the fact is that retail investors accounted for 99.54 per cent of total accounts at the end of 2001.

Current institutional investors are represented by the proprietary trading departments of securities firms and various other non-bank financial institutions such as trust and investment companies, securities investment funds, and insurance companies. Corporate investors also trade in the market from time to time when regulations permit. Despite double-digit annual growth for years, the institutional accounts at the two exchanges still amount to a small percentage of total accounts as shown in Table 2.9. The two exchanges have nearly equal numbers of accounts, approximately 33 million in SZSE and 35 million in SSE. Without question there is considerable overlap. A survey conducted by SZSE shows the overlapped proportion is about 91.29 per cent of the total accounts.

Table 2.9   Summary of investor accounts (SSE, December 2001)

Individuals (10,000)	A share investors (10,000)	%	B share investors (10,000)	%	Institutional investors (million)	%
3429.6	3326.93	97.09	92.97	2.71	15.87	0.46

Source: SSE Fact Book, 2001, http://www.sse.com.cn.

Perhaps in total there were only 33.6-34 million A-share individuals with share accounts across China at the end of 2001 or 26 individuals out of 1000 people.[33] They represent citizens living predominantly in China's developed and wealthy coastal provinces. In the Shanghai Market, Shanghai investors hold nearly 14.36 per cent of the total A-share accounts. After Shanghai, Guangdong is the second with more than 9.62 per cent followed by Jiangsu at 9.45 per cent, Sichuan at 6.89 per cent, and Shandong at 6.23 per cent. The regional character is slightly different for the Shenzhen market where Guangdong accounts for 22.13 per cent, followed by Jiangsu at 8.54 per cent, Shanghai at 8.5 per cent, and Sichuan at 7.61 per cent (Table 2.10). Overall, the top ten provinces' account holders in both markets account for over 70 per cent of all accounts and the same provinces comprise the top ten for each market. This is not surprising since these ten provinces or cities are among the most prosperous in China, representing nearly 25 per cent of China's population and half of the country's GDP.

Table 2.10   Regional composition of A share accounts (31 December 2001)

Top ten	SSE Accounts	SZSE Accounts	SSE (%)	SZSE (%)	All (%)
Shanghai	4 790 545	2 690 784	14.36	8.50	22.86
Guangdong	3 210 992	7 005 144	9.62	22.13	31.78
Beijing	1 469 822	1 436 130	4.41	4.54	8.95
Jiangsu	3 154 461	2 701 746	9.45	8.54	17.99
Zhejiang	1 685 040	1 419 603	5.05	4.49	9.54
Shangdong	2 078 552	1 624 304	6.23	5.13	11.36
Sichuan	2 299 340	2 407 476	6.89	7.61	14.50
Liaoning	2 057 398	1 565 435	6.17	4.95	11.12
Hubei	1 131 604	1 338 423	3.39	4.23	7.62
Fujian	1 116 683	1 014 215	3.35	3.20	6.55
Sub-total	22 994 237	23 203 260	68.92	73.32	
Total	33 366 961	31 652 183	100.00	100.00	

Note: Sub-total - top ten provinces in terms of the number of the accounts.

Sources: SSE and SZSE market statistics, http://sse.com.cn and http://cninfo.com.cn.

The previous discussion has dealt with the current investor base for China's A share market. Obviously, the investor base for overseas listed Chinese shares and B shares is significantly different. Before February 2001 only offshore individuals and economic entities were permitted to trade them. Due to the lack of transparency and liquidity on this small B share market, few foreign institutional investors would trade in the market. Since holding B shares became permissible for domestic investors in 2001, retail investors, especially domestic individuals, have increased more rapidly than institutional investors. Table 2.11 illustrates the structure of B share investors for the Shenzhen exchange.

Table 2.11   Ownership of Shenzhen B share accounts by country (October 2001)

Country or area	Accounts	% of total	Individuals	Institutions
China mainland	436 215	81.379	435 994	215
Hong Kong	76 580	14.286	73 866	2 548
USA	5 432	1.013	3 030	214
Macao	3 559	0.663	3 539	18
Taiwan	2 742	0.511	273	9
Canada	1 833	0.341	1 502	12
Australia	1 649	0.307	1 417	66
United Kingdom	1 314	0.245	427	261
Singapore	930	0.173	733	106
Japan	768	0.143	593	34
New Zealand	544	0.101	533	1
Others	4 414	0.840	2 791	596
Total	535 980	100	527 157	4 080

Source: SZSE market statistic data, http://www.cninfo.com.cn.

In short, the current investor structure seems less mature than that of international markets, where investment funds, pension funds and insurance companies have become the major participants. For example, institutional investors trade 80 per cent of the total turnovers in New York Securities Exchange. Since the enactment of investment fund rules in 1997, the Chinese government has moved to encourage funds as a vehicle to broaden market participation. In addition, insurance companies were permitted to invest in shares indirectly in October 1999 and securities firms have gained access to the first level inter-bank market and to use shares as collateral for loans. China's participation in the WTO may also hasten this process since the government has agreed to permit foreign involvement in A share markets through joint ventures in the asset management industry. As noted previously, the social insurance fund will also participate in the purchase of non-tradable shares during the process of state shares reduction. All these efforts to broaden the market participants are to change the composition of the investors and will transform China's share market from the current emerging market status to one of the major players in the world in the coming decade.

2.6   CONCLUSION

This chapter has reviewed the development history of China's stock market, discussed its scale and structure, and shed some light on its prospects. The market's characteristics reflect the influence of three factors: (1) government policy; (2) investor sentiment about the performance of the Chinese economy and listed compannies, and (3) the deficiency of the market system. Generally speaking, China's stock market is still an emerging market with a structure which is still far from a mature market. A major obstacle to the further development of the Chinese share market, undoubtedly, is the poor liquidity – the issue of large numbers of non-tradable shares. Achieving greater liquidity of state shares will help to ensure an appropriate dispersal of equity, strengthen the corporate governance of listed companies and provide an exit route for state capital that conforms to market requirements. Thus, how to reduce state shares and solve the problem of state share liquidity is an urgent task for Chinese policy makers and regulators. In addition, the introduction of a comprehensive legal framework, the creation of an environment of fair and orderly market competition and the establishment of transparent "rules of the game" must play key roles in stock market development. The development of institutional investors and large securities firms will also help to establish a sound structure and effective operation of the market and increase the level of stability by reducing speculation.

NOTES

1.   See Chapter 3 for a comprehensive review of the empirical literature.
2.   After nearly a decade of experimentation, the Ministry of Agriculture promulgated "the provisional regulations on farmer shareholding cooperative enterprises" on 12 February 1990 in *Jinrong Falu Fagui Quanshu*, Vol, 3, pp.2826-30 (cited by Walter and Howie, 2001, p.226). Generally speaking, in the TVEs, farmers or villagers held non-tradable share certificates and allocated the dividends according to the respective proportion of the shares they held at the end of each year.
3.   The "shareholding co-operative" enterprises in a manner were similar to shareholding companies. In general, some small state-owned, collective and private enterprises were merged. The employees jointly operated the business and allocated the profits according to their work hours and the proportions of the shares they held. More details can be found in Li (1998, p.53).
4.   Shenzhen Municipal Government, "Provisional regulations on the pilot program for the transformation of state-owned enterprises into shareholding companies", 15 Oct 1986, *Jinrong Falu Fagui Quanshu*, Vol.3, pp.2815-18 (cited by Walter and Howie, 2001, p.25). The provision defined the restructuring of a SOE into a shareholding company as follows: "transforming the net asset value of a SOE into shares representing the state's equity ownership; then transferring a portion of the state's ownership to other enterprises and individuals or taking in new shares from the state, other enterprises or individuals; then transforming the original enterprises into a company limited by shares in which the state, other enterprises and individuals participate in the shareholding".
5.   See Walter and Howie (2001), pp.29-30.
6.   At the beginning, SSE and SZSE were called the Shanghai securities exchange and the Shenzhen securities exchange, see *Jinrong Falu Fagui Quanshu*, August 1990 and January 1991, Vol.3, pp.2746-58 (cited by Walter and Howie, 2001, p.232). Later the fact that the Shanghai securities exchange unilaterally changed its English name to the "Shanghai Stock Exchange" is an indication of its effort to establish an independent identity. Later Shenzhen followed this practice.
7.   In Shanghai the council director is nominated by the council and followed by PBOC Shanghai branch approval. Its general manager, deputy general manager and supervisory committee director are all nominated by PBOC Shanghai Branch and approved by PBOC headquarters in Beijing. Shenzhen seems more independent. There

the council director, general manager and the supervisory committee are nominated by their council subject to PBOC Shenzhen Branch approval (Walter and Howie, 2001, pp.76-77).

8. This figure is based on the retail price index. The rate is 24.1 per cent if the CPI is used.

9. The SSE composite index is a weighted index of the share prices of all listed companies on the Shanghai exchange. Its base value is 100 points in December 1990. The SZSE composite index has a similar structure but with a base date of April 1991.

10. Such draft regulations include "Provisional measures on the experiment with the shareholding system by enterprise", "Regulations on shareholding companies", "Regulations on limited liability companies" and the PBOC drafts including "Provisional measures for the administration of the issuance and trading of shares". These drafts were then submitted to the State Council for review and approval. But, due to the Tiananmen incident in June 1989, these measures were not taken up again until after Deng Xiaoping's trip (Walter and Howie, 2001, p.95).

11. The Standard Opinion, implemented in May 1992, was aimed at standardizing the procedures for creating shareholding companies. For SOEs there were two principal ways to be restructured into companies: the promoter method and the fundraising method. The Corporate Law was signed into effect in July 1994. It was a formal law to standardize the organization and behaviours of limited liability and companies limited by shares.

12. See the paper entitled "Different Types of Shares in China's Stock Market", http://www.cninfo.com.cn.

13. See the paper entitled "Reasons for the Introduction of State Shares and Legal Person Shares", http://www.cninfo.com.cn.

14. The four state-owned banks became state-owned commercial banks only after the enactment of the Commercial Bank Law in 1995.

15. The PBOC was not to become a normal central bank until after the enactment of the PBOC Law in 1995.

16. There are two categories of securities firms: (1) comprehensive securities firms; and (2) brokerage firms. The two are subject to different regulations and receive different licences. The former must have a minimum of 500 million yuan in capital to run brokerage and proprietary trading business.The latter need only 50 million yuan to run brokerge business only.

17. A Red chip company should have at least a 35 per cent shareholding directly held by either: a) mainland entities which are defined to include state-owned organizations, provincial or municipal authorities in mainland China; or b) listed or privately owned Hong Kong companies which are controlled by mainland entities. Moreover, the company should have at least a 12-month trading

record after having satisfied the above criteria (Walter and Howie, 2001, pp.164-165).

18.   The Securities Law is intended to provide a framework for rationalizing the great many extant, narrow rules, measures and regulations that touch on securities matters, which apply to the issue and trading of shares, corporate bonds and other securities.

19.   China Daily, 25 April 2001, "B Share Pushes Stock Market Slightly Higher".

20.   Data are drawn from http://www/csrc.com.cn.

21.   Data are taken from China Daily, 1 January 2002.

22.   Most companies issue only A or B shares although some with A shares were permitted to issue B or H shares (Table 2.5).

23.   See Walter and Howie (2001), pp.111-112.

24.   China's regional development policy is to first develop the coastal regions of eastern China. For example, the eastern coastal regions were the first to be opened up, receiving preferential treatment in attracting foreign capital and technology, foreign trade, and so on. In recent years more emphasis has been placed on the development of western regions to narrow the gap between the eastern and western regions.

25.   The selection of the sectors and listing companies is an extremely complex process in China. According to "the trial measures on the shareholding system", 15 May, 1992, in CSRC. Art.1, "Circular on certain issues relating to share issuance", 26 December, 1996, it begins with the State Planning Commission's financing plan for state enterprises in accordance with the national industry policy, then the CSRC allocates the listing quotas after a decision taken by the State Council. The success of an enterprise in obtaining a listing quota, particularly H shares, depends to a large extent on its owner, whether a local government, a provincial government or the central government. Generally the central and provincial enterprises are favoured. Finally the selected companies receive listing approval from CSRC (Walter and Howie, 2001, pp.112-129).

26.   Since 1996 Chinese share types have been divided into promoter shares (including state-owned shares, domestic legal person, foreign legal person shares and so on), social legal person shares, employee shares, preferred and other shares. Legal person shares are created when a company uses state assets to invest in a company limited by shares. Overseas legal person shares represent the investment by properly authorized overseas Chinese state-owned enterprises. Social legal person shares represent investment by third party legal persons in the public offering of a company. Internal shares represent investment by internal staff or employees.

27.   Data are drawn from the web page http://www.sse.com.cn.

28. P/E (Price-earning ratio) is the price per share divided by the company's earning per share. In the early 1990s the average P/E ratio at issuance was 9-13 times and decided by the CSRC. During 1995-Febrary 1999 the offering price was set at taxed profits multiplied by average P/E ratio (14.5-20 times). After the pricing reform in March 1999 the offer price was based on additional factors such as the industry prospects, the company's performance, the P/E ratio in the secondary market and so on. During 2000-2001 higher P/E ratios were observed: 29.9-31 times in Shanghai and 31.72 times in Shenzhen.

29. In Beijing Zhongguancun there were 300 million legal person shares and 187 million A shares. The calculation was summarized as adding the total market capitalization of the company (A shares and legal person shares) to the funds raised through the rights offering and dividing by the new total number of shares as follows. $[(187+300)\times33.8 + (187\times5.78)] / (187+300+187)=26.025$ yuan (Walter and Howie, 2001, p. 57).

30. The calculation is $[(187\times33.8) + (187\times5.78)] / (187+187)=19.79$ yuan (Walter and Howie, 2001, p.58).

31. An approximation of this 20-25 per cent valuation can be arrived at by assuming that only the market capitalization of trade shares is real as shown in the example below:
Share market capitalization = US$200 billion. If a total of 100 billion shares have been issued, then the implied price per share = US$2 per share. If 30 per cent of shares are freely tradable A shares they have a value of US$60 billion. If all issued shares are floated on the market the price is US$0.6 per share. So, if all non-tradable shares were listed, their value is roughly 30 per cent of the current market price. The value 30 per cent is close to the official's estimate (Walter and Howie, 2001, p. 59).

32. Data are drawn from http://www1.chinadaily.com.cn, China Daily, 5 November 2002.

33. Based on a 2001 survey by the Shenzhen securities exchange of individual investors in China's stock market. See http://www.cninfo.com.cn or http://www.sse.com.cn.

3. Empirical studies: a survey

In this chapter we survey empirical work on the Chinese stock market. Since the stock market in China has existed for only a relatively short period, it is not surprising that empirical work has appeared only in the past decade, starting with the paper by Bailey (1994).

Most of the empirical literature on the Chinese market can be seen as a response to the peculiar features of the market; in particular, its rapidly emerging nature, its segregation into A and B markets and its isolation from stock markets in other countries. Its emerging nature makes it a natural subject for the study of market efficiency – the presumption is that the more recently emerging the market, the less efficient it is likely to be. The segregation of the main stock market into markets for A and B shares has been the subject of a number of empirical studies since it provides a unique opportunity to examine the way in which share prices react to information about the fundamental forces which underlie share value. Similarly, the relative isolation of the Chinese market for much of its history combined with the distinction between A and B shares has made it an ideal subject for those interested in the way in which information is transmitted across markets.

We consider literature addressing each of these three issues in turn in Sections 3.1, 3.2 and 3.3. Sections 3.4 and 3.5 comprise a brief review of two areas which have been extensively researched for overseas markets and are beginning to be examined using Chinese data, viz., the nature of volatility and the relationship between returns and volume. Concluding comments are offered in Section 3.6.

3.1 MARKET EFFICIENCY

3.1.1 The Efficient Markets Hypothesis

Market efficiency has a specific meaning in the jargon of financial economics. Following the work of Fama (1970, 1991) it has come to mean the speed and completeness with which relevant information is absorbed into asset prices. A market is said to be efficient, or the Efficient Markets Hypothesis (EMH), is said to hold if asset prices immediately and completely incorporate relevant information. It is common to distinguish three forms of the EMH depending on the content of "relevant information": if the information set includes only past returns, the weak form of the EMH is said to hold; if the information set includes all publicly-available information, the EMH is said to hold in semi-strong form; and if the information set also includes information which is not publicly available, the strong EMH is said to hold.

The EMH is based on an arbitrage argument: if information is not immediately and completely incorporated into returns, it must be the case that returns adjust gradually to information so that future returns can be predicted and a profit could be made by exploiting such information. It is assumed that in equilibrium all arbitrage profits are exploited.

An implication of the EMH which is often tested is that asset returns are not predictable since predictability implies profitable arbitrage opportunities (in the absence of transactions costs which are generally ignored in empirical work). To test the weak EMH it is common to estimate the autocorrelation function of returns or to regress current returns on past returns and examine the significance of autocorrelations or regression coefficients as the case may be. The semi-strong EMH is typically assessed by examining the reaction of returns to changes in variables other than past returns themselves. Thus, event studies have been a popular method of testing the semi-strong EMH – in these studies, particular company-related events such as earnings announcements are identified and the behaviour of returns around these events is examined, with the EMH predicting that prices will not gradually adjust to the information after it has been made available but will adjust completely and immediately.

Alternatively, returns may be regressed on a variety of variables which may be relevant to the pricing of assets such as dividends, earnings or macroeconomic variables such as inflation or interest rates and the predictive ability of such equations assessed. If these variables have predictive power for the returns, the semi-strong version of the EMH is considered to be violated. Studies which examine the inter-relationships between different national stock markets may be seen as contributing to tests of the semi-strong EMH (although this is often not their stated purpose) since returns in one market predicting returns in another is inconsistent with the EMH.

3.1.2 Predictability

As mentioned above, the paper by Bailey (1994) was one of the earliest in the empirical literature on the Chinese market (see Table 3.1). He set out to examine the operation of the then newly established Chinese stock market and certain of his tests can be seen to throw light on the EMH. Following on from an earlier paper on Pacific-basin stock markets, Bailey, Stulz and Yen (1990) in which autocorrelations and cross-market correlations were examined to test the efficiency of nine markets, Bailey (1994) focuses on the B share market given the paucity of data on A share prices in the early period of the Chinese stock market. He uses weekly data for a number of individual

B shares for the period March 1992 to March 1993 and computes autocorrelation coefficients for each but finds few significant, consistent with the weak EMH. He also provides evidence on the semi-strong EMH when he regresses B share returns on a number of lagged global financial variables many of which prove to have predictive ability, thus violating the EMH and providing early evidence of the integration of the B share component of the Chinese stock market into global financial markets.

Another paper which focused on traditional tests of the EMH and used data for the early 1990s is the one by Mookerjee and Yu (1999a) which used a sample ending in December 1993. They used daily data for both Shanghai and Shenzhen exchanges but restricted their analysis to indexes for A shares. Their analysis includes both autocorrelation functions and regression of returns on their own past values. They find general evidence of significant autocorrelation in the returns, suggesting the failure of the weak EMH for this period. This conclusion is confirmed by the evidence from the regression analysis. Estimation of equations with both lagged returns and lagged errors shows that for both markets the news captured by the errors takes time to be fully incorporated into returns, thus undermining the weak EMH.

Another paper based on data for the first half of the 1990s is one by Xu (2000) who uses a sample running from the beginning of 1993 to the end of 1995, thus avoiding the early turbulent years of the market. He restricts his data to that from the Shanghai exchange, using both the composite index (covering both A and B shares) and a separate B share index. He examines autocorrelations for both indexes but finds significant effects only for the B share index which exhibits strong positive autocorrelation at the first two lags (using daily data). A regression of current returns on past returns and day-of-the-week (DoW) dummy variables shows no significant autoregressive coefficients for the composite index but a significant first-order autoregressive coefficient for the B share index, consistent with the findings based on the autocorrelation function. The absence of significant autocorrelations for the composite index is puzzling in the light of Mokerjee and Yu's findings who find such autocorrelations for the Shanghai A index (which dominates the composite index) after May 1992. It is possible that the later sample period used by Xu is influential: Xu omits the early years of Mookerjee and Yu's sample as well as extending the sample to 1995.

3.1.3   Tests of the Random Walk Hypothesis

Liu, Song and Romilly (1997), Long, Payne and Feng (1999) and Darrat and Zhong (2000) test an alternative implication of the weak EMH which is that the (log of) stock prices follow a random walk.[1] Liu, Song and Romilly use daily data for both exchanges (presumably composite indexes) for the period May 1992 to December 1995 and test for a unit root in the log price process using an augmented Dickey-Fuller (ADF) test and then for cointegration

Table 3.1 A summary of empirical literature

Authors(year)	Topic(s)	Data	Method	Results
Bailey (1994)	EMH, SMI	Weekly, individual B share prices, March 1992-March 1993	Correlation coefficients, regression of B returns on global variables	Little autocorrelation; global variables have predictive power
Ma (1996)	A/B	Weekly, 38 companies, August 1992- August 1994	Cross-section and time-series regression	Risk, liquidity and expectations of regulatory changes explain A premium
Hu, Chen, Fok and Huang (1997)	EMH, volatility, SMI	Daily data for ShA and SzA, other markets	Estimate univariate GARCH; test for causality in variance	Little evidence of volatility spillover; China relatively isolated
Liu, Song and Romilly (1997)	EMH	Daily ShC and SzC, May 1992- December 1995	ADF tests, Johansen test and VECM	Cross-market predictability
Chakravarty, Sarkar and Wu (1998)	A/B	Daily matched A, B data for 39 companies, 1994-96	Cross-section regression	Support for asymmetric information explanation of B share discount

Table 3.1 (continued)

Authors(year)	Topic(s)	Data	Method	Results
Chui and Kwok (1998)	EMH, A/B	Daily matched A, B data for 46 firms, January 1993-August 1996	Regression analysis of intertemporal relationship A and B returns	Bi-directional flows but stronger from B to A shares
Mok and Hui (1998)	EMH, A/B	87 A and 22 B IPOs, Shanghai	Regression of underpricing on firms characteristics	Underpricing for A and B but larger for A; partly explained by firm characteristics
Su and Fleisher (1998)	EMH, volatility	Daily, ShA, ShB, SzA, SzB, 1992-December 1996	Autocorrelations, regression of returns on various variables; univariate GARCH Models	Significant autocorrelations and predictability of returns by global financial variables; time-varying volatility
Ang and Ma (1999)	EMH	50 earnings forecasters, 100 stocks, 1993-1995	Compute earnings forecast errors	Errors larger than Hong Kong market
Abdel-Khalik, Wong and Wu (1999)	EMH,A/B	Individual A, B share price data, 1993-95, Shanghai and Shenzhen	Event-study of price reaction to earnings announcement, descriptive analysis of information process	Both A and B shares show lagged adjustment, A share more like foreign markets

Study	Topic	Data	Method	Findings
Chow, Fan and Hu (1999)	EMH	Time series on 47 individual stocks, 1993-1998	Estimate dividend-discount model with adaptive expectations	Prices react to past prices and past dividends
Long, Payne and Feng (1999)	EMH, price-volume	Weekly ShA, ShB, February 1992-January 1994	Tests for random walk, price-volume regressions	Weak EMH consistent with the data, volume has weak predictive ability, strong contemporaneous price-volume relationship
Mookerjee and Yu (1999a)	EMH	Daily ShA and SzA to end 1993	Tests for autocorrelation and seasonality	Significant autocorrelation in returns, seasonality in Shenzhen and in Shanghai after 1992
Mookerjee and Yu (1999b)	EMH	Daily ShC and SzC to April 1994	Test for seasonalities	No consistent evidence of seasonal effects
Su and Fleisher (1999)	A/B, volatility	Daily matched A and B share prices for 24 firms	Estimate mixture of distribution models for each A and B return	Find A shares more volatile, related to intensity of information arrival
Darrat and Zhong (2000)	EMH	Weekly ShA, ShB, SzA, SzB, 1990-1998	Test for random-walk hypothesis using variance-ratio and forecast tests	Variance-ratio tests support random walk but forecast tests do not

Table 3.1 (continued)

Authors(year)	Topic(s)	Data	Method	Results
Huang, Yang and Hu (2000)	SMI	Daily data for ShA, SzA, Taiwan, Hong Kong, Japan, US 1992- June 1997	Pairwise cointegration tests and Granger causality tests	Only ShA and SzA are cointegrated; evidence of Granger causality particularly from the US
Lee and Rui (2000)	Returns/ volume	Daily data to December 1997 on ShA, ShB, SzA and SzB	Regression of returns on volume and lagged volume; also uses US and Hong Kong data	Strong contemporaneous relationship returns and volume; only weak predictability of returns on the basis of volume
Poon and Fung (2000)	volatility	Daily data 1994-June 1997 ShC, SzC, red chip and H shares	Estimate univariate and multivariate GACH models	Asymmetry in volatility response to good and bad news but little evidence of volatility spillover
Sjöö and Zhang (2000)	A/B	Weekly data on 41 matched A and B shares, 1993-1997	Cointegration and VECM between A and B share indexes for Shanghai and Shenzhen	Cointegration; long-run information flow from B to A in Shanghai and A to B in Shenzhen
Chen, Kwok and Rui (2001)	EMH	Daily data for ShA, ShB, SzA, SzB 1992 -1999	Regressions to test for DoW effects	Some evidence for negative Tues effects but sensitive to model and sample

Study	Topic	Method	Findings
Sun and Tong (2000)	A/B	Panel regression for B share discount	Support for the differential-demand hypothesis but other factors also significant (risk, liquidity and macro factors)
Xu (2000)	EMH, return/volume, volatility/volume	Autoregressions and DoW for returns and volatility; regression of volatility on volume	Strong autoregression in volatility but not in returns, bi-directional causality between volume and volatility for ShC but not for ShB
Yeh and Lee (2000)	SMI, volatility	VARs in cross-country returns; country-by-country GJR- GARCH	Evidence of asymmetric response to good and bad news; evidence of interrelationships in returns with HK
Chen, Lee and Rui (2001)	A/B	Dynamic panel model for B share discount depending on risk, liquidity and supply differences, decompose share prices into fundamental and non-fundamental components	Discount depends on all three factors, B share prices move closer to fundamentals than A shares do; A shares are over-priced

Table 3.1 (continued)

Authors(year)	Topic(s)	Data	Method	Results
Bergstrom and Tang (2001)	A/B	Quarterly data 1995-August 1999 for 79 matched A, B shares	Panel model of B share discount in terms of variables for liquidity, information, diversification, size and share supplies	All variables found to be significant
Fernald and Rogers (2002)	A/B	Annual data for 57 matched A and B shares, 1993-1997	Panel model for various measures of B share discount	Discount can be explained by differences in discount rates between domestic and foreign investors as well as more conventional factors such as risk and liquidity
Johnson and Soenen (2002)	SMI	Daily data for 13 Asian stock markets including China for 1988-1998	Compute measures of contemporaneous relations which are explained by macroeconomic variables in pooled regression	Relation measure influenced by inflation, growth, trade, interest rates and foreign direct investment but not exchange rates
Kang, Liu and Ni (2002)	EMH	Weekly data for 268 individual firms for 1993-2000	Forms portfolios based on past returns and assess subsequent profitability	Evidence that 30% of portfolios show profits based on contrarian or momentum strategies

Friedmann and Sanddorf-Kohle (2002)	volatility	Daily data for 1992-1999 for ShA, ShB, ShC, SzA, SzB, SzC	Estimate EGARCH and GJR-GARCH models of asymmetric volatility	Both models fit well but different parameter values reflect market segmentation
Pretorius (2002)	SMI	Quarterly data, 10 emerging markets including China, 1995-2000	Compute pairwise correlation coefficients which are then regressed on macro variables	Differences in correlations depend on trade and differences in growth rates
Jun, Marathe and Shawky (2003)	return-turnover	Monthly data for 27 countries (including China) for 1992-1999	Individual country regression and panel regression of return on various measures of liquidity including volume and turnover	Strong positive relation between return and liquidity
van der Hart, Slagter and van Dijk (2003)	EMH	Monthly data for 32 emerging markets (including China) 1985-1999	Forms portfolios on the basis of past values of factors such as P/E, book-to-market and size and assess subsequent profitability	Many of the standard factors such as P/E book-to-market and size are predictors of future profitability

Notes: EMH = Efficient Markets hypothesis, SMI = share market interrelationships, A/B = relationship between A and B share prices or returns, ShA = index of Shanghai A share prices, ShB = index of Shanghai B share prices, ShC = Shanghai composite share price index, SzA = index of Shenzhen A share prices, SzB = index of Shenzhen B share prices, SzC = Shenzhen composite share price index.

using the Johansen procedure. They find that the price process for each market contains a unit root and that the two price series are cointegrated. They subsequently estimate a vector error-correction model which they use for testing causation between returns in one market and returns in the other. They find that there is causation in both directions. The univariate (unit-root) results support the weak form of the EMH (although, as Darrat and Zhong point out, a unit root is only a necessary and not a sufficient condition for a random walk), while the causality results are inconsistent with the semi-strong form of the EMH since they imply that current returns can be forecast using lagged returns from the other market.

The work by Long, Payne and Feng (1999) also uses data from the early history of the Chinese market – for Shanghai from early 1992 until January of 1994, using weekly data on A and B shares. They test for a random walk using both the ADF test and the variance-ratio test of Lo and MacKinlay (1988). They find some weak evidence of departures from the EMH at short lags but conclude that overall the EMH in its weak form is not inconsistent with the data. This is confirmed by other (unreported) tests: a runs test and a regression of returns on their own past values also fails to reject the weak EMH.

Darrat and Zhong (2000) use daily data for only A shares for both Shanghai and Shenzhen for the period till October 1998. They use the daily data to construct weekly indexes to avoid the problems of thin trading which they argue may bias results in daily data. They approach the testing of the random-walk hypothesis in two ways. First they use the variance-ratio test both with and without adjustment for heteroskedasticity. At short lags they find evidence of departures from a random walk although this evidence disappears at longer lags, a conclusion which is consistent with that reached by Long, Payne and Feng for an earlier sample period. Darrat and Zhong conclude that the variance-ratio test results are ambiguous and do not constitute convincing evidence against the EMH and go on to a more direct test, viz., one based on prediction: if the random-walk hypothesis is true then the best predictor of next period's return is the current return. Darrat and Zhong therefore confront this (naïve) prediction model with more sophisticated ones: autoregressive-integrated-moving-average (ARIMA), generalized-autoregressive-conditional-heteroskedasticity (GARCH) and artificial-neural-network (ANN) models. They find that particularly the ANN model can consistently out-predict the naïve model so providing evidence against the random-walk version of the weak EMH.

3.1.4 Seasonality

A second set of tests carried out by Mookerjee and Yu (1999a) and one that has been extensively applied to other stock markets is to test for seasonalities which occur when returns are systematically greater or smaller on certain days of the week, weeks or months of the year, or around public holidays.

These seasonal effects are inconsistent with the weak EMH since they can be used to predict excess returns from which profits could be made. Mookerjee and Yu find significant weekend and holiday effects for the Shenzhen market but not for returns based on the Shanghai A share index although the finding for Shanghai is restricted to the period of price limits – when the tests are run for the period after price limits were removed (after May 1992) they found significant evidence of all three effects: weekend, holiday and January effects. Thus during this early period of the development of the two Chinese stock exchanges there was pervasive evidence of departures from the weak EMH. In contrast to these findings, Xu (2000), who used somewhat later data, found no significant DoW effects in his autoregressions of returns for either the B share index or the composite index.

Mookerjee and Yu (1999b), in a companion paper to their paper discussed above, examine the question of seasonal effects more thoroughly. They examine daily data for a longer period (ending April, 1994) and consider both exchanges, using data for the composite index in each case. They estimate DoW, monthly and quarterly effects in a regression framework. They find only mixed evidence for a DoW effect with the highest returns occurring on Thursdays; Shanghai shows no significant DoW effects before May 1992 and Shenzhen exhibits only a weak Thursday effect for the whole period. They find no evidence of a turn-of-the-month or turn-of-the-quarter effects for either market. Thus, their more thorough examination of seasonalities in Chinese stock market data for the early 1990s shows little evidence for the two composite indexes and this is consistent with Xu's findings discussed above and there is little to suggest that, as far as seasonalities are concerned, there are significant departures from the weak EMH.

The DoW seasonality was further examined by Chen, Kwok and Rui (2001) who used daily data for both exchanges from the beginning of 1992 to the end of 1997 and examined both A and B share indexes separately rather than using the less satisfactory composite index.[2] They find little evidence of the DoW effect before 1995 but there is generally some evidence of a negative Tuesday effect after 1995. This result is confirmed when only the Tuesday dummy variable is retained but is weakened when a GARCH effect is allowed for in the residuals of the testing equation to account for non-normality which undermines the standard tests. It is further weakened when US and Hong Kong stock prices are allowed to influence Chinese stock prices on the argument that the negative Tuesday effect in China may simply reflect the negative Monday effect in overseas markets. Chen, Kwok and Rui conclude that while there is evidence of a DoW effect in Chinese stock returns, this effect is not very robust, particularly to the introduction of the influence of foreign stock markets. It may, therefore, simply reflect Chinese reaction to overseas events and the finding that the DoW effect is apparently stronger after 1995 suggests that Chinese integration into world financial markets has gained pace over the decade. Chen, Kwok and Rui conclude that there is little robust evidence for a DoW effect and that such effect as there is would certainly not provide the basis for profitable trading after taking transactions costs into account.

3.1.5   Tests of Trading Rules

A newly emerging literature which also throws light on the EMH includes papers which evaluate stock trading rules which, according to the EMH should not generate excess returns. These studies require time-series data on individual share prices and, in some cases, firm characteristics. Such a substantial data requirement probably accounts for the slower emergence of these studies. These papers are of two types. The first uses past return performance to form portfolios, the returns from which are then evaluated against some benchmark – these follow the work of Lo and MacKinlay (1990). The second uses information on firm characteristics such as past earnings/price ratios and follow the seminal paper by Fama and French (1993) which evaluated portfolios formed on the basis of firm characteristics other than its beta coefficient. While such studies are generally not included in the EMH category but are generally seen as tests of asset-pricing models, in particular the capital asset-pricing model (CAPM), they can be seen as throwing light on the weak and semi-strong EMH since they test whether publicly available information can be used to predict stock prices and therefore make returns in excess of the market return.

The paper by Kang, Liu and Ni (2002) is of the first type. They form portfolios on the basis of firms' past performance to test a contrarian trading strategy that portfolios composed of stocks which have performed poorly in the past will outperform the market over some future holding period and the momentum strategy that stocks which have performed well in the past will continue to perform better than the market. They use weekly data from January 1993 to January 2000 on A share prices for up to 268 firms per year and compute tests over a variety of initialization and holding periods. They follow Lo and MacKinlay (1990) in forming portfolios of individual shares according to their recent performance, with winner portfolios being formed from those stocks which over the recent past have performed in excess of the market and loser portfolios being composed of those which have performed poorly over the recent past. They find that there are significant differences between returns to winner and loser portfolios at some horizons – approximately 30 per cent of various combinations of ranking and holding horizons show significant differences with contrarian strategies being successful at short horizons (previous losers outperforming winners) and momentum strategies being successful at intermediate horizons (previous winners continuing to outperform the market). These results are in violation of the weak form of the EMH in that they show that past performance can be used to form profitable portfolios although the evidence is relatively weak in that at many horizons performance between winners and losers was insignificant.

A study of the second type is the one by van der Hart, Slagter and van Dijk (2003) which is more extensive than the Kang, Liu and Ni work, both in that it covers a large number of emerging markets (including China) and in that a number of firm characteristics are used as the basis for portfolio formation rather than relying only on information on past performance. They use monthly data for 32 emerging markets from 1985 to 1999 to form portfolios chosen from stocks from all countries on the basis of past values of firm-specific characteristics which have been found successful in studies of developed markets such as earnings/price ratios, book-to-market ratios and firm size as well as past performance. They show that many of these factors which have been found to be relevant for stock pricing in developed markets are also priced in emerging markets although, when country-specific results are shown, the strategies prove not to be significantly profitable if choice is restricted to Chinese stocks. Nevertheless, from our perspective of the EMH, they show that the semi-strong form of the EMH is violated in these markets as a whole.

3.1.6 Miscellaneous Tests

A paper which is only indirectly related to market efficiency is one by Ang and Ma (1999) which assesses the transparency of the Chinese stock market, i.e., the facility with which information about firms is available and can be processed by market participants. They do this by comparing the forecast errors made by analysts forecasting Chinese firms' earnings to those made in forecasting earnings on related emerging markets of the Asia-Pacific region. They use data on forecasts by 50 forecasters for 100 stocks listed on the Chinese stock exchanges over the period 1993-1995 and compare forecast errors to those for Hong Kong and other countries reported by other researchers. They find that the errors in forecasts made by Chinese analysts of Chinese firms' earnings are approximately twice as large as those for the control group, suggesting a much less informationally efficient Chinese market.

The paper by Chow, Fan and Hu (1999) takes a different tack to the ones reviewed so far and attacks the EMH only indirectly. Their purpose is to test the explanatory power of the dividend-discount model using time-series data for a set of 47 stocks listed on the Shanghai exchange for various years from 1993 to 1998. While the dividend-discount model explains stock prices in terms of discounted expected future dividends, Chow, Fan and Hu assumed adaptive expectations so that eventually the real stock price was explained in terms of past prices and past dividends. This makes the results relevant to the semi-strong form of the EMH since, in their formulation of the dividend-discount model, stock prices are explained by their own past values as well as the past values of dividends, information on both of which is readily available. They find strong support for their model implying the violation of both the weak and semi-strong forms of the EMH. This finding must be discounted, however, in the light of the authors' ignoring the issue of stationarity. It is well known that stock prices and dividends are non-stationary so that regressions of stock prices on their own past values and on dividends are likely to be contaminated by common non-stationarity, making the interpretation problematic.

The paper by Abdel-Khalik, Wong and Wu (1999) approaches the EMH via the event-study route. The main focus of this paper is in the tradition of the evaluation of the information content of accounting numbers spawned by Ball and Brown (1968) and is therefore generally outside the scope of this survey. In the course of their discussion, however, they design an event study using Chinese stock market data for 1994 and 1995 to test the reaction of stock prices to the release of accounting information; in particular, information concerning earnings. They hypothesise that since, in contrast to the A share market, the B share market is open to foreign investors and has stricter reporting requirements, information available to investors is likely to be of superior quality so it is more likely to behave in a manner similar to that of developed foreign markets than the A share market is. Stock returns for A and B shares on both the Shanghai and Shenzhen exchanges were observed separately during a window of 32 trading days around an earnings announcement. They found that there was considerable evidence of lagged adjustment to earnings announcements in both markets and for both share types, although the evidence seemed stronger for the Shanghai market. In general, for the years they analysed there was evidence that adjustment to information contained in earnings announcements was not immediate and complete as required by the semi-strong EMH.

Another paper with a different approach which may also be considered to reflect on the EMH is one by Mok and Hui (1998) which analyses the pricing of initial public offerings (IPOs) on the Chinese stock market. IPOs have been the subject of considerable study in the literature on the developed markets. The main puzzle has been the systematic underpricing of IPOs in the sense that in a short period after the IPO begins to trade, predictable returns are generally earned. The work by Mok and Hui shows that this underpricing is very strong on Chinese markets – using information on 87 new issues of A shares and 22 new B share issues over the 1990-93 period, they find that average underpricing of A shares was 289 per cent and that for B shares was 26 per cent. Subsequent regression analysis was able to explain the variation of some but not all of this underpricing across firms; factors which influenced the extent of underpricing are the high equity retention by the state, the long period between offer and listing so that the conclusion must be that, while much of the excess returns are in fact returns to high risk, predictable risk-adjusted excess returns to IPOs could be obtained in violation of the EMH.

In addition to the papers so far surveyed which may be considered to focus largely on the EMH, many other empirical papers include results relevant to the EMH. These are of two types. The first is where evidence relevant to the EMH is incidental to the purpose of the paper such as where initial summary statistics for the data are provided and these summary statistics have implications for the EMH. For example, Su and Fleisher (1998) focus on the nature of volatility in the Chinese stock market but begin with a presentation of summary statistics for the data they use, included in which are Q*(p)*-statistics for tests of the joint significance of the first *p* autocorrelations. Su and Fleisher present Q(12) statistics which show that there is significant autocorrelation in all of Shanghai A and B and Shenzhen A and B share returns at a daily frequency for the period running from the beginning of trading in each market to the end of 1996. Moreover, they show that A and B share returns are significantly related to a range of lagged global financial variables, suggesting a violation of the semi-strong EMH. Many other papers report similar evidence.[3]

The other type which provides evidence relevant to the EMH includes papers for which the main finding may be interpreted in the light of the EMH. Thus papers which explore the intertemporal inter-relationships between the prices of A and B shares may be seen as relating to the semi-strong version of the EMH since a finding that, e.g., A share price changes lead to B share price changes is inconsistent with the semi-strong EMH.[4] Similarly, the literature which examines the relationship between the two Chinese markets and other stock markets in Asia and elsewhere may be seen in the light of the EMH where they find that returns in one market Granger-cause returns in another since such a finding is inconsistent with the no-predictability implication of the EMH.[5] Such papers will be reported under their own respective headings where the implications for the EMH will be briefly drawn out.

To sum up, traditional tests based on autocorrelations, regressions of returns on their own past values and seasonal effects produce only scattered evidence of predictability and, moreover, such predictability as is also commonly observed in developed markets. Standard tests of the random-walk version of the weak EMH are relatively weak tests and, moreover, show mixed results although the forecast-based tests of Darrat and Zhong (2000) provide more convincing evidence on predictability. Similarly, the miscellaneous papers on trading rules, event studies and IPOs are not extensive enough to warrant firm conclusions. Added to these mixed results is the criticism, which also plagues most studies of developed markets, that transactions costs have not been taken into account; in particular Fama (1991) emphasized the arbitrage basis of the EMH and that profits in excess of transactions costs must be adduced to overturn the EMH. Given that transactions costs in China are likely to have been high in the first decade of its operation and particularly so in the first years, there is no convincing evidence of substantial violation of the EMH in this market and, such evidence as there is, is certainly no stronger than exists for more developed markets.

3.2   THE RELATIONSHIP BETWEEN A AND B SHARE PRICES

The strict separation of the markets for A and B shares has been the feature of the Chinese stock market which has arguably attracted the most attention since it has provided a unique opportunity to analyse price formation for ostensibly identical assets in strictly segregated markets.[6]

The main question prompted by the A-B market segregation is whether shares in the same company traded on the two markets command the same price as they should under the simple dividend-discount model of share-pricing in which the price of the share is the present discounted value of expected future dividends. Since the rights attached to the shares are the same whether they are traded as A or B shares (but it's not always clear what these rights are!) they should trade for the same price in the two markets. But they do not. Indeed, there is a well documented, persistent and substantial discount for B shares or premium for A shares: e.g., Bergstrom and Tang (2001) report that the B share discount was around 40 per cent in mid-1997 although it had fallen to around 25 per cent by the end of the 1990s.

There has been theoretical (and empirical) work on pricing in segregated asset markets that pre-dates the Chinese stock market (see, e.g., Errunza and Losq, 1985; Eun and Janakiramanan, 1986; and Alexander, Eun and Janakiramanan, 1987). Explanations which have been offered for price differentials include an equilibrium argument that foreign and domestic owners have different diversification opportunities and therefore different discount rates; the argument that the investors in the two markets have different tastes for risk; the argument that the premium reflects different demand elasticities for shares by the two classes of buyers so that firms price-discriminate; and that the different classes of buyers have different information about the firms' prospects and so value the shares differently. The availability of data for this tightly segregated market provided the ideal opportunity for testing these hypotheses.

Other questions raised in the context of the segregated market concern the information diffusion between the two markets, the different behaviour of IPO prices in the A and B markets and, more recently, the behaviour of volatility in the two markets. We consider empirical work that has contributed to the analysis of each of these questions in turn.

3.2.1   The Determinants of the A-B Differential

Ma (1996) addressed the question of the explanation for the A share premium within the context of a model that permits five explanations for the price differential: costs of capital differences, different risk attitudes, differences in liquidity in the two markets, differences in diversification possibilities for the two groups of investors and different reactions to possible future regulatory changes. He confronts this model with weekly data for 38 companies which list both A and B shares for the two-year period, August 1992 to August 1994. He carries out both cross-section and time-series analysis. In the cross-section analysis he regresses the average price differential on variables which are designed to capture risk and liquidity, both of which play some part in the explanation of the price differential although significance is often marginal. In the time-series model he investigates the intertemporal behaviour of the A premium; he finds that there is a strong correlation between individual company A share premia over time, that the premia are non-stationary (although he uses only two years of data) and that the premium shifted when the Chinese government implemented regulatory changes. Thus, there is evidence (although relatively weak) that risk and liquidity differences and expectations of future regulatory changes influenced the A share premium for the 1992-1994 period.

Chakravarty, Sarkar and Wu (1998) use daily data for 39 matched A and B shares for the period 1994-1996 to test the hypothesis that the A share premium reflects informational asymmetries. They observe that, for their sample period, the discount for B shares averaged about 60 per cent, that correlations between returns to A shares on the two exchanges was high and that the correlation between returns on B shares was lower although significant but that there was little correlation of B share returns with foreign share returns such as those on the Hong Kong, Japanese and US exchanges. In their cross-section analysis they regress the B share discount on a range of variables designed to capture the implication of their model that explains the discount in terms of informational asymmetries as well as control variables for other characteristics of the two share classes. Their informational asymmetry hypothesis is that B shares trade at a discount because there is better information available to foreign investors than to domestic investors and they test this hypothesis by constructing a variable which measures the frequency of a company's being mentioned in the Wall Street Journal. They find that this information variable has a significant effect on the B discount but that other variables also have a significant impact, viz., variables which reflect the different risk characteristics of the two classes of shares, company size and the relative numbers of A and B shares outstanding. It is clear therefore that there are multiple explanations, of which the informational asymmetry argument championed by Chakravarty, Sarkar and Wu is only one.

Sun and Tong (2000) find evidence of the differential demand explanation of the B share discount, i.e., that the lower price simply reflects a smaller demand (relative to supply) by foreign buyers than by domestic buyers for shares in the same company. They investigate this hypothesis by noting that foreigners have alternative means to gain exposure to Chinese stocks, viz., H and "Red-Chip" shares where the former are shares in Chinese companies listed on the Hong Kong exchange and Red-Chip shares are shares in Hong Kong companies (listed on the Hong Kong exchange) which have a substantial part of their business in mainland China. Sun and Tong use monthly data over the period April 1994 to February 1998 for 40 H share firms, 38 Red-Chip share firms, 10 firms which list both A and H shares and 45 firms which list both A and B shares. Using a panel approach they find that the B share discount deepens when there are more substitute shares listed on the Hong Kong exchange thus supporting their differential-demand hypothesis. However, they also find a role for liquidity (relative trading volumes), risk differentials (measured by the ratio of standard deviations in the returns of A and B shares) and differential sensitivities to macro risk factors which may reflect different information flows to domestic and foreign investors.

Bergstrom and Tang (2001) report a comprehensive study on the A-B share price differential. They use quarterly data for the period January 1995 to August 1999 for 79 companies which have both A and B shares listed. In a panel data analysis they include a large number of variables encompassing most of the variables used in the earlier literature: two information variables (following Chakravarty, Sarkar and Wu, 1998), liquidity differences (in terms of both trading volume and spread differentials), differences in the scope for foreign and domestic investors to diversify, size and relative supplies of each type of share. All of these influences are found to contribute significantly to the B share discount.

Chen, Lee and Rui (2001) report work based on panel data for A and B shares for the period 1992-1997 although, in contrast to the study by Bergstrom and Tang, they use daily observations and estimate a dynamic panel model which includes a lagged dependent variable. Further, they use a generalized methods of moments (GMM) estimator rather than the commonly used ordinary least squares (OLS) estimator. They include a range of variables, although not as wide a range as used in some of the earlier papers, including relative supplies to test the differential demand hypothesis, relative trading volumes to test the liquidity hypothesis and relative volatilities to test the differential risk hypothesis. They find empirical support for all hypotheses except for the last although they point out that since the relative volatility variable is a generated regressor, the t-statistic should be interpreted with caution since the coefficient will be biased towards zero. Chen, Lee and Rui go on to an interesting extension in which they decompose share prices for A and B shares into fundamental and non-fundamental components using a decomposition based on work by Campbell and Shiller (1989) and Campbell (1991) in order to answer the question of whether A or B share prices are closer to their fundamentals.[7] They find that B-share prices move closer to their fundamentals suggesting that A shares are over-priced or that the price differential is an A-share premium rather than a B-share discount.

Fernald and Rogers (2002) use data for 57 companies over a sample period similar to the one used by Chen, Lee and Rui, viz. 1993-1997, although the Fernald and Rogers analysis is based on annual rather than daily data. They assert that the magnitude of the A share premium can be explained by plausible differences (of the order of 4 percentage points) in expected rates of return by the two classes of investors, where domestic investors have a lower rate of return than foreign investors because of the limited range of alternative investments available to domestic Chinese investors. In a panel study they find that market location and time dummy variables can explain over 50 per cent of the variation in the relative B share/A share price. They also add a limited number of variables used in previous work and find that risk variables are not significant but that state ownership, and turnover variables are significant, although their introduction does not affect their earlier conclusions.

3.2.2 Information Flows between A and B Shares

All the above papers focused on the question of what determines the differential between prices at which A and comparable B shares trade. Other papers (as well as some of the above) address the related question of the information flows between A and B shares; in particular, whether A share prices cause (usually in the Granger sense) B share prices or vice versa or both. Chen, Lee and Rui (2001) argue that the two issues are related in that if the information asymmetry explanation of the B-share discount is valid, information should flow from the better informed investors (domestic in their case although this choice is not unambiguous) to the less well-informed investors so that the direction of causation is from A to B shares. Chakravarty, Sarkar and Wu (1998), in analysing causation for individual pairs of A and B shares, find evidence of two-way causation between A and B shares although there is a preponderance of flows from A to B shares which they argue is consistent with the asymmetric information flows hypothesis. In contrast, Chui and Kwok (1998) find the opposite and explain this by asserting that foreign investors are better informed than domestic investors. They use daily data for 46 shares from January 1993 to August 1994 and find information flows in both directions but stronger from B to A. Chen, Lee and Rui also test causation (using a standard Granger-causation framework) for individual shares and also find a preponderance of cases where the A price causes the B price again claiming this to be consistent with the asymmetric information hypothesis of the A-B price differential. Sjöö and Zhang (2000) devote their paper to the question of direction of causation. They use a sample period similar to Fernald and Rogers (2002) and Chen, Lee and Rui, viz., 1993-1997, using weekly data on 41 matched A and B shares. Rather than a standard Granger-causation framework in returns, Sjöö and Zhang test for cointegration in average A and B share prices and, finding them to be cointegrated, estimate a vector error-correction model (VECM) from which they conclude that in the long run the information flow is from B to A prices in the Shanghai but from A to B in Shenzhen. Hence, it appears that foreign investors are better informed than domestic investors in the

Shanghai market but vice versa in the smaller and less liquid Shenzhen market.

Another focus on the A-B share differential concentrates on volatility differences between the two markets and the intertemporal relationship, if any, between the volatility for the two classes of shares. Chen, Lee and Rui (2001) also contribute to this question. They see this work as a further test of the asymmetric information hypothesis since volatility has been used in earlier literature to measure the arrival of information. Thus volatility spillover between A and B markets may be indicative of sequential arrival of information. Their test for volatility spillover is similar to that for Granger-causality between returns (although they don't seem to say how the volatility is computed) but their findings are different – they find relatively little evidence of causality in volatility but such causation as there is runs from B to A rather than A to B as they found for returns.

Su and Fleisher (1999) observe that there is a distinct difference in the volatility of A share and B share prices. While other studies have taken this for granted and examined the relationship between the volatilities, Su and Fleisher use a modified mixture of distributions model in returns and trading volume for A and B shares to explain the volatility differences as the result of differences in intensity of information arrival. They use daily data on prices and trading volume for 24 matched companies for a sample period similar to one used in numerous other studies – 1993-1997. They set out a theoretical model of returns and volume and show that differences in information arrival will be reflected in differences in volatility. They therefore use the estimated parameters of the model to explain the greater volatility found in the A share returns.

Furthermore, two papers already surveyed in the previous section throw additional light on A and B share differences. The paper by Mok and Hui (1998) on IPO underpricing compares the extent of underpricing between A and B shares and finds it vastly larger for A shares, even after controlling for various factors that influence the extent of underpricing in both markets. The paper by Abdel-Khalik, Wong and Wu (1999) compares the information environment for A and B shares from the perspective of the literature dealing with the information content of accounting numbers. Their largely descriptive analysis finds that the information environment of B shares is significantly superior to that of A shares. The environment for A shares is informal, unstructured and relies on informal communication between market participants, while that for B shares conforms more to international standards in accounting practices, disclosure, auditing and information dissemination. Moreover, the large financial institutions which purchase B shares are more effective monitors of market events than the many small investors in the A share market.

Finally, Zou (2002) applied a CAPM model to examine market integration between the A and B shares in China. Zou's findings generally reject the hypothesis that the A and B share markets are segmented. However, Zou's conclusions are sensitive to (1) the period during which returns are calculated and (2) whether the companies issue both A and B shares.

In conclusion, the two main issues addressed in the literature surveyed in this section are the determinants of the B share price discount and the related question of the direction of information flows between the two markets. On the first there is a good deal of effective agreement: the important variables are risk differences, liquidity differences, demand differences, discount rate differences, differences in the extent of state ownership and the size of the market. There was some suggestion that in later papers the importance of risk was waning.

On the second question, there are conflicting results with some studies finding bi-directional causation between the two markets, some finding causation from A to B and others from B to A. Moreover, one study found that the direction was different for the Shanghai market than for the Shenzhen market. Such work as there is on the causality of volatility suggest that there is only weak evidence of volatility spillover and that it runs from B to A. The divergence in results no doubt reflects the fact that almost all work involves samples of individual companies and in many cases samples include different companies.

3.3   THE RELATIONSHIPS BETWEEN THE CHINESE STOCK MARKET AND OTHER STOCK MARKETS

There has been an explosion of empirical work which analyses the interrelationships between national share markets since early studies such as those by Eun and Shim (1989) over a decade ago. The information afforded by such studies is of interest not only in its own right but it also throws light on the semi-strong EMH since if there is causation running from one stock market to another there is predictability on the basis of publicly-available information which, *prima facie*, is evidence against the EMH. Moreover, the gains from international diversification are crucially dependent on the extent to which stock markets move together, thus providing another impetus to the study of such inter-relationships. The study of the relationships between the Chinese exchanges and the rest of the world financial market is of further interest since the Chinese market has been relatively isolated – foreign investors and domestic investors were until recently strictly segregated so that there were relatively few opportunities for the sort of arbitrage activity which is commonly seen as connecting other national stock markets. This raises the question of whether this has resulted in only weak relationships between the Chinese and other markets or whether the ingenuity of international investors has managed to circumvent the restrictions. These questions concern mainly the relationships between returns in different markets. Recent work has also examined the relationship between volatilities in related markets and we also briefly examine these.

3.3.1   Relationships between Returns

The earliest paper in this area is Bailey (1994). As discussed above, he considers the one-way dependence of Chinese stock returns on past values of a set of global financial variables and finds that the latter have significant predictive content for a range of B share returns, indicating that at least the B shares are not completely isolated from world financial markets even in the early years of the Chinese stock market development .

More recently, Huang, Yang and Hu (2000) use the tools of cointegration and Granger causality to examine the inter-relationships between the stock markets of the US, Japan and the "South China Growth Triangle" consisting of Shanghai, Shenzhen, Hong Kong and Taiwan. They examine the relationships between the A share indexes for the two mainland Chinese exchanges and those for Hong Kong and Taiwan using daily data for the period October 1992 to June 1997. They begin by testing for unit roots in all (log) price series using the ADF method as modified by Zivot and Andrews (1992) which allows for breaks in trend and level at points in the sample which need not be pre-specified. They find that with the exception of Taiwan the prices are all integrated of order 1, i.e. I(1). Pairwise tests for cointegration lead them to conclude that no pairs of indexes are cointegrated with the exception of the Shanghai and Shenzhen. Consequently, they proceed to an analysis of Granger causality in terms of returns except when considering Shanghai and Shenzhen together. Their results indicate that there is causation from the US to both Hong Kong and Taiwan (but not to Shanghai) and from Hong Kong to Taiwan. Thus Shanghai does not appear to have a causal effect on any of the other markets or to be affected by them in turn, suggesting relative isolation from world stock markets. For the two cointegrated markets of Shanghai and Shenzhen, the authors estimate a vector error-correction model (VECM) which indicates a two-way relationship between returns in the two markets. The results show that the two Chinese markets are closely integrated but relatively isolated from the rest of the world (as measured by the US and Japanese markets).

In an interesting recent paper Pretorius (2002) not only asks whether there have been interrelationships between stock markets but examines the economic determinants of such interdependence. He uses quarterly stock price index data for 10 emerging markets including China for the period 1995-2002. He estimates quarterly correlation coefficients for each pair of countries and uses these in a second stage panel estimation of the correlations on a range of macroeconomic variables. He finds the correlations to vary across countries and over time and that the variation depends on the extent of bilateral trade between the two countries, the differential in growth rates of industrial production and regional dummy variables with the model explaining approximately 40 per cent of the variation in correlations.

A paper with a partly similar aim is one by Johnson and Soenen (2002). They use daily data for the period 1988-1998 for 13 Asian markets including a single index for China to examine the extent to which these markets are integrated with the Japanese market as the dominant developed market in the region and the factors which determine the extent of integration. Rather than using the correlation measure of integration used by Pretorius or measures of causality based on the vector-autoregressive (VAR) model commonly used in the literature, Johnson and Soenen use a measure of contemporaneous relation due to Geweke (1982). They then use annual measures of integration for each country pair to run a pooled cross-section-time-series regression on a range of macroeconomic variables including ones measuring the importance of each country in the other's trade, inflation differentials, interest rate differentials, exchange rate variations, exchange rate volatility, growth rate differentials and the importance of foreign direct investment in the pair's relationship. They find that most of these variables are significant determinants of the extent of integration – the main exceptions are the two exchange rate variables.

3.3.2 Relationships between Volatilities

Empirical work on the inter-relationships between the Chinese market and other markets has considered not only the relationship between returns but also between volatilities. A paper which straddles both of these strands of the literature is the one by Yeh and Lee (2000) which estimates and compares single-country models of volatility (concentrating on asymmetric responses to good and bad news) and then estimates standard VARs in returns to assess the inter-relationship between returns (but not volatilities). Their subject is the "greater China" region comprising Taiwan, Hong Kong, Shanghai and Shenzhen. They use daily data for the period May 1992 to August 1996 and for the Chinese markets they use both the composite indexes (including both A and B shares) as well as the B share indexes separately. For each index they estimate a univariate generalized autoregressive conditional heteroskedasticity (GARCH) model modified along the lines of Glosten, Jagannathan and Runkle (GJR) (1993) to allow for the asymmetric response of volatility to positive and negative errors (good and bad news). They find evidence of asymmetric responses to good and bad news across the region but, interestingly, that the Chinese markets behave differently to the others – while Hong Kong and Taiwan show greater volatility responses to bad news, the Chinese markets respond more strongly to good news. The second part of their analysis consists of a standard VAR analysis of the returns of the four markets, using the B share indexes for the Chinese markets. They find that Hong Kong is the dominant market in the group.

The paper by Poon and Fung (2000) extends the analysis of the type carried out by Yeh and Lee (2000) by not only estimating univariate volatility models but also their multivariate counterparts to assess the extent of volatility spillover. Like Yeh and Lee, they also allow for asymmetry in the GARCH model although they do this not by using the GJR variant but the exponential GARCH (EGARCH) model. Also, in contrast to the Yeh and Lee analysis, they concentrate on Hong Kong-based H shares and Red Chip shares as the foreign shares. For China they use the Shanghai and Shenzhen composite indexes. Data used is daily from August 1994 to June 1997. The volatility spillover is modelled in a multivariate EGARCH model using a two-stage estimation procedure. There is only limited evidence of spillover or volatility from one market to another although there is widespread evidence that returns in one market affect those in another as has been found in earlier research.

Finally in this group of papers, the study by Hu, Chen, Fok and Huang (1997) uses a technique devised by Cheung and Ng (1996) to test for causality in variance (in contrast to causality in mean or return) between the two developed markets of the US and Japan and the four markets of the South China Growth Triangular (*sic*) comprising Hong Kong, Taiwan, Shanghai and Shenzhen (for the last two using A share price indexes). They begin, as many other studies do, by examining the behaviour of returns in individual markets, in this case the autocorrelation function and the stationarity of the individual series as well as estimating a GARCH model for each market individually. They then apply the Cheung and Ng test for causality in the variance. They find only limited evidence of causality in the second moments; in particular, there is no causality from any market to either of the two mainland Chinese markets and in only one case does a Chinese variance cause one in another market which is from the Shanghai market to the Hong Kong market at a lag of three days. Indeed, of the 150 t-statistics for significant causation in variance reported, only 6 (or 4 per cent) are significant, not much more than the nominal size of the test.

In conclusion, there have been relatively few studies of the inter-relationships between the Chinese stock exchanges and those in the rest of the world. Early work by Bailey (1994) showed strong evidence of a response of Chinese returns to foreign financial variables but this has not found support in subsequent work, explained, no doubt, by the fact that Bailey used data only for B shares which are traded by foreign investors and which are thus more likely to be influenced by global factors. Two studies of volatility spillover confirm the conclusion of the relative isolation of the Chinese exchanges for the first decade of their existence and it will be interesting to observe whether these results change as the strict segregation begins to break down in the second decade of their operation.

3.4   VOLATILITY

In this section we will look specifically at papers which focus on volatility in the Chinese stock market. Several papers have already been mentioned which analyse volatility either in conjunction with another topic or in the context of volatility spillovers from one market to another. Thus, both Su and Fleisher (1998) and Su and Fleisher (1999) have been mentioned above, the first as making a contribution to the analysis of the EMH and the second throwing light on the relationship between A and B share returns. Both papers also consider volatility. The Su and Fleisher (1998) paper focuses on the estimation of time-varying volatility using a GARCH framework and uses the model to investigate the effect on volatility of changes in the regulatory environment of the Chinese stock market. They found evidence that the removal of daily price limits significantly increased volatility but there is little evidence that other regulatory changes had a significant effect on volatility in either market.

The Su and Fleisher (1999) paper has been discussed in the context of the relationship between A and B shares since it focuses on the difference in volatilities of the two markets which it explains in terms of differences in the intensity of information arrival. So, also the Chen, Lee and Rui (2001) study examines the causal relationship between volatility in China's A and B markets. They find little causation in volatility for individual shares across the two markets although such causation as there is tends to be from the B market to the A market suggesting that price movements start in the market more open to foreign influences.

In addition, the paper by Friedman and Sanddorf-Kohle (2002) appears to be the only one which focuses solely on volatility. It estimates two variants of the ubiquitous GARCH model to capture time-varying volatility, viz. the exponential GARCH (EGARCH) and the variant due to Glosten, Jagannathan and Runkle (1993), the GJRGARCH both of which allow for asymmetric volatility effects so that the conditional variance can respond differently to positive innovations (good news) and negative innovations (bad news). They used daily data for an A share index, a B share index and a composite index for each case of the two markets for the period May 1992 to September 1999. They find that both models are suitable for the characterization of the data for the two markets but that the series for the two markets produce quite different parameter estimates reflecting the market segmentation between the A and B shares.

Song, Jiang and Li (2003) present a study of volatility in the Shenzhen market. It is one of the main studies conducted by researchers inside China. Song et al. applied a GARCH(1,1) model and found that, while the practice of daily price limits reduced volatility in the Shenzhen market, the increase in stamp duty and the floating of insurance companies increases volatility in the market. This conclusion is also drawn in Wu and Xu (2002), another report released inside China. Song et al. also compared the Shenzhen index with S&P500 index and concluded that, after 1997, volatility tended to fall in the Shenzhen market but rise in the S&P500 index. However, in general and in accordance with expectations, the S&P500 index is less volatile than the Shenzhen index.

In conclusion, there is evidence of time-varying volatility in the two markets and differences in the nature of volatility but there is little evidence of spillover of volatility from A to B shares or vice versa. Several studies have used asymmetric volatility models and found strong support for the conjecture that volatility reacts differently to good and bad news.

3.5 PRICE-VOLUME STUDIES

Long, Payne and Feng (1999) carry out two exercises in the price-volume area. As indicated above, they use data only for the Shanghai market but use index data for both A and B shares for the period February 1992 to January 1994. In all cases their price variable is the log first difference in price (and so a continuously compounded return) and the volume measure is the change in log volume and so represents the growth in volume. They run regressions both in lagged form and in contemporaneous form. In running the lagged regressions their intention is to test for causality between price and volume. They find only weak evidence of causality in either direction. They run contemporaneous regressions between price and volume to compare results to similar work for the US. They discover a strong contemporaneous relationship for both A and B shares which is stronger than that usually found in the US.

The paper by Xu (2000) also uses data only on the Shanghai market using the composite index and a B share price index. While Xu does not investigate price-volume relationships, he does consider the effect of volume on volatility in the hope of discovering whether increased trading volume leads to greater volatility. Volatility is measured as the absolute value of the residual from an AR(12) model in returns and this is regressed first on lagged values of itself and current volume. He finds that his measure of volatility has strong DoW effects and modest autoregressive properties, especially at short lags and that for both indexes used, volatility responds positively to current volume even in the presence of autoregressive and DoW terms. As to causation, the results for the composite and B share indexes are strikingly different: for the composite index, there is bi-directional causation between volatility and volume whereas for the B share index there is no causation in either direction.

Lee and Rui (2000) also examine the return-volume relationship. They use daily data from the beginning of the stock exchanges to the end of 1997 for Shanghai A and B and Shenzhen A and B indexes. They first regress returns on contemporaneous volume and find a consistently strong relationship for all series. They then examine the question of whether volume can be used to predict return or vice versa. For these causality tests they also use US and Hong Kong volume data to assess whether they can be used to forecast Chinese returns. They find little evidence of predictability of returns by volume or vice versa either within the Chinese market or in combination with the two overseas markets considered. They conclude that the Chinese market is relatively isolated from the other markets considered.

The paper by Jun, Marathe and Shawky (2003) examines the relationship between stock returns and liquidity where the latter variable is measured in several ways: turnover, trading value and the ratio of turnover to volume. They examine this relationship for a range of 27 emerging markets (including China) using monthly data for the period 1992-1999. They find that, in a panel regression, each of the three measures of liquidity significantly influences returns even after other influences such as the world market return and the exchange rate are taken into account, although the turnover variant has the greatest explanatory power. Both the cross-section and time-series variation in the panel data set appear to contribute to the positive relation between return and turnover when they estimate separate cross-section and time-series regressions.

Thus, in conclusion, return and volume are strongly related contemporaneously but there is little evidence that either can be used to predict the other. There is only mixed evidence of a causal relationship between volume and volatility.

3.6   CONCLUSIONS

This chapter has surveyed the empirical literature on the Chinese stock market, focusing on that dealing with the EMH, the relationship between prices of A and B shares and the relationship of Chinese stock prices to those in other markets.

There is some evidence that the EMH is violated, both in its weak and semi-strong forms, in the Chinese market. However, the evidence is far from unanimous and not greatly different from that found in established markets. Besides, there is no evidence that the inefficiencies observed would produce profitable trading opportunities in the face of transactions costs.

The relationship between the prices of A and B shares was found to be a complex one. In the first place, there has been a substantial and persistent discount for B shares of the order of 20 to 40 per cent depending on the date at which the discount is measured. The discount has been the subject of extensive investigation and the literature indicates that many factors are required to explain it: risk differences, discount rate differences, liquidity differences, differences in the extent of state ownership and size differences.

It will be interesting to observe the development of the discount as the segregation between the markets gradually disappears over time.

The direction of informational flows between A and B markets is not clear, with considerable conflict in the evidence produced, deriving presumably from the differences in the samples of companies covered and the dates over which the prices were observed.

The surveyed literature which dealt with the inter-relationships between the Chinese market and foreign markets indicates that on the whole the Chinese markets have been quite isolated from events in the rest of the global financial environment.

Finally, price-volume studies indicate that there has been a strong contemporaneous relationship between these variables but that there is little in the way of predictability of one by the other.

NOTES

1. That a random walk for (log) stock prices is an implication of the weak EMH is true only under certain simplifying assumptions; see LeRoy (1989).
2. We have shown in the previous chapter that the market structure, liquidity and capitalization of the A and B shares is quite different in both Shanghai and Shenzhen markets. The reasonable prior must therefore be that A and B share prices will behave differently so that it seems unsatisfactory to combine them in a composite index, until, at least, it has been shown that they do behave in a similar manner and can therefore be treated as one.
3. See Huang, Yang and Hu (2000), Poon and Fung (2000) and Hu, Chen, Fok and Huang (1997) *inter alia*.
4. See, e.g., Chakravarty, Sarkar and Wu (1998), Chui and Kwok (1998), Sjöö and Zhang (2000) and Chen, Lee and Rui (2001).
5. See, e.g., Huang, Yang and Hu (2000).
6. See Chapter 2, pp 12-13, for a detailed description of the difference between A and B shares.
7. See also similar analysis for share prices for a range of countries in earlier work by Lee (1995, 1998), Chung and Lee (1998) and Hess and Lee (1999), for instance.

4. Market efficiency

4.1 INTRODUCTION

There is a growing literature demonstrating the importance of the financial system in the process of economic development. The financial system provides a mechanism whereby the resources available for financing new capital expenditure (domestic saving and net capital inflow from abroad) are distributed among competing ends.[1] Competing projects differ both in their expected returns as well as in risk and it has long been a central tenet of financial economics that an efficiently operating financial market optimally balances risk and return in funds allocation. Thus the investigation of the efficiency of financial markets has been an important preoccupation of empirical financial economics and much of the literature has focused on the efficiency of the stock market.

China's stock market is a relatively new but increasingly important part of the Chinese financial system. This system is undergoing a structural shift from a heavily-regulated and almost exclusively bank-based system to one with a much greater diversity of institutions, including a vigorous and increasingly sophisticated stock market. Since their establishment, the two official stock exchanges, the Shanghai Exchange and the Shenzhen Exchange, have expanded rapidly and have operated in a continually changing regulatory environment. China's stock market is now the second largest in Asia, exceeded only by Japan. The speculation is that China's securities market has the potential to rank among the top four or five in the world within the coming decade (Ma and Folkerts-Landau, 2001).

In this chapter we investigate the efficiency of the Chinese stock market. In the literature of financial economics, efficiency has come to take on a specific meaning following, particularly, the work of Fama (1970, 1991). Fama defined efficiency as the ability of the market to rapidly digest new information so that securities' prices would at every point in time incorporate all relevant available information (see Chapter 3 for a review). This has become known as the Efficient Markets Hypothesis (EMH) and an arbitrage argument is used to show that the EMH implies the absence of predictability of asset prices – if prices were predictable, profits could be made on the basis of the predictability, and arbitrage would eliminate these profits in an efficiently operating market. It is this unpredictability implication of the EMH which is most commonly tested in the empirical literature.

In our investigation of the efficiency of the Chinese stock market, we focus on the interplay between market efficiency and changes in regulation. In particular, we examine the impact of the banks on market efficiency. This is an important question since the banks have a traditional and dominant place in the financial system and have for much of the 1990s been important sources of funds (and other influence) for the stock market. Interestingly, there have been two distinct changes of government policy in relation to the banks' role in the stock market and these provide a useful opportunity to assess the implication of the banks for the efficiency of the system in the Fama sense.

Our first objective is to re-examine the weak form of the efficient markets hypothesis (WEMH) using daily Chinese stock market data. While numerous studies have addressed issues in this area in the recent past, there is widespread evidence of departures from market efficiency in the Chinese stock market. This evidence, however, is not unambiguous and may even appear contradictory occasionally. No doubt a large part of the ambiguity is due to the different series used and the different sample periods over which the data were measured. We analyse daily data for seven share price indexes over the period 1992-2001. This large sample provides us with a greater variety of information and should reflect the dramatic changes that have taken place in China's securities sector in the past decade. An interesting component of our data set is the index for the 30 leading shares on the Shanghai exchange, the analysis of which allows us to throw light on the question of the influence of thin trading on efficiency tests.

Our second objective is to examine the effects of deregulation on the operation of the stock market. This is a recent and rapidly growing body of literature reflecting, no doubt, the rapid changes in the structure of financial sectors throughout the world. For example, Levine (1997) comprises a recent survey, and a broad cross-country analysis, typical of the literature is given in Beck, Levine and Loayza (2000). Recent work by Henry (2000a, 2000b) focuses on deregulation in the stock market but looks at effects which are more general than those on market efficiency. Only the recent paper by Kawakatsu and Morey (1999) examines the relationship between financial liberalization and the EMH. They examine a range of emerging markets which does not, however, include China. Moreover, they use mainly a simple AR(1) model as the framework for efficiency analysis. They find little evidence that deregulation improves the efficiency of the markets in the countries included in their sample.

The Chinese financial system has traditionally been dominated by the state banks and when stock exchanges were established in the early 1990s, the banks were dominant in share trading. Until 1996 banks had a dominant influence on the stock market. Before 1994 most Chinese banks served as brokers since these had yet to appear on the Chinese financial scene. Banks were allowed to set up departments or subsidiaries as brokers but as the Chinese stock markets expanded, the direct involvement of banks became risky and was considered inappropriate. Thus, in 1994 banks were required to quit their direct involvement in the stock market and bank stock-broking departments and subsidiaries became independent broker houses (Lan, 1997). However, banks continued to funnel large amounts of funds into the stock market thus providing substantial part of liquidity. In 1996, regulations were further tightened by preventing banks from offering loans for stock transactions. The aim of these was to encourage independent competitive firms as brokers and sources of funds such as mutual funds independent of the banks. In early 2000 the 1996 regulations were reversed and banks resumed their positions as important sources of funds for stock investment (Surry, 2000). It is likely that these changes in the regulations governing the relationship between the banks and the stock market had effects on the efficiency with which the markets processed information. In section 4.5, we will examine the impact of the changing role of the banks on the EMH. We do this by investigating efficiency over three different sub-periods in which banks were subject to different regulations in so far as their relationship to the stock market was concerned.

Tests of weak efficiency which we use include autocorrelation tests and autoregressive models which are extended to include day-of-the-week (DoW) effects and holiday effects. We also test the random-walk version of the EMH by testing the log of the share price indexes for stationarity.[2] The technical details of these tests are presented in the following section.

4.2 MODELLING ISSUES

Market efficiency has traditionally been associated with the absence of predictability of returns on the grounds that if returns are predictable, profit opportunities exist which profit-maximizing investors will exploit until the predictability disappears. This argument ignores transactions costs since in their presence not all predictability is exploitable. Some authors, therefore, qualify their definition of efficiency to account for this aspect; see, e.g., Fama (1991). A further qualification arises from the potential predictability of the "required return" component of share returns, so that the definition may be couched in terms of predictability of "excess" or "abnormal" returns.

In practice, however, transactions costs and predictability of required returns are typically ignored in tests of the EMH and, for the most part, the work reported below follows this pattern. The relationship between the EMH and tests for predictability is developed using Sharpe's (1983) formulation.

Write the one-period return to an asset, R_t, as the sum of two components, the equilibrium return expected last period (the "required return"), $E_{t-1}(R^e)$, and an unexpected or "abnormal" component, Z_t, i.e.

$$R_t = E_{t-1}(R^e_t) + Z_t \tag{4.1}$$

where

$$E_{t-1}(R^e_t) = E(R^e_t / \psi_{t-1}) \tag{4.2}$$

where Ψ_{t-1} denotes the set of information available to agents at period $t-1$. The condition for market efficiency is then:

$$E(Z_t / \psi_{t-1}) = 0 \tag{4.3}$$

If Ψ_{t-1} contains only past returns, (4.3) becomes

$$E(Z_t / R_{t-1}, \dots, R_{t-n}) = 0 \tag{4.4}$$

and the market is said to be weakly efficient. If Ψ_{t-1} also contains other publicly available information, X (which excludes R), then (4.3) becomes a statement of semi-strong efficiency:

$$E(Z_t / R_{t-1}, \dots, R_{t-n}; X_{t-1}, \dots, X_{t-n}) = 0 \tag{4.5}$$

Finally, if Ψ_{t-1} also contains information, I, which is not publicly available the market is called strongly efficient and (4.3) is written as

$$E(Z_t / R_{t-1}, \dots, R_{t-n}; X_{t-1}, \dots, X_{t-n}; I) = 0 \tag{4.6}$$

This chapter reports tests of both weak and semi-strong efficiency. Consider tests of weak efficiency first. Equation (4.4) suggests an investigation of the relationship between Z_t and past returns. However, Z_t is unobservable, being defined in terms of the unobservable $E_{t-1}(R^e)$ and, as frequently pointed out, all tests of efficiency are necessarily joint tests of a theory of $E_{t-1}(R^e)$ and the EMH. A common and convenient assumption is that $E_{t-1}(R^e) = c$, a constant which enables (4.4) to be written as:

$$E(R_t - c / R_{t-1}, R_{t-2}, \dots, R_{t-n}) = 0 \tag{4.7}$$

This suggests tests of the weak EMH based on an investigation of the intertemporal properties of the series R_t, $R_{t-1}, \dots, R_{t-n}$. We present the results of two such tests which are in essence equivalent. The first involves the autocorrelations of the R process – we report both individual autocorrelations and the Box-Pierce-Ljung portmanteau test that the first p autocorrelations of the R_t process are zero. The second test is based on the regression of R_t on $R_{t-1}, \dots, R_{t-p}$. Both approaches address the question of whether past returns are useful in predicting the current return and therefore clearly fall in Fama's (1991) category of "tests for return predictability". Within the regression framework we also test the DoW effect and the holiday effect since these are common sources of return predictability.

An alternative test of the weak EMH is based on the random-walk property of share prices implied by the EMH and the assumption of constant expected returns.[3] Equation (4.7) allows the model generating R_t to be written:

$$R_t = c + \varepsilon_t \qquad (4.8)$$

Where ε_t is a random error term with $E_{t-1}(\varepsilon_t) = 0$. Writing R_t as the log difference of the price index, P_t, (4.8) becomes:

$$\ln P_t = c + \ln P_{t-1} + \varepsilon_t \qquad (4.9)$$

which, if we further assume that ε_t is white noise, is simply a random walk with drift and suggests the use of a test for a unit root in the $\ln P_t$ process. Two such tests are reported: the augmented Dickey-Fuller (ADF) test and the Phillips-Perron (PP) test[4] which differ only in the way in which they adjust for autocorrelation in the error process of the "Dickey-Fuller equation". We test both a random walk against a stationary alternative and a random walk with drift against the alternative of a trend-stationary process. In the first case we maintain $\beta_2 = 0$ under both H_0 and H_A and test $H_0 : \beta_1 = 0$ and in the second case we test $H_0 : \beta_1 = 0$ and $\beta_2 = 0$ in:

$$\Delta \ln P_t = \beta_0 + \beta_1 \ln P_{t-1} + \beta_2 t + \varepsilon_t \qquad (4.10)$$

4.3   THE DATA

This study uses share-price index data for Chinese stock exchanges in Shanghai and Shenzhen. In particular, we use daily data for closing prices for the following indexes for the indicated sample periods:

(a)   Shanghai A (PSAA), 2/1/1992 – 28/2/2001
(b)   Shanghai B (PSAB), 2/1/1992 – 28/2/2001
(c)   Shanghai 30 Leaders (PSA30), 1/7/96 – 28/2/2001
(d)   Shanghai Composite (PSAC), 3/5/1993 – 28/2/2001
(e)   Shenzhen A (PSEA), 4/10/1992 – 28/2/2001
(f)   Shenzhen B (PSEB), 6/10/1992 – 28/2/2001
(g)   Shenzhen Composite (PSEC), 20/7/1994 – 28/2/2001

The logs of the price indexes are denoted LPSAA, LPSAB, etc.; returns are computed as continuously compounded and denoted RSAA, RSAB. Observations for non-trading days are dropped.

Summary statistics for returns are reported for each of the indexes in Table 4.1. There is considerable variation in average returns across the indexes. Comparing the returns to the two Shanghai shares, RSAA and RSAB, the first is relatively high while the second is actually negative – the index was lower at the end of the sample than it was at the beginning. The higher return to A shares has been commonly observed and various studies have focused on explaining this difference – see, e.g., Chakravarty, Sarkar and Wu (1998) and Chen, Lee and Rui (2001). In contrast, the two Shenzhen shares have approximately equal mean returns of about 0.04 per cent per day, with the A returns actually marginally smaller than the B returns. It is interesting that the Shanghai 30 index has a considerably lower mean return than all A shares for Shanghai suggesting that an important part of the return computed for Shanghai A shares is for small (infrequently traded) shares. This also suggests that the risk (in terms of the standard deviation) associated with these small shares is higher since the standard deviation for RSAA is considerably higher than that for RSA30. We ought to keep in mind, however, that the sample period for the 30 leaders index for Shanghai is considerably shorter than that for all A shares. If we recompute the mean return and standard deviation for the RSAA for the shorter (RSA30) sample period, we obtain a mean of 0.0848 per cent per day and a standard deviation of 1.8891. So, over the common sample period, the full A share return has a considerably higher mean and lower standard deviation that the 30 leaders.

Table 4.1   Summary statistics for returns

Variable	Mean (% daily)	SD (% daily)	Skewness	Excess Kurtosis	Normality (GF)
RSAA	0.0796	3.4870	103.2563	992.4011	1169.1472
RSAB	-0.0139	2.3150	7.7457	49.9392	872.0143
RSEA	0.0426	2.7790	17.0353	133.7490	557.5302
RSEB	0.0402	2.4000	8.4731	71.0714	1762.5728
SA30	0.0584	1.9630	-1.6502	32.7960	327.1039
RSAC	0.0208	2.8920	29.1928	190.6270	874.5896
RSEC	0.0953	2.7860	13.3822	92.9406	498.6027

Notes: The Skewness and Excess Kurtosis statistics are standard-normally distributed under the null of normally distributed returns. The GF statistic is a goodness-of-fit statistic for a test of normality. It is χ^2 distributed with 57 degrees of freedom. The 5% critical value is 79.0819.

The remainder of the columns in Table 4.1 relate to tests of normality of the returns. The skewness and excess kurtosis statistics are standard-normally distributed. All but RSA30 show evidence of significant positive skewness and all returns are leptokurtic. It is not surprising that the GF statistic for normality shows that all the returns are non-normal. This is a common feature of financial data.

4.4 TESTING THE EMH

We begin our examination by presenting the first five autocorrelations (ρ_i) for the returns computed from each of the indexes. They are reported in Table 4.2. Clearly there is significant autocorrelation in the returns although there is considerable variety amongst the indexes. Only in the 30 Leaders index is there no evidence of autocorrelation, this presumably reflects the high liquidity of these stocks. The two A returns show some evidence of autocorrelation but it is relatively weak, with the autocorrelation coefficient never exceeding 5 per cent. The B returns, on the other hand, show much stronger evidence of autocorrelation with the correlation at the first lag being approximately 20 per cent for both indexes. There is further autocorrelation at longer lags particularly for the Shenzhen index. Finally, the two composite indexes exhibit autocorrelation behaviour similar to that of the A shares as one would expect given that the composite indexes cover both A and B stocks. A comparison of the results suggests that the autocorrelation could well be the result of thin trading since it is most evident in the indexes for the most illiquid stocks (the two B stocks) and absent altogether for the 30 leaders on the Shanghai exchange.

The autocorrelations reported above are generally considerably smaller than those reported for the US and Asian countries by Bailey et al. (1990) where first-order autocorrelations in daily data of the order of 0.1 to 0.3 are common although these were for an earlier time period and for shorter periods. The autocorrelations reported in Table 4.2 are confirmed by the regression results in Table 4.3 where we report the results of estimating an AR(5) model for each of the returns.

As with the autocorrelations, there is by far the most predictability in the returns for the B shares – both RSAB and RSEB have coefficients of around 0.2 on the first lagged value with very high t-ratios, and in both cases at least one subsequent lag is significant. Despite this, the value of R^2 is quite low at about 5%. There is some evidence of significant predictability for the A returns but both the estimated lag coefficients and the values of R^2 are lower. There is no evidence of predictability in the return for the 30 leaders for Shanghai. The sum of the lag coefficients is significant for all but the 30 leaders index and (surprisingly) the composite index for the Shanghai exchange. Regressions with longer lags show very similar results – most of the predictability appears to occur at short lags.

A common violation of the weak EMH is the presence of a DoW effect or the "holiday effect" and the next question we address is whether these effects are present in any of our seven indexes. We begin by adding DoW dummy variables to the regressions reported in Table 4.3. The DoW dummy variables are defined as: "Monday" =1 on Mondays and 0 otherwise etc. Since

Table 4.2   Autocorrelations

Return	ρ_1	ρ_2	ρ_3	ρ_4	ρ_5	Q(5)
RSAA	0.05 (0.02)	0.05 (0.02)	0.04 (0.02)	0.03 (0.02)	0.04 (0.02)	20.99 (0.001)
RSAB	0.19 (0.02)	0.00 (0.02)	0.05 (0.02)	0.01 (0.02)	-0.01 (0.02)	87.69 (0.000)
RSEA	0.02 (0.02)	0.05 (0.02)	0.01 (0.02)	0.05 (0.02)	0.03 (0.02)	14.69 (0.012)
RSEB	0.20 (0.02)	0.07 (0.02)	0.11 (0.02)	0.09 (0.02)	0.05 (0.02)	135.40 (0.000)
RSA30	0.02 (0.03)	-0.01 (0.03)	0.02 (0.03)	0.04 (0.03)	0.01 (0.03)	2.80 (0.73)
RSAC	-0.02 (0.02)	0.03 (0.02)	0.03 (0.02)	0.02 (0.02)	0.03 (0.02)	6.23 (0.284)
RSEC	0.06 (0.02)	0.04 (0.02)	0.03 (0.02)	0.01 (0.02)	0.07 (0.02)	18.57 (0.002)

Note: The numbers in parentheses under the autocorrelations are standard errors and under the Q statistics are *p-values*.

Table 4.3 *Regression tests of weak efficiency*

Regressor	Dependent Variable						
	RSAA	RSAB	RSEA	RSEB	RSA30	RSAC	RSEC
Lag 1	0.0471	0.2025	0.0152	0.1814	0.0116	-0.0177	0.0573
	(2.22)	(9.50)	(0.69)	(8.20)	(0.39)	(0.78)	(2.31)
Lag 2	0.0464	-0.0504	0.0487	0.0106	-0.0110	0.0193	0.0362
	(2.18)	(2.32)	(2.21)	(0.47)	(0.37)	(0.85)	(1.46)
Lag 3	0.0335	0.0616	0.0069	0.0822	0.0080	0.0283	0.0229
	(1.57)	(2.84)	(0.31)	(3.67)	(0.27)	(1.25)	(0.93)
Lag 4	0.0180	-0.0063	0.0490	0.0482	0.0421	0.0145	-0.0025
	(0.82)	(0.29)	(2.22)	(2.14)	(1.43)	(0.64)	(0.10)
Lag 5	0.0321	-0.0054	0.0319	0.0211	0.0042	0.0301	0.0704
	(1.51)	(0.25)	(1.45)	(0.95)	(0.14)	(1.33)	(2.85)
Constant	0.0006	-0.0001	0.0004	0.0003	0.0004	0.0003	0.0008
	(0.88)	(0.16)	(0.59)	(0.57)	(0.69)	(0.49)	(1.11)
Sum	0.1771	0.2020	0.1517	0.3436	0.0549	0.0744	0.1843
	(4.09)	(5.03)	(3.26)	(8.78)	(0.85)	(1.50)	(3.61)
R^2	0.0080	0.0417	0.0066	0.0506	0.0022	0.0026	0.0109

Notes: Figures in parentheses under the estimated coefficients are absolute values of the t-ratios. The figure in the "Sum" row is the sum of the lag coefficients and its t-statistic relates to a test of the hypothesis that the sum of these coefficients is zero.

Table 4.4 Day-of-the-week effect

Regressor	Dependent Variable						
	RSAA	RSAB	RSEA	RSEB	RSA30	RSAC	RSEC
Lag 1	0.0471	0.2037	0.0173	0.1823	0.0195	-0.0138	0.0634
	(2.22)	(9.54)	(0.78)	(8.23)	(0.65)	(0.61)	(2.56)
Lag 2	0.0501	-0.0496	0.0496	0.0125	-0.0131	0.0190	0.0350
	(2.36)	(2.28)	(2.25)	(0.56)	(0.44)	(0.83)	(1.40)
Lag 3	0.0363	0.0619	0.0065	0.0854	0.0061	0.0269	0.0221
	(1.71)	(2.85)	(0.29)	(3.80)	(0.21)	(1.19)	(0.90)
Lag 4	0.0172	-0.0055	0.0507	0.0487	0.0486	0.0187	0.0018
	(0.81)	(0.25)	(2.30)	(2.16)	(1.64)	(0.82)	(0.07)
Lag 5	0.0256	-0.0083	0.0277	0.0148	-0.0057	0.0239	0.0630
	(1.20)	(0.39)	(1.26)	(0.66)	(0.19)	(1.06)	(2.55)
Monday	-0.0044	-0.0008	-0.0028	0.0012	-0.0031	-0.0047	-0.0025
	(1.88)	(0.53)	(1.44)	(0.76)	(1.71)	(2.29)	(1.16)
Tuesday	-0.0063	-0.0024	-0.0050	-0.0038	-0.0051	-0.0054	-0.0057
	(2.70)	(1.61)	(2.62)	(2.35)	(2.81))	(2.63)	(2.66)
Thursday	-0.0006	-0.0014	-0.0025	-0.0004	-0.0045	-0.0046	-0.0050
	(0.24)	(0.92)	(1.29)	(0.25)	(2.46)	(2.24)	(2.31)
Friday	0.0017	0.0015	-0.0003	0.0017	-0.0008	-0.0004	0.0010
	(0.71)	(0.98)	(0.13)	(1.03)	(0.45)	(0.17)	(0.43)
Constant	0.0026	0.0006	0.0025	0.0006	0.0031	0.0034	0.0033
	(1.58)	(0.54)	(1.84)	(0.51)	(2.44)	(2.31)	(2.14)

Regressor	Dependent Variable							
	RSAA	RSAB	RSEA	RSEB	RSA30	RSAC	RSEC
Sum	0.1763	0.2022	0.1518	0.3438	0.0553	0.0746	0.1851
	(4.08)	(5.03)	(3.27)	(8.81)	(0.86)	(1.50)	(3.64)
R^2	0.0150	0.0450	0.0110	0.0570	0.0128	0.0091	0.0198
DoW	0.003	0.112	0.058	0.007	0.019	0.013	0.006

Notes: Figures in parentheses under the estimated coefficients are absolute values of the t-ratios. The figure in the "Sum" row is the sum of the lag coefficients and its t-statistic relates to a test of the hypothesis that the sum of these coefficients is zero. The number in the "DoW" row is the prob value for an F-test of the joint significance of the DoW dummy variables.

Wednesday is left out, all DoW dummy variables measure the intercept relative to Wednesday. The results are reported in Table 4.4.

From the table it is clear that the introduction of the DoW variables has had little effect on the lag coefficients – the sum of the lagged coefficients and their t-statistics have been little altered by the addition of the DoW dummies and the individual coefficients are similar across the two tables. The R^2 figures have increased only marginally. Generally, both the Monday and Tuesday dummy variables are significant although the former only weakly in most cases and they are jointly significant at the 5 per cent for five of the seven series analysed as indicated by the marginal significance level. Rather surprisingly, the DoW effect seems to be weaker for the B shares than for the A shares and the effect for the 30 leaders index is about the same as that for the Shanghai A shares as a whole. So, there is clear evidence of a widespread DoW effect but it is not the common weekend effect since it occurs most strongly on Tuesdays. The results are, however, consistent with earlier work reported for China by Xu (2000) although his results are statistically weaker than ours. This may be due to his shorter and earlier sample period as we show below when we repeat some of these tests for sub-periods.

A second source of predictability in share returns is the holiday effect where returns are predictably different before or after a public holiday. We identified four main holidays affecting the stock exchanges – the Chinese New Year in January or February, the May Day holiday in early May, the National Day holiday in early October and the New Year holiday.

We experimented with various forms of dummy variables which we used to capture the holiday effects – separate dummy variables before and after each holiday period, a single dummy variable for each holiday, a single dummy variable for all holidays combined and two dummy variables, one before all holidays and one after all holidays. The results of the investigation are that the holiday effect is very weak – only when a dummy variable combined the before and after effects of the Chinese New Year holiday was it significant; all other variables and combinations were insignificant. The results for the Shanghai and Shenzhen A shares are reported in Table 4.5. These results are consistent with those obtained by Mookerjee and Yu (1999b) for Shanghai although they used data only for the early 1990s.

An alternative test for the EMH is to test the (log) share price index for a unit root. The random walk version of the EMH requires the variables to be I(1). In Table 4.6 we report ADF and PP tests of a unit root in the log share price indexes. Tests are reported both with and without a trend in the "Dickey-Fuller equation". In the equation without a trend the null hypothesis is that the log price process has a unit root and the alternative is that the process is stationary while in the case where a trend is included we test trend-stationarity against difference-stationarity. The equation with trend seems more sensible given the strong upward trend present in most share price indexes. Tests are reported for five lags. Since results are occasionally sensitive to lag length, we also re-ran some of the tests with longer lags. They are not reported but produce the same conclusions.

Generally the results are consistent with the hypothesis of a unit root in the log price process and therefore with weak efficiency of the share market. The

Table 4.5   Holiday effect

Regressor	Dependent Variable	
	RSAA	RSEA
Lag 1	0.0461 (2.17)	0.0141 (0.64)
Lag 2	0.0493 (2.32)	0.0483 (2.19)
Lag 3	0.0366 (1.72)	0.0066 (0.30)
Lag 4	0.0186 (0.88)	0.0515 (2.34)
Lag 5	0.0268 (1.26)	0.0295 (1.34)
Monday	-0.0040 (1.69)	-0.0032 (1.64)
Tuesday	-0.0059 (2.55)	-0.0051 (2.66)
Thursday	-0.0005 (0.21)	-0.0025 (1.31)
Friday	0.0018 (0.76)	-0.0005 (0.27)
Chinese New Year	0.0174 (2.11)	0.0185 (2.80)
Constant	0.0022 (1.36)	0.0025 (1.83)
Sum	0.1775 (4.11)	0.1500 (3.24)
R^2	0.0165	0.0148

Notes: Figures in parentheses under the estimated coefficients are absolute values of the t-ratios. The figure in the "Sum" row is the sum of the lag coefficients and its t-statistic relates to a test of the hypothesis that the sum of these coefficients is zero.

Table 4.6   Unit root tests

Variable	Without Trend		With Trend	
	ADF	PP	ADF	PP
LPSAA	-2.70	-2.56	6.88	5.93
LPSAB	-2.19	-2.30	2.42	2.71
LPSEA	-0.97	-0.82	3.01	2.86
LPSEB	-1.23	-0.62	1.72	2.16
LPSA30	-2.24	-2.96	2.81	4.56
LPSAC	-1.27	-1.20	9.18	10.44
LPSEC	-1.73	-1.65	2.19	1.85

Notes: The tests without trend are t-tests and have a 10% critical value of -2.57; the tests with trend are for trend stationarity against difference stationarity and have a 10% critical value of 5.34.

main exception to this finding is the Shanghai A returns where three of the four reported results suggest stationarity. This is rather surprising in view of the earlier results that show little evidence of predictability of the returns for the Shanghai exchange.

We conclude that there is some evidence that the weak form of the EMH is violated although the strongest evidence is for the two B shares which are the least liquid so that the predictability may be spurious and reflect stale prices. This view is reinforced by the finding that there is no evidence of predictability for the 30 leaders index for the Shanghai exchange.

4.5   MARKET EFFICIENCY AND ROLE OF THE BANKS

Given the traditional importance of the banks in the Chinese financial system it is likely that changes in the role of the banks would have significant effects on the efficiency of the market. In section 4.2 we explained that there had been important changes in the relationship between the banks and the stock market in 1996 and 2000 although the changes were such that it is not clear whether they would have enhanced efficiency or not. It is likely that, in the long run, a competitive financial system which is not dominated by relatively few powerful banks would enhance the efficiency of the market. Conversely, the loss of liquidity when the banks were forced to withdraw might reduce efficiency, at least in the short run. We investigated these questions by rerunning our predictability tests for the Shanghai A and B shares and the Shenzhen A and B shares for the following sub-periods: 6/10/1992 – 30/6/1996, 1/7/1996 – 31/12/1999 and 1/1/2000 – 28/2/2001. The results for Shanghai are reported in Table 4.7 and the results for Shenzhen are reported in Table 4.8.

The results for Shanghai are mixed. The Q statistic shows a progressive decline over the three sub-periods, suggesting a fall in autocorrelation of the returns consistent with increasing efficiency as the market rules are changed. On the other hand, the value of R^2 increases progressively over the periods suggesting increased predictability. However, R^2 is not strictly comparable across the three sub-periods and if we look at the individual autocorrelation and regression statistics, there appears to be some evidence that efficiency improved after 1999 when banks were permitted to re-enter the stock market in 2000. The DoW dummy variables are stronger for the middle period of 1996-1999 although the Chinese New Year holiday effect has a progressively higher t-ratio. It is interesting that the DoW effect seems to have completely disappeared in the post-1999 period although this is the only period in which the CNY effect is significant.

The results for Shenzhen are also mixed. The Q statistic is clearly greatest for the period when the banks were excluded from the stock market, suggesting less efficiency during this period. On the other hand the predictability as measured by R^2 increases progressively over the sub-periods although, judging by the significance of the individual coefficients and that of the CNY dummy variable, most of this was the effect of the CNY variable. In fact, if this variable is omitted, the implications of R^2 match those of the Q statistic, i.e. efficiency was reduced when the banks were excluded in the middle sub-period. As was the case for the Shanghai exchange, the DoW effect seems to have completely disappeared after 1999 but the CNY effect is strongest then.

The results for Shenzhen and, to a lesser extent, those for Shanghai suggest that the exclusion of the banks has not improved the efficiency of the stock market in the sense of making returns less predictable. This is consistent with the liquidity explanation, that the banks are important sources of liquidity (and perhaps expertise). Therefore, excluding them from involvement in the stock market may make for a more competitive and diversified brokerage industry in the long run, but in the short run, it reduces the amount of trading in the market and consequently slows information diffusion.

4.6   CONCLUSIONS

This chapter has explored weak efficiency in the Shanghai and Shenzhen stock markets and the relationship between efficiency and changes in the regulations concerning the role of the banks in the stock exchanges. We found that there was evidence of departures from weak efficiency in the form of predictability of returns on the basis of their own past values, as well as systematic day-of-the-week and holiday effects. Over the period as a whole, predictability was most marked for the B shares in both the exchanges and absent altogether in the index for the 30 leading stocks on the Shanghai

Table 4.7   The efficiency effects of regulatory change: Shanghai

Variable/ Statistic	21/2/1992 – 28/2/2001	21/2/1992 – 30/6/1996	1/7/1996 – 31/12/1999	1/1/2000 – 28/2/2001
ρ_1	0.05	0.06	-0.01	0.08
	(0.02)	(0.03)	(0.03)	(0.06)
ρ_2	0.05	0.06	0.01	0.04
	(0.02)	(0.03)	(0.03)	(0.06)
ρ_3	0.04	0.04	0.09	-0.06
	(0.02)	(0.03)	(0.03)	(0.06)
ρ_4	0.03	0.02	0.04	-0.03
	(0.02)	(0.03)	(0.03)	(0.06)
ρ_5	0.04	0.04	0.03	-0.07
	(0.02)	(0.03)	(0.03)	(0.06)
Q(5)	20.99	12.11	8.57	5.00
	(0.001)	(0.033)	(0.128)	(0.415)
RSAA (-1)	0.0461	0.0528	-0.0069	0.0300
	(2.17)	(1.74)	(0.20)	(0.49)
RSAA (-2)	0.0493	0.0583	0.0175	0.0114
	(2.32)	(1.92)	(0.51)	(0.19)
RSAA (-3)	0.0366	0.0341	0.0853	-0.0756
	(1.72)	(1.12)	(2.49)	(1.26)
RSAA (-4)	0.0186	0.0142	0.0517	-0.0157
	(0.88)	(0.47)	(1.50)	(0.26)
RSAA (-5)	0.0268	0.0268	0.0123	-0.0565
	(1.26)	(0.88)	(0.36)	(0.95)
R^2	0.0165	0.0206	0.0259	0.0576
Mon	-0.0040	-0.0062	-0.0027	0.0022
	(1.69)	(1.41)	(1.25)	(0.83)
Tues	-0.0059	-0.0069	-0.0062	-0.0015
	(2.55)	(1.57)	(2.81)	(0.60)
Thurs	-0.0005	0.0028	-0.0050	-0.0001
	(0.21)	(0.64)	(2.24)	(0.02)
Fri	0.0018	0.0046	-0.0016	0.0009
	(0.76)	(1.05)	(0.72)	(0.33)
CNY	0.0174	0.0175	0.0147	0.0192
	(2.11)	(1.07)	(1.77)	(2.84)

Notes: ρ_i = autocorrelation for lag i. (standard errors in parentheses);
   Q(5) = Box-Pierce-Ljung portmanteau test for first- to fifth-order autocorrelation (p-values in parentheses);
   RSAA ($-i$) = coefficient of RSAA lagged i periods in a regression of RSAA on five lagged values of itself and a constant (absolute value of the t-ratio in parentheses);
   R^2 relates to the regression of RSAA on five lags of itself and a constant; and
   Mon, Tues, Thurs, Fri are DoW dummy variables and CNY is a Chinese New Year dummy variable in a regression including five lags of RSAA and a constant (absolute values of the t-ratio in parentheses).

Table 4.8   The efficiency effects of regulatory change: Shenzhen

Variable/ Statistic	6/10/1992– 29/3/2001	6/10/1992– 30/6/1996	1/7/1996– 31/12/1999	1/1/2000– 29/3/2001
ρ_1	0.02	0.01	0.02	0.05
	(0.02)	(0.03)	(0.03)	(0.06)
ρ_2	0.05	0.05	0.05	0.02
	(0.02)	(0.03)	(0.03)	(0.06)
ρ_3	0.01	-0.03	0.12	-0.04
	(0.02)	(0.03)	(0.03)	(0.06)
ρ_4	0.05	0.06	0.04	0.00
	(0.02)	(0.03)	(0.03)	(0.06)
ρ_5	0.03	0.04	0.03	-0.04
	(0.02)	(0.03)	(0.03)	(0.06)
Q(5)	14.69	8.31	16.32	2.04
	(0.012)	(0.140)	(0.007)	(0.84)
RSEA (-1)	0.0141	0.094	0.0122	0.0106
	(0.64)	(0.28)	(0.35)	(0.18)
RSEA (-2)	0.0483	0.0507	0.0470	0.0556
	(2.20)	(1.52)	(1.37)	(0.94)
RSEA (-3)	0.0066	-0.0327	0.1144	-0.0213
	(0.30)	(0.98)	(3.35)	(0.37)
RSEA (-4)	0.0515	0.0558	0.0478	0.0209
	(2.34)	(1.68)	(1.39)	(0.36)
RSEA (-5)	0.0295	0.0439	0.0061	-0.0407
	(1.34)	(1.32)	(0.18)	(0.71)
R^2	0.0148	0.0174	0.0324	0.0516
Mon	-0.0032	-0.0043	-0.0030	0.0012
	(1.64)	(1.19)	(1.22)	(0.49)
Tues	-0.0051	-0.0048	-0.0064	-0.0007
	(2.66)	(1.34)	(2.63)	(0.28)
Thurs	-0.0025	0.0004	-0.0063	-0.0019
	(1.30)	(0.11)	(2.55)	(0.77)
Fri	-0.0005	0.0006	-0.0022	0.0011
	(0.27)	(0.18)	(0.89)	(0.45)
CNY	0.0185	0.0226	0.0130	0.0210
	(2.80)	(1.83)	(1.39)	(3.15)

Notes: ρ_i = autocorrelation for lag i. (standard errors in parentheses);
Q(5) = Box-Pierce-Ljung portmanteau test for first- to fifth- order autocorrelation (*p*-values in parentheses);
RSEA (-*i*) = coefficient of RSEA lagged *i* periods in a regression of RSEA on five lagged values of itself and a constant (absolute value of the t-ratio in parentheses);
R^2 relates to the regression of RSEA on five lags of itself and a constant; and
Mon, Tues, Thurs and Fri are DoW dummy variables and CNY is a Chinese New Year dummy variable in a regression including five lagsof RSEA and a constant (absolute values of the t-ratio in parentheses).

market. These results suggest that much of the apparent predictability simply reflects thin trading so that there may be little, if any, unexploited profits in this predictability. Our finding on the day-of-the-week effect was consistent with what others have found before us, particularly that there are lower than average returns on Tuesdays. Interestingly, we found this effect to have completely disappeared in the 2000-2001 part of our sample period. We found little evidence of a holiday effect with only the Chinese New Year effect being significant and that only in the last of our three sub-samples.

We also found evidence that efficiency suffered when banks were excluded from the stock market in 1996 and efficiency improved when they were re-admitted in early 2000. We offered a tentative explanation in terms of liquidity given the traditionally dominant role played by the banks in the Chinese financial system – when the banks were excluded liquidity suffered and information transmission was less efficient; this process was reversed in 2000. Clearly this hypothesis needs further exploration with more disaggregated data.

NOTES

1. For recent evidence on the importance of the relationship between the financial system and development see, e.g., Levine (1997), Levine and Zervos (1998), Arestis and Demetriades (1999), Beck, Levine and Loayza (2000), Henry (2000a, 2000b), and Levine, Loayza and Beck (2000).

2. An interesting alternative approach to examining efficiency is that of Ang and Ma (1999) who interpret forecastability of earnings as a measure of transparency of the market and hence of the efficiency with which the market discloses and digests information.

3. LeRoy (1989) has pointed out the inaccuracy of the term "random walk" in this framework since the theory implies a weaker restriction, viz. a martingale. Moreover, in the presence of dividends it is not the (log) share price but the value of a particular type of mutual fund which satisfies the martingale restriction. In our case, these qualifications are not serious since only the martingale property is being tested and the data used in the tests ignores dividends. We therefore retain the conventional terminology.

4. See Dickey and Fuller (1981) and Phillips and Perron (1988).

5. Profitability and trading rules

5.1 INTRODUCTION

As discussed in the preceding chapters, the efficient markets hypothesis (EMH) is one of the mainstays of financial economics and is usually stated in terms of the predictability of financial asset returns on the basis of their own past values (the weak EMH), or other publicly available information (the semi-strong EMH) or any information, whether publicly available or not (the strong form of the EMH). The EMH has been widely tested, especially for share markets, and pervasive evidence of some inefficiency is often found. Concerns have been expressed about data-mining − if enough researchers work over a given data set or data for a given stock market, they are bound to find some predictability sooner or later.

One response to this concern of data-mining has been to extend the countries for which the tests are carried out and in the recent literature we find a growing number of studies of the EMH using data from emerging markets. Studies of emerging markets are also of interest in their own right since they allow us to address the question of whether efficiency improves as the institutional framework for the market takes shape and as trading volume increases.

In existing empirical work on the Chinese stock market (see Chapters 3 and 4), tests of the weak EMH most often involve the computation of autocorrelations or the estimation of regressions of current returns on their own past values. Significant autocorrelations or regression coefficients are then taken as evidence again the weak EMH. However the arbitrage argument underlying the EMH does not necessarily require that returns are unpredictable but rather that any predictability is unprofitable (see Fama, 1991). It is a logical extension of standard predictability tests of the EMH to test the profitability of trading rules based on the regressions used to test for predictability. Profitability tests can be more stringent since, properly formulated, they take into account only the information available to traders and they can account for transaction costs.

The objective of this chapter is to examine the profitability of different trading rules in the Chinese stock market. The remainder of the chapter is structured as follows. In section 5.2 we provide a brief background of recent empirical work on the Chinese stock market and continue in section 5.3 to describe the data used. In section 5.4 we report the results, starting with those based on daily data, then weekly and finally monthly. Conclusions are presented in the final section.

5.2 EMPIRICAL STUDIES

There is a considerable literature on tests of trading rules applied to stock markets as well as other markets, particularly foreign exchange markets (see section 3.1.5, Chapter 3). A seminal paper in this area is the one by Brock, Lakonishok and LeBaron (BLL) (1992) which used daily data on the Dow Jones Index from 1897 to 1986 to examine mechanical trading rules that rely on the comparison of moving averages of prices to formulate buy and sell signals. They evaluated the trading rules by comparing the average returns for the buy and sell periods and find that the returns during buy periods significantly exceed returns during sell periods, concluding on the basis of this that the rules have predictive capability. Subsequently, other researchers built on this initial study by applying the BLL procedure to a variety of other countries.[1] The general flavour of all these studies is that the mechanical rules have predictive power in many cases (although, surprisingly, not more so for emerging markets than for developed markets) but that profits after trading costs are very small or non-existent.

A feature of all the papers cited above is that they examine *mechanical* trading rules – generally ones based on the comparison of moving averages of share prices – rather than rules based on the regressions which are used in tests of the weak EMH. Further, their focus is generally not on the profitability of portfolios but they simply compare the average returns for buy and sell days and test whether, on average, the "buy returns" exceed the "sell returns". These rules avoid the problem of data-mining in evaluating rules which have been found after repeated econometric tests (they are claimed to be rules actually used by share traders) and also obviate the need for interest rate data. However, they are alternatives to standard weak EMH tests rather than natural extensions which address the question of whether the predictability found in the weak EMH tests are actually profitable.[2]

In contrast, in this chapter we report an extensive evaluation of trading rules based on econometric forecasting equations of the type typically used in the tests of the weak EMH. Moreover, we not only compute mean buy and sell returns but compare the end-of-sample accumulated values of portfolios based on trading rules to the value of a buy-and-hold portfolio and so examine profitability directly. We use data for A shares on the Shanghai stock exchange from 1992 to 2001.

We begin by evaluating five rules based on equations estimated using daily observations for the full sample period. The remainder of the chapter consists of an assessment of the robustness of these results. We begin by addressing the question of whether the differences between the performance of the rules and the buy-and-hold strategy are statistically significant. We first test the forecasting performance of the underlying equations using a Pesaran and Timmermann (1992) test for predictive accuracy. We also test the significance of the difference between the mean returns to the trading rules and the buy-and-hold strategies as well as between the buy and sell returns as carried out in the literature following BLL. We interpret the test statistics both by comparison to their theoretical critical values as well as to bootstrapped values given that the returns do not satisfy the classical assumptions underlying the standard t-tests.

Next we note that since the rules are based on forecasting equations estimated over the whole sample period, they use information which is not available to investors in practice and are therefore open to the charge of data-mining. We therefore go on to evaluate strategies based on recursive regressions to overcome this problem.

5.3 DATA

All our data are taken from the *Taiwan Economic Journal* data base. We use daily data on the index of A share prices on the Shanghai stock exchange from 2 January, 1992 to 29 March, 2001. These are illustrated in Figure 5.1. We also use the following interest rate data for the same period: the demand deposit rate, the five-year term deposit rate and the two-year term deposit rate. Unfortunately, daily interest rate data were unavailable for our sample period so that monthly data were used. However, an inspection of the data (see Figure 5.2) showed that even monthly data varied very little over the sample period; e.g. the demand deposit rate changed only nine times over the 12 years for which we have data. Hence we feel justified in using the monthly data on a daily basis on the assumption that demand deposits would have been available at the monthly rate on any trading day of the month.

We report some diagnostics for share prices at all three frequencies in Table 5.1. Given the limited nature of the interest rate data, we do not report similar statistics for them. The value of the statistics reported in Table 5.1 makes it clear that the share price index is non-stationary but the return is stationary at all frequencies. The returns show strong evidence of non-normality common in financial data; both skewness and excess kurtosis are clearly evident in the returns at all frequencies. The non-normality will affect the interpretation of standard statistical tests and provides a motivation for extending the usual tests to those based on bootstrapped critical values.

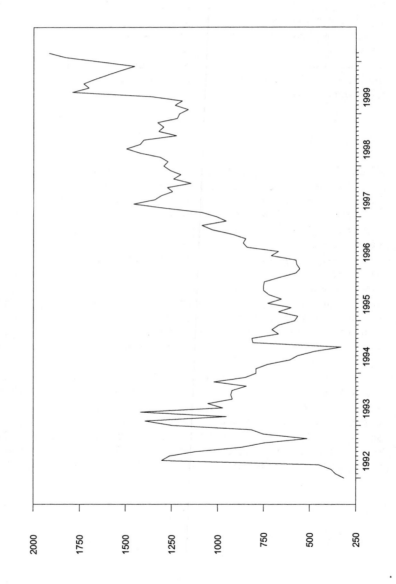

Figure 5.1   A Share price index, Shanghai (daily)

Figure 5.2 Interest rates (monthly)

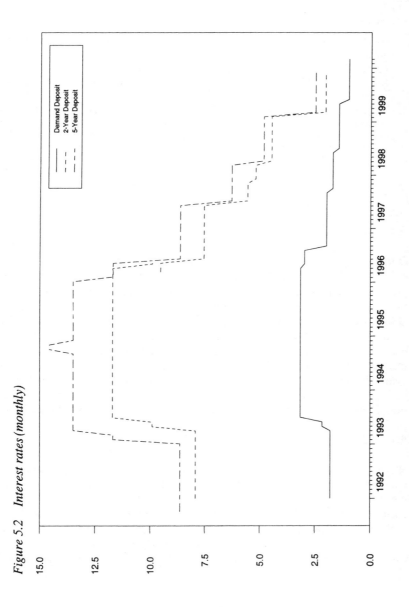

Table 5.1   Diagnostic statistics

Variable	ADF	PP	Skewness	Kurtosis	Normality
Daily					
Price	-1.3866	-1.3350			
Return	-6.9544	-45.296	214.8811	2798.96	1541.0099
Weekly					
Price	-1.4223	-1.4702			
Return	-6.2324	-20.272	73.3919	431.8718	380.0009
Monthly					
Price	0.1415	-1.3506			
Return	-3.3451	-11.158	20.1041	61.9534	63.4896

Notes: ADF = augmented Dickey-Fuller test for a unit root, 10% critical value = -2.57 (Dickey and Fuller, 1981); PP = Phillips-Perron test for a unit root, 10% critical value = -2.57 (Phillips and Perron, 1988); skewness and excess kurtosis statistics are both $N(0,1)$ under the null of normality and GF is the goodness-of-fit test for normality. For daily data is it distributed χ^2_{57} with a 5% critical value of 75.9048, for weekly data it is distributed χ^2_{27} under normality and has a 5% critical value of 40.1133 and for monthly data it is distributed χ^2_7 with a 5% critical value of 14.0671.

5.4   RESULTS

Our trading rule is a very simple risk-neutral one of the type explored by, e.g., Clare, Thomas and Wickens (1994): hold shares if the one-period-ahead predicted return exceeds the (known) return to cash; otherwise hold cash. Cash is a demand deposit. Assuming that the investor starts with a sum of US$1, we accumulate the portfolio at the implied return and compared its terminal value to that of three alternatives; the first is to buy and hold the market portfolio as measured by the index, the second is to hold cash as measured by the demand-deposit rate and the third is to hold the longest available (highest-yielding) term deposit. We report first a base case using daily data with the forecasting equation estimated over the whole of the sample period and then proceed to extensive robustness testing of the results.

5.4.1   Base Case

We begin with results based on a forecasting equation estimated using daily data over the entire sample. We begin the evaluation of the trading rules and the three alternative strategies six months into the sample to provide comparability with the results based on recursive regression presented below – there we allow six months for the initial estimation of the forecasting equation. It is recognized that using data for the entire sample period in the estimation of the forecasting equation involves the use of data not available to an investor but it follows most naturally from the standard regression-based tests of the weak EMH and will allow us to assess the value in terms of trading profits of using this sort of information.

Following results reported elsewhere in the literature, we experiment with a number of alternative forecasting equations beginning with an equation which explains the current return in terms of its own five lagged values – we feel that even in a relatively inefficient market shocks will have worked their way through within a week. We also use a two-lag version to assess the importance of the last three lags. We then add a set of day-of-the-week (DoW) dummy variables given the widespread evidence of the significance of their effects, and then a dummy variable for the Chinese New Year (CNY) holiday and finally use an equation with just the day-of-the-week dummies. The terminal value of the portfolio, the mean return and the standard deviation of the return for each rule are reported in Table 5.2.

Table 5.2 Trading rules based on full-sample forecasting equation

Rule	Portfolio Value	Mean Return (% per day)	Standard Deviation (% per day)
E B&H	1.7151	0.0745	3.2078
DD B&H	1.1995	0.0084	0.0034
TD B&H	1.9452	0.0292	0.0001
Regression Based:			
AR(5)	6.9493	0.1222	2.5915
AR(2)	3.3766	0.0889	2.6013
AR(5), DoW	18.7989	0.1659	2.4909
AR(5), DoW,CNY	16.9316	0.1604	2.4641
DoW	15.3093	0.1549	2.4422

Notes: E B&H = equity buy-and-hold, DD B&H = demand deposit buy-and-hold, TD B&H = term deposit buy-and-hold; DoW = day-of-the-week dummy variables, CNY = Chinese New Year dummy variable.

The first three lines in the table provide information on the three benchmark portfolios. The first is an equity buy-and-hold portfolio which has a terminal value of 1.7151 after approximately nine years. This compares to the amount of 1.1995 received from holding demand deposits over the period and an amount of 1.9452 received from holding two five-year term deposits. Of the three, holding a term deposit turned out to dominate the three benchmark strategies – it has a higher mean return/terminal value as well as a lower standard deviation since the only uncertainty (apart from default risk, which we ignore) in holding the term deposits is the rate at which the first five-year deposit can be rolled over. Holding a demand deposit is, not surprisingly, much less attractive although it, too, has a low risk compared to holding equity.

The return from the trading rule based on the simple five-period autoregressive model is considerably better than any return from benchmark portfolios – the terminal value of the portfolio based on this rule is approximately four times that of the equity buy-and-hold portfolio. In addition, it has a lower standard deviation of return over the period so that it dominates in both return and risk dimensions. The two-period forecasting equation also produces a higher terminal value (but by a multiple of only two) and has a lower risk as measured by the standard deviation of the daily return. Given the relative performance of the two- and five-lag equations, further experiments use only the latter.

The addition of the DoW dummy variables results in a considerable improvement in performance of the trading rule – the terminal value more than doubles and is now approximately 11 times that of the buy-and-hold portfolio and the risk falls marginally. Adding the CNY dummy has little value in terms of profit/return. Finally, the set of DoW dummy variables alone performs better than the five lags alone but not as well as the two sets of variables combined.

It appears, therefore, that considerable profits could have been made on the basis of predictions from a simple econometric forecasting equation of the type commonly used to test the weak EMH. This suggests that the forecasting equations have economic significance in addition to statistical significance. However, the results presented so far beg many questions which need to be addressed before taking them seriously. Questions we address in the remainder of this section are as follows:

- How sensitive are the results to choice of starting date? From Figure 5.1 it can be seen that the Shanghai market showed considerable fluctuations in its first two years of operation and it will be no surprise that the overall return to a buy-and-hold strategy will depend importantly on the starting date of the evaluation. It is not clear, however, how sensitive the comparison is to the choice of starting date, and we investigate this first.
- Are the differences between the performance of the rules statistically significant? It is possible that even though the differences in terminal values are substantial, they are not significant.
- We indicated earlier that the estimated coefficients of the forecasting equation incorporate data for the whole period which implicitly assumes that the trader has information covering the whole period when making trades, an assumption which is clearly not realistic and therefore is likely to exaggerate potential profits. We therefore proceed to re-compute our results basing the forecasting equation on a recursive estimation procedure which ensures that the hypothetical trader bases the forecasting equation only on information available at the time of making the forecast.

- Are the trading-rule portfolios still superior once we account for trading costs? As pointed out earlier in the chapter, ultimately the EMH revolves around profitability, not merely predictability and so we need to ask whether the superiority of the trading rules simply reflects the fact that they require frequent trading, the transactions costs of which have been ignored. To anticipate our results, we find that transaction costs wipe out all profits generated using the trading rules – it is clear that daily trading involves costs which greatly exceed the daily profits that can be generated by the trading rules. This leads us to our last question.
- Is less frequent trading more sensible from a profit point of view? We experiment with trading rules based on both weekly and monthly data.

5.4.2 Sensitivity to Starting Date

The results reported in Table 5.2 are all based on estimating the equation over the entire sample period and beginning the evaluation of the trading rules at day 130, approximately six months into the sample. As explained, this is to allow for comparison to the results generated using recursively estimated forecasting equations which need some time for start-up for which we allow 130 observations. However, inspection of the data for the share price index in Figure 5.1 makes clear that the behaviour of the index was very volatile for at least the first two years of the sample. Hence the choice of the start of the evaluation period will undoubtedly affect the mean return to the buy-and-hold portfolio but the interesting question for us is whether it affects the relationship between the trading-rule-based and the buy-and-hold portfolios.

We assess this issue by systematically shifting the start of the evaluation period from day 130 to the end of the sample. For each evaluation period we recompute the terminal values of the two portfolios, with the trading rule being based on the AR(5) forecasting equation, and take the ratio of the two. The resulting time series is shown as the solid line in Figure 5.3. Clearly, the choice of the starting point of the evaluation period is not an innocuous one, with the ratio being around 4-5 for a starting point early in the sample, then dropping rapidly to around 2 for much of the middle period before falling to around 1 if the evaluation period is restricted to the end of the 1990s. Part of this may simply reflect a shorter evaluation period – earlier research has shown that trading rules are less effective if evaluated over shorter periods than over long periods (see BLL, for example) – and part of it also has to do with the fact that the evaluation and estimation periods have less and less in common. If we correct for the latter effect by estimating over the same period as we use for the evaluation we obtain the broken line in Figure 5.3. We can see that this has a dramatic effect on the results – clearly rules which are based on equations estimated over the same period used for evaluating the

Figure 5.3   Ratio of AR(5) trading-rule portfolio to buy-and-hold portfolio

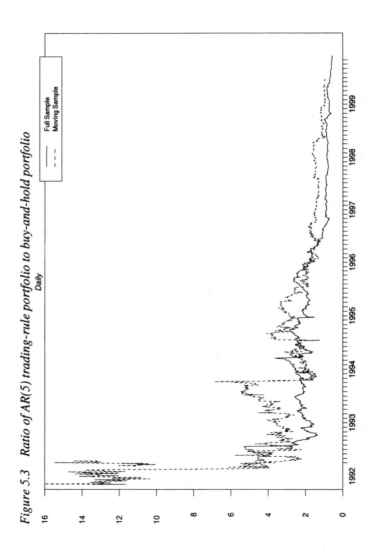

rule show much greater profitability. Seen from a different perspective, the use of data from the volatile beginning of the sample "messes up" the forecasting equation for quite some time; deleting the first 150-200 observations improves the performance of the trading rule up to threefold.

We can conclude that the period chosen for evaluating the comparative performance of the trading rule and the buy-and-hold strategy has an important effect on the outcome of the comparison, which makes the interpretation of the comparisons problematic. However, the appropriate resolution of this problem is not obvious and we continue with comparisons based on the original period which was, after all, chosen without regard to the resulting outcome.

5.4.3 Tests of Significance

We now turn to the question of whether the differences between the rule outcomes described in section 5.4.1 are significant in the statistical sense. We carried out several tests, the results of which are reported in Table 5.3.

Table 5.3   Statistical tests of superiority of trading rules

Rule	Terminal Portfolio Value	Portfolio/Buy-and-Hold Portfolio	Predictive Accuracy	Equality of Trading Rules and B-and-H	Equality of Buy and Sell
AR(5)	6.9493 [0.648]	4.0518 [0.056]	1.8684 (0.0309) [0.108]	0.5365 (0.2958) [0.064]	0.9456 (0.1722) [0.158]
AR(2)	3.3766 [0.736]	1.9687 [0.056]	-0.2449 (0.5967) [0.720]	0.1631 (0.4352) [0.074]	0.3958 (0.3595) [0.109]
AR(5), DoW	18.7989 [0.470]	10.9608 [0.044]	0.8966 (0.1849) [0.590]	1.0444 (0.1482) [0.032]	2.1941 (0.0141) [0.040]
AR(5), DoW, CNY	16.9316 [0.508]	9.8721 [0.052]	0.5681 (0.2849) [0.702]	0.9853 (0.1622) [0.040]	2.1475 (0.0159) [0.060]
DoW	15.3093 [0.458]	8.9262 [0.016]	1.4007 (0.0807) [0.260]	0.9264 (0.1771) [0.014]	2.1223 (0.0169) [0.008]

Notes: DoW = day-of-the-week dummy variables, CNY = Chinese New Year dummy variable. Figures in parentheses are *p*-values based on theoretical distributions of the test statistics and figures in square brackets are proportions based on a bootstrapping exercise.

The first column of numbers in Table 5.3 reproduces the terminal portfolio values from Table 5.3 with all numbers in brackets relating to a bootstrapping experiment to be described below. The next column reports the ratio of the terminal value of the rule-based portfolio to that of the buy-and-hold portfolio. The third column of figures relates to Pesaran and Timmermann's (1992) test of forecasting performance of the equations underlying the trading rules. The form of the test we use tests whether the sign of the predicted return relative to its sample mean matches that of the actual return relative to its sample mean. The test statistic is approximately standard-normally distributed under the null hypothesis of no predictive ability. Not surprisingly, the number of positive and negative signs was roughly 50 per cent but the number of cases where the sign was correctly predicted, was in most cases, only marginally above 50 per cent and in one case, the AR(2) rule, below 50 per cent. The numbers in parentheses are theoretical prob values for a one-tail test and they show that only the AR(5) rule has a significant predictive accuracy at 5 per cent while the DoW rule is significant at the 10 per cent level. The other rules do not have any significant predictive ability.

The second test is a standard equality of means test between the returns to the trading rule and the returns to the buy-and-hold strategy in each case. Again the figures in parentheses are theoretical p-values for a one-tail test and show that the mean returns were not significantly different for any of the rules at conventional significance levels; this is despite the very considerable differences in terminal values of the portfolios reported in the first column of figures.

The final test reported is a test of the equality of buy and sell returns. Each day is classified as either a buy or a sell day depending on whether the forecast equity return is larger or smaller than the (known) demand deposit rate and the returns on buy days are compared to those on sell days. This test is the standard one used in the trading rules literature to evaluate the predictive ability of the rule. For all rules the mean buy return is positive and the mean sell return is negative indicating some ability of the rules to distinguish good from bad days. For two of the rules (the AR(5) and AR(2) rules) the differences between the buy and sell returns are not significant at conventional level. However, for the last three rules the differences are significant at the 5 per cent level.

A comparison of the second and third tests suggests that the conventional test of equality of buy and sell returns may exaggerate the usefulness of the rules; after all, the question is whether an investor can make money using a rule based on the observed predictability which is most naturally tested by comparing the mean return to a rule-based portfolio to that obtainable from a buy-and-hold strategy.

The above tests are all based on assumptions of normality and independence of returns. The normality assumption is clearly violated in the present case, judging by the summary statistics reported in Table 5.1.

Moreover, the independence assumptions are also likely to be violated for the two tests of equality of returns. This is particularly the case for the test of the equality between the return based on the trading rules and the return obtained from a buy-and-hold portfolio since for all buy days the returns will be identical. For these reasons we carried out a bootstrapping exercise as follows.[3] We bootstrapped under the null hypothesis of a random walk so that we sampled the returns with replacement to generate an artificial return series. We generated 500 such series and computed the test statistics described above for each. In so doing we generated an empirical distribution for each of the statistics. The values of the test statistics which were computed for our actual data and reported in Table 5.3 were then compared to the empirical distributions based on the 500 replications.

The results of this exercise are captured by the figures in square brackets in Table 5.3. The bootstrapped figures in the terminal portfolio value column are the proportion of the 500 series which generated terminal portfolio values smaller than the observed value. Thus, in the 500 replications, 64.8 per cent of the series had terminal values less than 6.9493 using the AR(5) rule. Recall that the bootstrapping was carried out under a random walk null. Therefore, an alternative way to read the figure is that, even with random returns the AR(5) rule was able to generate a terminal portfolio value at least as great as 6.9493 in 35.2 per cent of the cases. Thus for all the rules there is a large number of cases where even larger portfolio values can be generated from random returns, which throws doubt on the strength of the evidence that the large portfolio values provide for predictability of returns. However, before dismissing this evidence, we should take into account that possibility that for the artificial series with a high rule-based portfolio value the buy-and-hold portfolio is also high. We take this into account by also bootstrapping the ratio of the rule-based portfolio to the buy-and-hold portfolio which is given in the next column. We see there that it seems indeed to be the case that high rule-based portfolios are associated with high buy-and-hold portfolios, so that the ratios of the former to the latter observed in the actual data are exceptionally high compared to the bootstrapped ones as indicated by the proportions reported in brackets in the second column of figures. This suggests that the rules have been able to exploit predictability to generate significant excess returns.

The bootstrapped *p*-values for the Pesaran and Timmermann test of predictive accuracy indicate that the theoretical *p*-values are overly supportive of the predictive ability of the forecasting equations – while the AR(5) rule had significant predictive ability at the 5 per cent level and the DoW rule at the 10 per cent level on the basis of the theoretical critical values, the bootstrapped results indicate that this exaggerates the significance of the rules – only the AR(5) rule comes close to being significant at the 10 per cent level.

The opposite is the case for the test of the equality of the rule-based returns and the buy-and-hold return. The bootstrapped results show that all rules have returns which are significantly different from the buy-and-hold alternative, despite that fact that with one exception all the t-ratios are below 1. This presumably reflects the lack of independence of the two return series on which the theoretical p-values are based.

Finally the bootstrapped p-values for the equality of buy and sell returns confirm the outcomes of the previous tests, although the p-values are somewhat different. The AR(5) and AR(2) produce buy and sell returns which are insignificantly different from each other while the last three rules all produce buy and sell returns which are significantly different from each other.

In summary, the initial results show that the use of trading rules based on forecasting equations can generate portfolio values substantially in excess of those resulting from a buy-and-hold strategy. But standard prediction tests and tests of equality of returns between the different portfolio returns indicate that much of this difference is not statistically significant although tests of the difference between buy and sell returns are more favourable to the trading rules. Standard tests ignore non-normalities and likely dependencies within the data and correcting for these using a bootstrapping procedure reverses the outcomes of the equality-of-returns tests and confirms the results of the buy-sell comparison tests so that once the characteristics of the data have been taken into account, there do appear to be significant gains to be had from the use of trading rules based on forecasting equations, even though these equations generally fail a predictive accuracy test.

We turn now to further tests of robustness of our original conclusions.

5.4.4   Comparisons based on Recursive Estimation

We have pointed out earlier that all the results obtained so far have used equations estimated using data for the whole period. This may be a legitimate way of modelling traders' unobservable knowledge of the operation of the market. However, if the estimation procedure is designed to model the way in which traders actually formulate trading rules it is clearly illegitimate since it assumes that they have access to future information which is not in fact available. We assess the importance of this information assumption by re-computing our results using a recursive estimation procedure in which the estimated equation used as the basis for the trading decision is re-estimated every period as a new observation becomes available. The results of this exercise are reported in Table 5.4.

Clearly, the profitability of all the trading rules based on regression equations has fallen substantially. This is a clear measure of the upward bias in the measures of profitability generated by the use of information from the whole sample which is not, in practice, available to traders. The rules based only on the AR models are now less profitable than a simple equity buy-and-hold procedure although the lower returns are matched by a lower standard deviation, making the choice between the two ambiguous for a risk-averse investor. Buying and holding a term deposit clearly dominates the AR trading rules in both return and risk dimensions. The rules which incorporate the calendar dummy variables are still considerably more profitable than the equity buy-and-hold, with terminal values as much as five times that of the latter. Besides, the standard deviations of the returns to the regression-based rules are lower. Hence, while the use of a recursive estimation technique considerably reduces the profitability of the trading rules, it is still considerably more profitable than all the benchmark strategies and less risky than the equity portfolio.

Table 5.4   Trading rules based on recursively estimated forecasting equation

Rule	Portfolio Value	Mean Return (% per day)	Standard Deviation (% per day)
E B&H	1.7151	0.0745	3.2078
DD B&H	1.1995	0.0084	0.0034
TD B&H	1.9452	0.0292	0.0001
Regression Based:			
AR(5)	1.3659	0.0528	2.8215
AR(2)	1.2936	0.0493	2.7842
AR(5), DoW	8.6579	0.1288	2.4503
AR(5), DoW,CNY	7.7595	0.1236	2.4431
DoW	6.7175	0.1156	2.3750

Notes: E B&H = equity buy-and-hold, DD B&H = demand deposit buy-and-hold, TD B&H = term deposit buy-and-hold; DoW = day-of-the-week dummy variables, CNY = Chinese New Year dummy variable.

5.4.5   Comparisons involving Transaction Costs

An important difference between the regression-based trading rules and the benchmark strategies is that the former require portfolio switches between cash and equity which in practice incur transaction costs, while the latter do not. A realistic comparison therefore requires some accounting for transaction costs. The literature on trading rules attests to the fact that trading costs are notoriously difficult to estimate, with the consequence that they are often not explicitly taken into account although their importance is invariably asserted. Alternatively, break-even transaction costs are calculated as the level of transaction costs which just erode the profit advantage of the trading rule relative to some benchmark strategy and the reader is left to decide whether the break-even costs are less or greater than actual transaction costs. We have no reliable information on trading costs in the Chinese market and, instead, recompute the outcomes of our trading strategies using two alternative estimates of likely transaction costs, viz, 1 per cent and 0.5 per cent of the value of the portfolio per transaction. With 1 per cent transaction costs the results in Table 5.4 change to those reported in Table 5.5 and with a cost level of 0.5 per cent (a 1 per cent round-trip cost), the results in Table 5.6 are obtained. Clearly, 1 per cent transaction costs not only wipe out the profits but effectively wipe out the value of the entire portfolio. The results using a 1 per cent round-trip transaction cost assumption are not substantially different as shown in Table 5.6.

Table 5.5   Trading rules using recursive estimation and 1 per cent transaction costs

Rule	Portfolio Value	Mean Return (% per day)	Standard Deviation (% per day)
E B&H	1.7151	0.0745	3.2078
DD B&H	1.1995	0.0084	0.0034
TD B&H	1.9452	0.0292	0.0001
Regression Based:			
AR(5)	0.0547	-0.0933	2.8610
AR(2)	0.0521	-0.0988	2.8176
AR(5), DoW	0.0019	-0.2618	2.5082
AR(5), DoW,CNY	0.0016	-0.2679	2.4982
DoW	0.0012	-0.2843	2.4220

Notes: E B&H = equity buy-and-hold, DD B&H = demand deposit buy-and-hold, TD B&H = term deposit buy-and-hold; DoW = day-of-the-week dummy variables, CNY = Chinese New Year dummy variable.

Table 5.6   Trading rules using recursive estimation and 0.5 per cent transaction costs

Rule	Portfolio Value	Mean Return (% per day)	Standard Deviation (% per day)
E B&H	1.7151	0.0745	3.2078
DD B&H	1.1995	0.0084	0.0034
TD B&H	1.9452	0.0292	0.0001
Regression Based:			
AR(5)	0.2746	-0.0212	2.8357
AR(2)	0.2606	-0.0248	2.7953
AR(5), DoW	0.1279	-0.0665	2.4674
AR(5), DoW,CNY	0.1136	-0.0722	2.4588
DoW	0.0901	-0.0843	2.3860

Notes: E B&H = equity buy-and-hold, DD B&H = demand deposit buy-and-hold, TD B&H = term deposit buy-and-hold; DoW = day-of-the-week dummy variables, CNY = Chinese New Year dummy variable.

A variation on the above results is based on the observation that in the presence of transaction costs the rational investor will switch from one asset to the other only if the predicted excess return exceeds the transaction costs. If we adjust the trading rule to take this effect into account we obtain the results reported in Tables 5.7 and 5.8, based on 1 per cent and 0.5 per cent transaction costs respectively.

Table 5.7   Conditional trading rules based on recursive estimation and 1 per cent transaction costs

Rule	Portfolio Value	Mean Return (% per day)	Standard Deviation (% per day)
E B&H	1.7151	0.0745	3.2078
DD B&H	1.1995	0.0084	0.0034
TD B&H	1.9452	0.0292	0.0001
Regression Based:			
AR(5)	0.5470	-0.0115	2.8799
AR(2)	1.2674	0.0490	2.8051
AR(5), DoW	0.1612	-0.0524	2.5755
AR(5), DoW,CNY	0.3084	-0.0162	2.8018
DoW	0.9976	0.0464	3.1939

Notes: E B&H = equity buy-and-hold, DD B&H = demand deposit buy-and-hold, TD B&H = term deposit buy-and-hold; DoW = day-of-the-week dummy variables, CNY = Chinese New Year dummy variable.

Table 5.8   Conditional trading rules based on recursive estimation and 0.5 per cent transaction costs

Rule	Portfolio Value	Mean Return (% per day)	Standard Deviation (% per day)
E B&H	1.7151	0.0745	3.2078
DD B&H	1.1995	0.0084	0.0034
TD B&H	1.9452	0.0292	0.0001
Regression Based:			
AR(2)	0.4024	-0.0030	2.8479
AR(2)	1.6521	0.0619	2.8246
AR(5), DoW	0.5772	0.0074	2.6199
AR(5),DoW,CNY	0.6079	0.0094	2.6054
DoW	0.7171	0.0208	2.7164

Notes: E B&H = equity buy-and-hold, DD B&H = demand deposit buy-and-hold, TD B&H = term deposit buy-and-hold; DoW = day-of-the-week dummy variables, CNY = Chinese New Year dummy variable.

As expected, the change in the trading rule makes switches less frequent and therefore reduces the losses incurred by using the rule. However, the losses are not so far reversed as to make the rules profitable except for the AR(2)-based rule and even there the rule is not more profitable than the equity buy-and-hold benchmark strategy. The results are not dependent on whether transaction costs are assumed to be 1 per cent or 0.5 per cent.

5.4.6   Comparisons using Weekly and Monthly Data

Based on daily data we found that the apparent profitability of the trading rules is more than completely eroded by what are probably modest transaction costs for an emerging market such as China. It is possible, however, that the application of the rule less frequently than daily would reverse the results since it is clear that 1 per cent trading costs completely swamp the small daily return advantages accruing from the rules. We therefore proceed to a re-examination of the rules using first weekly and then monthly data.

The results for various cases using weekly data are reported in Table 5.9. We again first report the results for three benchmark portfolios: buy-and-hold equity, buy-and-hold demand deposit and buy-and-hold term deposit. We then report the outcomes of a variety of trading rules depending on whether recursive estimation is used or not, and depending on the level of transaction costs and how they are taken into account. All regression results are based on an equation which explains the current return in terms of two lagged returns, the DoW dummy variables being irrelevant to weekly returns and our previous results showing that the Chinese New Year holiday dummy is of little forecasting value.

It will be noted that the terminal values of, and the mean returns to, the benchmark portfolios are marginally different to those computed using daily data and reported in previous tables; this reflects the slightly different sample period used for the weekly data as well as the use of weekly rather than daily compounding. We see that, again, the holding of a 5-year term deposit out-performs the equity buy-and-hold strategy in terms of both return and risk.

The results confirm our conjecture that, while daily trading with 1 per cent transaction costs results in the transaction costs completely swamping the small daily excess return available from the use of a regression-based trading rule, this is not the case when using lower frequency data (and so, making less frequent trades). Using weekly data, the regression-based rule outperforms the equity buy-and-hold strategy even with 1 per cent transaction costs. It is interesting to observe that the use of the conditional rule reduces profits while in the case of daily data the use of the conditional rule considerably improved the profits (reduced the losses) generated by the rule.

Table 5.9   Profitability of trading rules using weekly data

Rule	Portfolio Value	Mean Return (% per week)	Standard Deviation (% per week)
E B&H	1.7983	0.4402	8.8584
DD B&H	1.1941	0.0407	0.1625
TD B&H	1.8686	0.1463	0.0352
Regression Based:			
Full-sample	5.2367	0.6643	8.6241
Recursive	2.3964	0.4987	8.7819
Recursive, TC = 1%	2.0770	0.4643	8.7493
Recursive, TC = 0.5%	2.2314	0.4815	8.7651
Conditional, TC = 1%	1.6764	0.4239	8.8579
Conditional, TC = 0.5%	1.7193	0.4297	8.8570

Notes: E B&H = equity buy-and-hold, DD B&H = demand deposit buy-and-hold, TD B&H = term deposit buy-and-hold; TC = transactions costs as percentage of portfolio value.

The results using monthly data are reported in Table 5.10. They are all based on equations with two lagged returns and all accumulations started 34 months into the sample to allow for lags and 30 months for the initialization of the recursive procedure. The longer initialization time explains the difference in the characteristics of the benchmark portfolios. Not surprisingly, the term deposit and demand deposit portfolios have a lower terminal value than they had when we used weekly and daily data, reflecting the shorter accumulation period. However, the equity portfolio has a higher value and corresponding mean return, reflecting the very poor returns in the beginning of the sample which are avoided by the later starting period for the accumulation of the portfolios.

If we use a forecasting equation estimated over the entire sample, the trading rule returns a higher sum at the end of the accumulation period than the benchmark portfolios as well as a lower standard deviation than the equity buy-and-hold strategy. Once we use recursive estimation to more closely approximate the information available to a trader, the excess return to the trading rule disappears; in fact, the trading rule portfolio has the same terminal value as the equity buy-and-hold portfolio. This reflects the fact that there are no portfolio switches in this case – the forecasting equation always forecasts a higher return for equity than the return to cash so that there is an initial purchase of equity which is held for the remainder of the sample. The same is true once we take transaction costs into account; the small fall in the terminal value simply reflects the initial transaction cost of purchasing shares.

Table 5.10   Profitability of trading rules using monthly data

Rule	Portfolio Value	Mean Return (% per month)	Standard Deviation (% per month)
E B&H	2.7085	1.6905	9.2817
DD B&H	1.1355	01608	0.0705
TD B&H	1.6856	0.7018	0.1140
Regression Based:			
Full-sample	3.3039	1.9222	9.0103
Recursive	2.7085	1.6905	9.2817
Recursive, TC = 1%	2.6755	1.6778	9.3096
Recursive, TC = 0.5%	2.6920	1.6841	9.2955
Conditional, TC = 1%	2.6755	1.6778	9.9306
Conditional, TC = 0.5%	2.6920	1.6841	9.2955

Notes: E B&H = equity buy-and-hold, DD B&H = demand deposit buy-and-hold, TD B&H = term deposit buy-and-hold; TC = transactions costs as percentage of portfolio value.

A comparison of the results for the three cases considered – daily, weekly and monthly – suggests that, once transaction costs are taken into account, daily trading profits are too small to offset trading costs, but that a weekly trading frequency allows the trader to make a profit based on regression equation forecasts. Finally, monthly trading is not profitable due to the poor performance of the forecasting equation – it always forecasts equity to have a superior return compared to cash so that the decision is always to hold equity, and the trading-rule and equity buy-and-hold portfolios have the same return.

5.5   CONCLUSION

This chapter emerges from the literature which reports tests of efficiency of the newly emerging Chinese stock market. There have been a number of recent studies which observe deviations from the weak EMH in the form of predictability in stock returns on the basis of their own past values. None, however, have taken the extra step to test the economic significance of the observed predictability by asking whether it is economically significant, i.e. could a trader make profits from the predictability.

In this chapter we have carried out this step by examining the profitability of trading rules based on regression equations of the type commonly used to test the weak EMH. Using daily data and forecasting equations estimated over the entire sample period, we found that portfolios based on trading rules substantially outperform an equity buy-and-hold strategy – the terminal value of the trading-rule-based portfolio is up to 11 times as large as that resulting from simply holding the market index. We subjected these conclusions to a number of robustness tests.

First, we showed that the results were sensitive to the choice of the beginning of the evaluation period as well as to the length of the period over which the forecasting equation is estimated.

Next, statistical tests were carried out to see whether the differences between the rule outcomes were significant. Tests based on standard critical values proved not to be very encouraging for the rules. However, we argued that there were reasons to be cautious about these conclusions since standard critical values may be inappropriate due to the violation of important underlying assumptions. To account for these we used a bootstrapping procedure to generate alternative critical values and found that using these we could conclude that the differences between the rule and buy-and-hold portfolios are significant.

Further results involved using recursive estimation to more closely approximate the actual information likely to be available to a trader, as well as taking into account transaction costs. These modifications considerably reduced the advantage of using a trading rule; this was particularly the case when modest trading costs were imposed on the exercise – trading according to the forecasting rule actually lost money as small daily excess returns were more than completely eroded by transaction costs. This was generally not the case however, when we used weekly or monthly data so that trading was restricted to occur at weekly or monthly intervals. With less frequent trades, some rules returned a better end result than a buy-and-hold strategy.

NOTES

1. Hudson, Dempsey and Keasey (1996) apply the BLL procedure to UK stock prices and arrive at broadly similar conclusions. Others have examined trading rules for emerging markets – Bessembinder and Chan (1995) apply the BLL procedure to Asian stock markets, Ratner and Leal (1999) apply it to several markets in Asia and Latin America and Gunasekarage and Power (2001) also apply the BLL procedure to four emerging South Asian stock markets.

2. An interesting example of an alternative way to avoid data-mining in rule choice where regression-based forecasting equations drive the trading rule is the work by Pesaran and Timmermann (1995, 2000). They not only re-estimate the forecasting equation after each new data point becomes available but also re-run the specification search for the form of the forecasting equation at each point.

3. For general descriptions of bootstrapping see Efron and Tibshirani (1993) and Li and Maddala (1996).

6.   Stock returns and market turnover

The relationship between stock price changes (returns) and trading volume (market turnover) has been subject to extensive research.[1] Earlier empirical studies focus primarily on well-developed financial markets (such as New York and London) and are concerned mainly with contemporaneous correlations rather than dynamic causal relationships.[2] Granger and Morgenstern (1963), Godfrey, Granger and Morgenstern (1964), Crouch (1970a, 1970b), Rogalski (1978) and Epps (1975, 1977), among others, are representative of earlier literature that finds either no significant correlation or a positive contemporaneous correlation between returns and trading volume. Since the early 1990s, however, there has been an increasing number of studies that investigate the relationship between stock returns and trading volume in the emerging markets.[3] Moreover, the resurgent empirical studies on the topic emphasize lead-lag causal relationships and cross-markets spillovers rather than simple contemporaneous correlations.

The recent interest in the emerging financial markets reflects both the increasing importance of these markets in the world financial scene and concerns that unique characteristics of these markets may shed more light on the return-volume relationship. A good example is China's stock market. Since its establishment in the early 1990s, China's stock market has expanded rapidly in terms of capitalization, turnover and number of firms listed (see Chapter 2 for a review). Furthermore, China's stock market, similar to other emerging financial markets, faces a distinctive institutional and regulatory environment compared to those of the well-developed financial markets. Such disparities are likely to give rise to information flows that are different from those of the well-developed financial markets, which will, in turn, affect their return-volume relationship.

This chapter has two objectives. First, we are able to access the *Taiwan Economic Journal (TEJ) Mainland China Database* that provides updated and consistent calculations of price indices and trading volumes for the Chinese stock exchanges in Shanghai and Shenzhen. No existing study on China's stock market has used as long a sample period or more consistently defined variables from a common source than the current study. The importance of using the most updated data is clear with the onset of the Asian financial crisis and the return of Hong Kong to Chinese rule in 1997, events which may be expected to have affected the relationship between China's stock market and the Hong Kong market.

The second objective of this chapter is to focus on the dynamic causal relationship between returns and turnover for individual markets and cross-markets spillovers. The resurgence of empirical research on the emerging markets (in particular on China's financial markets) almost exclusively focuses on price movements in an individual market and/or price co-movements across different markets. These studies ignore information contained in trading volume that provides predictive power for stock returns. As reviewed in Chapter 3, Bailey (1994), Ma (1996), Yeh and Lee (2000) and Xu (2000) are some examples of studies on price movements and co-movements of China's financial markets. Lee and Rui (2000) is the only study that emphasizes both contemporaneous correlations and dynamic causal relationships between returns and trading volume for the Chinese market. Unfortunately, their sample only runs until the end of 1997 and thus neglects important changes in the institutional and regulatory framework facing the investors since then.

The remainder of this chapter is organized into four main sections. Section 6.1 reviews both the empirical and theoretical literature. Section 6.2 describes the data. Testing procedures and results are discussed in each of the six sub-sections of section 6.3, followed by discussion and conclusion in section 6.4.

6.1 LITERATURE REVIEW

Early empirical studies such as Granger and Morgenstern (1963) and Godfrey, Granger and Morgenstern (1964) find no relationship between weekly price changes and volume. Rather, they find that price changes follow a random walk. Later, Crouch (1970a, 1970b) finds a positive correlation between volume and the absolute value of returns. Rogalski (1978) finds a positive contemporaneous correlation between volume and returns using monthly stock and warrant data, while Epps (1975, 1977) finds the same relationship using transactions data. Smirlock and Starks (1985) find evidence of asymmetry in the relationship between returns and volume. More specifically, they find that the response of volume to returns is greater for price increases than for price decreases.

More recent research examines the lead-lag relationship between returns and volume. Smirlock and Starks (1988) find a strong positive lagged relationship between volume and absolute price changes using individual stock transactions data. Bhagat and Bhatia (1996), using daily data, test causality in both mean and variance and report that returns cause volume, rather than that volume causes returns. A non-linear Granger causality test was performed by Hiemstra and Jones (1994); they conclude that there is a significant positive relation going in both directions between volume and returns.

There is an extensive literature on the theoretical groundings for a positive correlation between trading volume and returns. Wang (1994) develops a model of competitive stock trading in which investors are heterogeneous in their information and private investment opportunities and rationally trade for both informational and non-informational motives. It is found that volume is positively correlated with absolute changes in prices. One stream of theoretical model relies on asymmetric information or differences in opinion about a security's value to explain trading volume. The extent of disagreement among traders is reflected in the trading volume. Consequently, there is a positive relation between volume and absolute price changes (Epps and Epps, 1976). Blume, Easley and O'Hara (1994) present a model in which volume contains valuable information about past price movements, and traders who include a volume measure in their technical analysis perform better in the market than those who do not. Kramer (1999) constructs a model of a rational trader who operates in a market with transaction costs and noise trading. The level of trading affects the rational trader's marginal cost of transacting; as a result, trading volume is a source of risk.

A considerable number of empirical studies focus on the empirical relationship between returns and volume in emerging markets. Ratner and Leal (2001) study emerging markets in Latin America and Asia and find that a positive contemporaneous relationship exists between returns and volume in all countries except India. Bi-directional Granger-causality is observed between returns and volume and asymmetry tests indicate that returns relate most consistently to volume across all countries during rising rather than falling stock market returns. Saatcioglu and Starks (1998) use monthly return and market turnover series from six Latin American stock markets to test the relation and find a positive relation between volume and both magnitude of price change and price change itself, a finding reported by many for developed markets. They also find evidence of a causal relationship running from volume to stock price changes, but not the opposite. Basci, Suheyla and Kursat (1996) use weekly data on 29 individual stocks in Turkey and find that the price level and volume are cointegrated, as predicted by their theoretical model. Silvapulle and Choi (1999) study the linear and non-linear causality between stock price and trading volume using daily Korean Composite Stock Index data and conclude that there is evidence of significant bi-directional linear and non-linear causality between these two series.

An increasing number of studies on the Chinese stock market have been published in recent years. However, most of these studies do not directly consider the relationship between returns and volume, but focus on the price movements alone (see the survey in Chapter 3). An earlier paper that is similar to our current work is the study by Lee and Rui (2000). They use daily data from 12 December 1990 to 31 December 1997 to examine contemporaneous and causal relationships between volume, stock returns and return volatility for both A and B share price indexes on both of China's two stock exchanges. They also examine cross-market causality, including in their sample not only data for the four Chinese series but also indexes for the Hong Kong and US stock markets. They find no evidence that volume Granger-causes returns for individual Chinese markets, but in cross-market analysis, they find considerable evidence of inter-relationships amongst the Chinese markets although they find little predictive ability of the Hong Kong or US markets for the Chinese market.

Our analysis may be seen as an extension of the work of Lee and Rui (2000). In the first place we extend the sample from 1997 to 2002 and thus encompass a period of dramatic events in the Asian financial market. While China's relatively closed economy may have insulated it from outside events during this period, the closer economic relationships between China and Hong Kong may well have had an important effect on the inter-relationships between the markets of the two economies. In any event, only empirical tests will tell whether China's stock market has become more sensitive to movements in the market of its closest neighbour. We address this question directly by an analysis of both the whole sample as well as sub-samples split at 1997.

In addition to extending their sample period, we also extend and sharpen the tests used by Lee and Rui. We sharpen our tests by concentrating on the relationships between volume and returns (leaving aside the effects of volatility) and on the relationships between the four Chinese series and the Hong Kong stock price index, thus leaving aside the influence of the US market. We extend their tests by looking more closely at the contemporaneous relationship between stock prices and volume, including an analysis of asymmetry in this relationship.

6.2   DATA

We obtained the stock price indices and market turnover data for the Chinese market from the *Taiwan Economic Journal (TEJ) Mainland China Database*. Price-index data for Hong Kong (stock price index, total market value and value of shares traded) are from *Datastream*. The following are the daily indices used in the current study:

1.   Shanghai A shares - daily price index (code: SHA, sources: *TEJ*)
2.   Shanghai B shares - daily price index (code: SHB, source: *TEJ*)
3.   Shenzhen A shares - daily price index (code: SZA, source: *TEJ*)
4.   Shenzhen B shares - daily price index (code: SZB, source: *TEJ*)
5.   Hong Kong Total Market - daily price index (code: HK, source: *Datastream*)

The sample period for all series runs from 6 October 1992, which is the earliest date available for the Chinese data from *TEJ*, to 27 June 2002. We use a balanced dataset, meaning all return and turnover series for the five stock exchanges under study have the same number of observations (N = 2279) in the sample period. Since the Chinese stock market closes for more days due to longer public holidays (such as the Chinese New Year and National Day holidays) than the Hong Kong market, we delete a number of the Chinese non-trading days from the Hong Kong data series. The deletion of these sample observations does not affect any of our results for individual markets.

Furthermore, in our analysis we split the entire sample period into two sub-periods to test whether a structural change has taken place in the dynamic relationship between returns and trading volume since the onset of the Asian financial crisis and the establishment of the Hong Kong SAR in 1997. We thus set the first sub-period from 6 October 1992 to 31 December 1997 and the second sub-period from 1 January 1998 to 27 June 2002 to coincide with these events.

In this chapter, returns are calculated as the percentage change of the closing price indices with the formula: $RET_t = [\ln(P_t) - \ln(P_{t-1})]*100$, where $\ln(P_t)$ denotes the natural logarithm of the closing index at time t. We use market turnover rather than the raw volume of shares traded to measure trading volume. Turnover has an advantage over volume of shares traded in events such as stock splits or right issues which would increase the number of shares outstanding, but leave turnover relatively unaffected. Consequently, using the number of shares traded as a measure of trading volume without making appropriate adjustments renders the data series non-comparable before and after the event occurrence. Data on market turnover (TO_t) for the Chinese markets are directly available from *TEJ* and defined as:

$$TO_t = \frac{Volume_t}{Outstanding\ Shares_t} * 100\% \tag{6.1}$$

where Volume is the number of shares traded at day t and Outstanding shares is the number of shares held by the public, which excludes State shares. For Hong Kong, *Datastream* does not directly give data on market turnover so we calculate it by using the total market value and the value of shares traded on each day as:

$$TO_t = \frac{Value\ of\ Shares\ Traded_t}{Total\ Market\ Value_t} * 100\% \tag{6.2}$$

In Table 6.1, we report the mean, standard deviation, skewness and excess kurtosis statistics for the return series, and mean and standard deviation for the turnover series. The daily mean returns are roughly the same for both

Shanghai A and B shares at around 0.04 per cent per day. However, the standard deviation of returns is 3.01 per cent for Shanghai A compared to 2.45 per cent for Shanghai B. The daily mean returns for Shenzhen A and B and Hong Kong are similar at around 0.02 per cent, with Hong Kong showing the smallest standard deviation at 1.88 per cent. The skewness and excess kurtosis statistics show that all are most positively skewed and leptokurtic, indicating the non-normality common in financial data. The means and standard deviations of the turnover series are shown in the last two columns of Table 6.1. The figures show that on average turnover for A shares is approximately four to five times higher than that of B shares, but A shares' turnover is two to three times more volatile than that of B shares. Hong Kong daily turnover is similar to that of A shares, but volatility is approximately midway between that of A and B shares.

Table 6.1   Summary statistics for return and turnover

Variable	No. of observations	Return (%)				Turnover (%)	
		Mean	SD	Skewness	Kurtosis	Mean	SD
Shanghai A	2279	0.041	3.010	35.805	200.124	2.301	2.344
Shanghai B	2279	0.040	2.449	9.569	40.768	0.538	0.881
Shenzhen A	2279	0.029	2.712	18.400	143.334	2.048	2.185
Shenzhen B	2279	0.023	2.482	6.891	62.038	0.390	0.860
Hong Kong	2279	0.026	1.878	8.443	127.419	1.870	1.329

Notes: The skewness and excess kurtosis statistics are $N(0,1)$-distributed under the null hypothesis of normally distributed returns. Returns are calculated as the first difference of the log of daily closing price indices, multiplied by 100. Turnover is the percentage of outstanding shares traded in a day for the Chinese indices, and is the percentage of total market value traded in a day for Hong Kong.

6.3   EMPIRICAL TESTS

6.3.1   Tests for the Presence of a Unit Root

We begin our investigation by testing the stationarity of the return and turnover series for all indices under study. In Table 6.2 we report the Dickey-Fuller (DF) and Augmented Dickey-Fuller (ADF) statistics with and without a trend for the return and turnover series.

All the DF and ADF test statistics in Table 6.2 take considerably larger (negative) values than the critical values at the 5 per cent significance level. Thus, we can reject the null hypothesis of the presence of a unit root in these series and conclude that they are stationary. The test results are clearly not sensitive to the number of lags or to the presence of a trend.

Table 6.2　Unit roots tests for stationarity

Variable	With Trend		Without Trend	
	DF	ADF(1)	DF	ADF(1)
Returns				
Shanghai A	-46.688	-32.000	-46.698	-32.007
Shanghai B	-40.267	-31.426	-40.256	-31.410
Shenzhen A	-46.734	-32.036	-46.739	-32.038
Shenzhen B	-40.109	-30.160	-40.081	-30.130
Hong Kong	-45.675	-33.662	-45.653	-33.633
Turnover				
Shanghai A	-14.053	-12.719	-13.174	-11.867
Shanghai B	-18.840	-13.381	-18.044	-12.780
Shenzhen A	-11.801	-9.6521	-11.640	-9.5107
Shenzhen B	-12.769	-9.0648	-12.169	-8.6266
Hong Kong	-26.454	-19.773	-26.460	-19.777

Notes:　DF and ADF denote Dickey-Fuller and Augmented Dickey-Fuller τ-statistics, respectively. The 5% critical value is -3.414 (with trend) and -2.863 (without trend).

6.3.2　Contemporaneous Relationship between Return and Turnover

In Figure 6.1, we show the scatter plots of turnover versus returns for the four indices. While it is difficult to make any definitive statement about the strength of the contemporaneous relationship between returns and turnover by looking only at the scatter plots, they appear to be consistent with the V-shape commonly reported by previous studies.

We now test formally the direction and strength of the contemporaneous relationship between turnover and returns by using the following regressions:

$$TO_t = \beta_0 + \beta_1 RET_t + \epsilon_t \tag{6.3}$$

$$TO_t = \beta_0 + \beta_1 \mid RET_t \mid + \epsilon_t \tag{6.4}$$

where TO_t and RET_t are turnover and returns at time period t, respectively and ϵ_t is a random error term. In equation (6.3), we test whether returns and turnover are contemporaneously associated, whereas equation (6.4) tests whether the absolute value of returns and turnover are contemporaneously associated. Thus, equation (6.3) conjectures a positive linear relationship while equation (6.4) conjectures a V-shape relationship between returns and turnover. We report the test results in Table 6.3.[4]

The results in Table 6.3 show that the contemporaneous relationship is positive and significant for all four Chinese markets but not for Hong Kong. Even for the Chinese market, however, the degree of explanation is low, judging by the value of the adjusted R^2s. According to the table, the relationship is much stronger between the absolute value of returns and turnover; in this form it is clearly significant for all markets, providing strong evidence that the relationship between these variables is non-linear and supporting the V-shaped pattern evident in Figure 6.1 between returns and turnover.

Table 6.3   Regression results

Daily Index	Number of observations	β_0	β_1	Adjusted R^2
Panel A: $TO_t = \beta_0 + \beta_1 RET_t + \epsilon_t$				
Shanghai A	2279	2.2934***	17.720***	0.0513
		(47.94)	(11.15)	
Shanghai B	2279	0.5361***	4.6193***	0.0161
		(29.28)	(6.18)	
Shenzhen A	2279	2.0441***	14.984***	0.0342
		(45.43)	(9.03)	
Shenzhen B	2279	0.3888***	5.0122***	0.0205
		(21.81)	(6.98)	
Hong Kong	2279	1.8799***	-0.2676	-0.0004
		(67.50)	(0.18)	
Panel B: $TO_t = \beta_0 + \beta_1 \mid RET_t \mid + \epsilon_t$				
Shanghai A	2279	1.5490***	42.295***	0.1917
		(28.31)	(23.26)	
Shanghai B	2279	0.2989***	14.787***	0.0950
		(12.79)	(15.50)	
Shenzhen A	2279	1.4268***	35.465***	0.1124
		(25.24)	(17.02)	
Shenzhen B	2279	0.1419***	16.407***	0.1407
		(6.741)	(19.34)	
Hong Kong	2279	1.4237***	35.927***	0.1396
		(40.62)	(19.25)	

Notes: *t*-statistics are in parentheses and *** denotes statistical significance at the 1 per cent level.

Interpretations of the estimated coefficients can be made. For example, results for Shanghai A in panel A of Table 6.3 suggest that turnover is on average roughly 2.3 per cent when returns are zero and increases by around 18 percentage points for every one percentage point rise in returns. Comparing these results to panel B of Table 6.3, we find that the estimated intercept and slope for Shanghai A are roughly 1.6 per cent and 42 per cent, respectively, reconfirming that the V-shape contemporaneous relationship is more pronounced than the positive linear contemporaneous relationship.

6.3.3   Further Asymmetry Testing

From the test results above, the data suggest that the relationship between returns and turnover is a V-shaped one. This is a particular form of asymmetry which restricts the coefficient of the negative returns to be equal

Figure 6.1 Scatter plots of turnover and returns

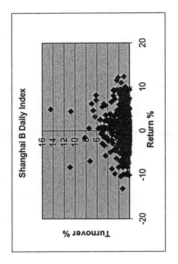

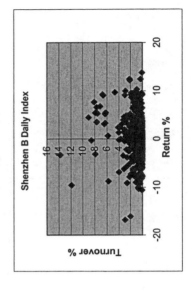

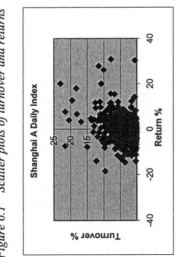

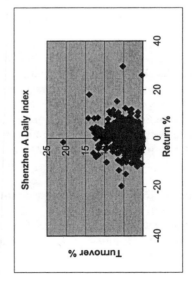

to, but of opposite sign, that of the positive returns. In their study of the emerging markets in Latin America and Asia, Ratner and Leal (2001, p.5) report that: "Asymmetry tests indicate that stock returns relate most consistently to volume across all countries during rising rather than falling stock market returns", thus suggesting that this restriction may not be supported in practice. We therefore go on to relax the restriction on the form of asymmetry embedded in equation (6.4) and test the five indices for asymmetry by using the following regression:

$$TO_t = \beta_0 + \beta_1 RET_t^{(+)} + \beta_2 RET_t^{(-)} + \epsilon_t \qquad (6.5)$$

where $RET_t^{(+)} = RET_t$ if $RET_t > 0$, 0 otherwise and $RET_t^{(-)} = RET_t$ if $RET_t < 0$, 0 otherwise. The simple linear relationship (6.3) is a special case where $\beta_1 = \beta_2$. The form of the asymmetry in equation (6.4) is captured by the restriction that $\beta_1 = -\beta_2$, both of which can be tested in the framework of equation (6.5). We report t-statistics for both tests in Table 6.4. Since the slope coefficients β_1 and β_2 represent the response by turnover to either rising returns or falling returns, respectively, the Ratner and Leal (2001) finding would suggest β_1 positive and β_2 negative and, furthermore, the absolute value of the estimate for β_1 larger than that of β_2.

Table 6.4 contains asymmetry test results for the five indices. The results show that all estimated coefficients are statistically significant at the 1 per cent level and that all estimated β_1 are positive and estimated β_2 negative, as expected. More importantly, estimated β_1 are larger in absolute size than estimated β_2 in all cases except Hong Kong where we see the opposite is true. In the last two columns of Table 6.4, we present the results of a *t*-test for the null hypotheses of $\beta_1 = \beta_2$ and $\beta_1 = -\beta_2$. Not surprisingly, in light of the results reported in Tables 6.2 and 6.3, the tests reject the null hypothesis of equality between β_1 and β_2, indicating a significant asymmetric V-shape relationship between turnover and returns. However, for all but Hong Kong the tests also decisively reject the restriction on asymmetry implicit in the equation which uses the absolute value of returns as the regressor and supports the Ratner and Leal result that the response to an upswing is stronger than that to a downturn in returns.

6.3.4 Causality Testing: Individual Markets Analysis

Tests for the contemporaneous relationship between returns and turnover that have been conducted so far do not consider the dynamic causal relationship between the two variables. In this section, we turn to tests of whether returns "cause" turnover or turnover "causes" return over time. Of course, the causation can be running both ways in which we see a bi-directional or feedback relationship between returns and turnover. We employ the following bivariate vector autoregression (VAR) for the causality testing:

$$
\begin{aligned}
x_t &= \delta_0 + \sum_{i=1}^{m} \delta_i x_{t-i} + \sum_{i=1}^{n} \lambda_i y_{t-i} + \varepsilon_{1t} \\
y_t &= \gamma_0 + \sum_{i=1}^{m} \gamma_i x_{t-i} + \sum_{i=1}^{n} \beta_i y_{t-i} + \varepsilon_{2t}
\end{aligned}
\tag{6.6}
$$

where x_t and y_t are returns and turnover at time t, respectively. The bivariate VAR in equation (6.6) tests causality by implementing the propositions that 1) the future cannot cause the present or the past; 2) an event x can only cause y if it occurs before y; and 3) the prediction of y can be made more accurate given the occurrence of x. These basic intuitions underline the widely used Granger (1969) causality test. Formally, x Granger-causes y if the mean square error associated with the prediction of y_t given the information set I_{t-i}, $\sigma^2 (y_t \mid I_{t-i})$, is smaller than the mean square error associated with the prediction of y_t given the information set that does not include past, $\sigma^2 (y_t \mid I_{t-i} - x_{t-i})$. In the framework set out above we use an information set consisting of only past x and past y. Thus, in the first equation of (6.6), if the joint effect of the y_{t-i} is significant in predicting x_t, then we can say that y Granger-causes x. An F-test with the null hypothesis that all the λ_i jointly equal zero is appropriate in this context. Similarly, to test whether x Granger-causes y, we can conduct an F-test with the null hypothesis that all the γ_i jointly equal zero in the second equation of (6.6). In case of a rejection resulting from both F-tests in (6.6), we have a bi-directional causality or a feedback relationship between x and y (or between returns and turnover).

Table 6.4   Asymmetry tests results

Daily Index	β_0	β_1	β_2	Adjusted R-square	t-statistic $\beta_1 = \beta_2$	t-statistic $\beta_1 = -\beta_2$
Shanghai A	1.5976	49.729	-28.918	0.2082	21.2653	6.9723
	(29.26)	(23.78)	(10.99)		[0.000]	[0.000]
Shanghai B	0.3080	16.990	-11.318	0.1007	14.6698	3.9117
	(13.16)	(15.37)	(8.70)		[0.000]	[0.000]
Shenzhen A	1.4566	45.428	-21.711	0.1334	16.1787	7.4898
	(26.02)	(18.53)	(7.87)		[0.000]	[0.000]
Shenzhen B	0.1493	19.313	-12.419	0.1501	18.6569	5.1117
	(7.11)	(18.98)	(10.81)		[0.000]	[0.000]
Hong Kong	1.4236	35.041	-36.873	0.1393	19.2559	-06656
	(40.61)	(15.29)	(15.71)		[0.000]	[0.506]

Notes: t-statistics are in parentheses under the estimated coefficients. Figures in the square brackets under the t-statistics in the last two columns are P-values.

Table 6.5 shows regression results for the first equation of (6.6) that indicate whether turnover Granger-causes returns for the five indices under study. In all cases the value of R^2 indicates that there is little explanatory power in the returns equations which is consistent with the efficient markets hypothesis which states that returns are not predictable with publicly-available information. Nevertheless, turnover has significant incremental explanatory power for returns in both Shenzhen B and Hong Kong, the latter surprisingly so since it would commonly be judged the most efficient of the four markets. The results indicate that turnover Granger-causes returns on Shenzhen B and Hong Kong. In addition the results for Shanghai A are marginally significant. Thus there is some evidence of Granger-causality between turnover and returns in our five markets.

Table 6.6 shows similar results for the second equation of (6.6) which indicate whether returns Granger-cause turnover for the five indices under study. In this case explanatory power is very much higher, indicating that a larger proportion of movement in turnover is predictable using past turnover and returns. The F-test results show that returns contribute significantly to this explanatory power for all markets except Hong Kong, so that returns Granger-cause turnover on all markets except Hong Kong.

In short, the results of causality testing for the individual markets indicate that turnover Granger-causes returns on Hong Kong, while returns Granger-cause turnover on Shanghai A, Shanghai B and Shenzhen A and a feedback relationship between returns and turnover on Shenzhen B. These results are in some contrast to those reported by Lee and Rui (2000) for an earlier period – they do not report separate results for Hong Kong and find that for all four Chinese markets returns Granger-cause volume, and volume fails to cause returns, even using a 10 per cent significance level.

6.3.5 Causality Testing: Cross-markets Analysis

In this section we extend the analysis by considering the cross-market causal linkages in returns and turnover. We use the bivariate VAR in equation (6.6) with returns and turnover in different markets. This procedure is in contrast to the procedure used by Lee and Rui (2000) in their earlier study. In all their cross-market tests they use six variables in the information set – returns, volume and volatility in each of two markets. Since our focus is solely on the relationship between returns in one market and turnover in another, we find that restricting the information set to lags of two variables, rather than six, sharpens the test by excluding potentially irrelevant variables – in the limit it is always possible to specify a sufficiently broad information set that the omission of any particular element will have insignificant effects on the explanatory power of the prediction equation. On the other hand, it may be argued that by leaving out

Table 6.5 *Granger causality test results (individual market analysis I)*

Indices	δ_0	δ_1	δ_2	δ_3	δ_4	δ_5	λ_1	λ_2	λ_3	λ_4	λ_5	F-stat	Adjusted R^2
Shanghai A	0.0006	0.0022	0.0286	0.0667	0.0180	0.0347	0.0012	0.0011	0.0003	0.0011	0.0016	2.3819	0.0103
	(0.64)	(0.10)	(1.19)	(2.78)	(0.76)	(1.54)	(1.95)	(1.50)	(0.36)	(1.52)	(2.78)	[0.036]	
Shanghai B	0.0002	0.1742	0.0292	0.0553	0.0065	0.0322	0.0007	0.0007	0.0002	0.0008	0.0000	0.6725	0.0301
	(0.28)	(8.23)	(1.34)	(2.54)	(0.30)	(1.51)	(0.73)	(0.70)	(0.15)	(0.78)	(0.02)	[0.644]	
Shenzhen A	0.0004	0.0113	0.0272	0.0059	0.0357	0.0373	0.0006	0.0002	0.0008	0.0015	0.0007	1.1585	0.0028
	(0.50)	(0.51)	(1.13)	(0.25)	(1.50)	(1.65)	(0.90)	(0.21)	(1.01)	(2.03)	(1.06)	[0.327]	
Shenzhen B	0.0004	0.1575	0.0107	0.0655	0.0491	0.0041	0.0029	0.0013	0.0034	0.0042	0.0049	5.4942	0.0465
	(0.73)	(7.49)	(0.49)	(3.00)	(2.24)	(0.19)	(2.13)	(0.86)	(2.15)	(2.72)	(3.68)	[0.000]	
Hong Kong	0.0006	0.0450	0.0195	0.0732	0.0477	0.0320	0.0007	0.0011	0.0007	0.0003	0.0006	4.1838	0.0154
	(0.75)	(2.14)	(0.93)	(3.50)	(2.28)	(1.53)	(2.10)	(2.73)	(1.73)	(0.77)	(1.76)	[0.001]	

Notes: The results are from regression $x_t = \delta_0 + \sum_{i=1}^{m} \delta_i x_{t-i} + \sum_{i=1}^{n} \lambda_i y_{t-i} + \varepsilon_{1t}$. x_t and y_t are returns and turnover at time t, respectively. Figures in

parentheses below estimated coefficients are t-statistics. Figures in square brackets below F-statistics are p-values. The F-test is for the hypothesis that λ_i ($i=1,\ldots,5$) are zero, i.e. that y does not Granger-cause x.

Table 6.6   Granger causality test results (individual market analysis II)

Indices	Γ_0	Γ_1	Γ_2	Γ_3	Γ_4	Γ_5	β_1	β_2	β_3	β_4	β_5	F-stat	Adjusted R^2
Shanghai A	0.2699	0.6833	0.0268	0.0871	0.1054	0.0207	12.821	2.1590	1.4137	0.6313	3.0699	52.903	0.7708
	(7.40)	(29.99)	(0.98)	(3.20)	(3.88)	(0.97)	(15.00)	(2.40)	(1.57)	(0.71)	(3.62)	[0.000]	
Shanghai B	0.0699	0.4172	0.1248	0.1464	0.0473	0.1312	4.1728	1.0943	0.5267	0.6633	0.0685	19.744	0.6356
	(5.09)	(19.86)	(5.47)	(6.45)	(2.08)	(6.32)	(8.94)	(2.28)	(1.10)	(1.38)	(0.15)	[0.000]	
Shenzhen A	0.1842	0.5992	0.1223	0.1375	0.0532	0.0028	13.739	0.7221	1.3868	1.4523	0.8650	71.323	0.8253
	(6.50)	(26.85)	(4.72)	(5.32)	(2.07)	(0.14)	(18.29)	(0.89)	(1.72)	(1.82)	(1.14)	[0.000]	
Shenzhen B	0.0375	0.5294	0.2215	0.0734	0.0665	0.0107	4.1771	0.4020	0.4972	0.8968	0.3543	38.327	0.8096
	(4.24)	(25.07)	(9.30)	(3.03)	(2.80)	(0.52)	(12.82)	(1.18)	(1.47)	(2.64)	(1.06)	[0.000]	
Hong Kong	0.5384	0.4027	0.0720	0.1071	0.0855	0.0464	0.0111	0.7515	0.2400	1.7301	2.1211	1.077	0.3226
	(10.85)	(19.19)	(3.19)	(4.75)	(3.78)	(2.20)	(0.01)	(0.61)	(0.20)	(1.41)	(1.73)	[0.371]	

Notes: The results are from regression $y_t = \gamma_0 + \sum_{i=1}^{m} \gamma_i x_{t-i} + \sum_{i=1}^{n} \beta_i y_{t-i} + \varepsilon_{2t}$. x_t and y_t are returns and turnover at time t, respectively. Figures in parentheses below estimated coefficients are t-statistics. Figures in square brackets below F-statistics are p-values. The F-test is for the hypothesis that γ_i ($i=1,\ldots,5$) are zero, i.e. that x does not Granger-cause y.

possibly relevant variables, our results may suffer from omitted variable bias. However, since there is no widely accepted model for stock returns or turnover, it is not possible to specify which variables are relevant or not; certainly Lee and Rui do not specify a model to justify their choice of variables. Hence we confine our test equations to the two variables of interest.

Table 6.7 shows the F-statistics with their corresponding P-values for every regression involving cross-markets returns and turnover. The large number of summary statistics in Table 6.7 is summarized in the second (whole sample period) column of Table 6.8. The notation $x \rightarrow y$ stands for x Granger-causes y and $x \leftrightarrow y$ for a feedback relationship (two-way causation) between x and y.

We start by looking at the results of the whole sample in the second column of Table 6.8. The first noticeable feature of this column is that Hong Kong appears almost completely disconnected from the four mainland Chinese markets, as evidenced by the number of 'No Links' between Hong Kong and the Chinese market. The only direct influence is that Hong Kong returns Granger-cause returns for Shanghai B shares. A second feature is that there is a strong relationship between the two A shares and between the two B shares. We consider each of these features in turn.

It is surprising to find little linkage between Hong Kong and the B market since shares on these markets may be owned by the same investors and therefore possibilities for arbitrage exist. We argue that it is possible that there are indirect linkages between Hong Kong and the four Chinese markets. The Hong Kong market exerts extensive influences on the Chinese market indirectly via Shanghai B because returns on Shanghai B directly or indirectly Granger- cause other returns and turnovers on the Chinese markets. Thus, for example, Hong Kong returns Granger cause Shanghai B returns which, in turn, Granger cause turnover in Shenzhen A shares which, in turn, Granger cause turnover in Shanghai A shares and so on. We summarize the direct and indirect impacts of the Hong Kong market on the Chinese markets in Table 6.9 for the whole sample.

It is clear from Table 6.9 that Hong Kong returns, directly or indirectly, affect returns on Shanghai B and Shenzhen B as well as turnover on all Chinese markets. Note that Hong Kong returns do not help predict returns on either Shanghai A or Shenzhen A. This is hardly surprising since A shares in Shanghai and Shenzhen are strictly for local investors and are denominated in Chinese yuan. Moreover, given that returns are Granger-caused by turnover on the Hong Kong market, Hong Kong turnover then helps predict directly or indirectly returns and turnovers on all Chinese markets, excluding returns on Shanghai A and Shenzhen A.

Table 6.7 *Granger causality test results (cross-markets analysis)*

		Shanghai A		Shanghai B		Shenzhen A		Shenzhen B		Hong Kong	
		RET	TO	RET	TO	RET	TO	RET	TO	RET	TO
Full sample: 6 October 1992 to 27 June 2002											
Shanghai A	RET	NA	NA	0.4216 [0.834]	1.9302 [0.086]	3.7440 [0.002]	32.8564 [0.000]	1.1557 [0.329]	1.3380 [0.245]	1.2908 [0.265]	0.8560 [0.510]
	TO	NA	NA	1.0782 [0.370]	0.2946 [0.916]	1.8520 [0.100]	4.9107 [0.000]	2.4894 [0.029]	0.6377 [0.671]	0.5357 [0.749]	0.2663 [0.932]
Shanghai B	RET	0.4661 [0.802]	1.7801 [0.114]	NA	NA	1.7656 [0.117]	4.4077 [0.001]	0.7182 [0.610]	14.6639 [0.000]	0.5080 [0.770]	0.5830 [0.713]
	TO	0.4839 [0.788]	0.5212 [0.760]	NA	NA	0.5196 [0.762]	0.8265 [0.531]	1.4897 [0.190]	100.3200 [0.000]	0.3111 [0.907]	0.4122 [0.841]
Shenzhen A	RET	3.9837 [0.001]	36.4176 [0.000]	0.8340 [0.525]	3.4730 [0.004]	NA	NA	0.5577 [0.733]	1.1124 [0.352]	1.3124 [0.256]	1.0652 [0.378]
	TO	0.4230 [0.833]	3.4536 [0.004]	0.4232 [0.833]	0.9702 [0.435]	NA	NA	1.5391 [0.174]	0.7129 [0.614]	0.7602 [0.579]	0.5653 [0.727]
Shenzhen B	RET	0.5789 [0.716]	4.0816 [0.001]	2.3705 [0.037]	21.8154 [0.000]	1.2744 [0.272]	5.1408 [0.000]	NA	NA	0.5958 [0.703]	0.4032 [0.847]
	TO	0.2782 [0.925]	0.2529 [0.938]	3.9492 [0.001]	11.6235 [0.000]	0.2795 [0.925]	0.1573 [0.978]	NA	NA	0.3877 [0.858]	0.2342 [0.948]
Hong Kong	RET	1.2829 [0.268]	1.1488 [0.332]	5.2250 [0.000]	1.2731 [0.273]	1.0643 [0.378]	0.7270 [0.603]	1.5573 [0.169]	1.0940 [0.362]	NA	NA
	TO	0.2672 [0.931]	0.0879 [0.994]	1.4252 [0.212]	0.0420 [0.999]	0.2775 [0.926]	0.1968 [0.964]	1.3839 [0.227]	0.3376 [0.890]	NA	NA

Table 6.7 (continued)

Sub-sample: 6 October 1992 to 31 December 1997

		Shanghai A		Shanghai B		Shenzhen A		Shenzhen B		Hong Kong	
		RET	TO	RET	TO	RET	TO	RET	TO	RET	TO
Shanghai A	RET	NA		0.7408	1.6376	2.4916	16.3135	2.8295	1.5851	1.2721	1.4982
				[0.593]	[0.1471]	[0.030]	[0.000]	[0.015]	[0.161]	[0.273]	[0.1875]
	TO		NA	2.4317	2.4443	1.2397	2.6977	4.3904	1.7468	0.3960	0.5404
				[0.033]	[0.032]	[0.288]	[0.020]	[0.0006]	[0.121]	[0.852]	[0.746]
Shanghai B	RET	0.4493	0.7900	NA		2.1259	2.9793	0.9945	8.7598	2.1289	1.1684
		[0.814]	[0.557]			[0.060]	[0.011]	[0.420]	[0.000]	[0.060]	[0.323]
	TO	0.5045	0.1706		NA	0.8209	0.7013	0.5869	0.4972	0.3159	0.3143
		[0.773]	[0.973]			[0.535]	[0.622]	[0.710]	[0.779]	[0.904]	[0.905]
Shenzhen A	RET	2.5014	19.2206	0.9277	3.3681	NA		0.9824	1.7547	1.1557	1.4434
		[0.029]	[0.000]	[0.462]	[0.005]			[0.427]	[0.119]	[0.3291]	[0.206]
	TO	0.3353	1.5585	0.6341	1.4905		NA	2.9043	4.6652	0.9826	1.8758
		[0.892]	[0.169]	[0.674]	[0.190]			[0.013]	[0.000]	[0.427]	[0.096]
Shenzhen B	RET	0.6679	2.3552	5.4109	7.8425	1.1452	2.4818	NA		1.0034	0.6548
		[0.648]	[0.039]	[0.000]	[0.000]	[0.334]	[0.030]			[0.414]	[0.658]
	TO	0.6546	0.2384	4.5160	6.2451	0.5708	0.4931		NA	0.4313	0.4105
		[0.658]	[0.946]	[0.000]	[0.000]	[0.722]	[0.782]			[0.827]	[0.842]
Hong Kong	RET	1.5019	0.8128	5.2846	1.4764	0.8493	0.3481	0.7406	0.3234	NA	
		[0.186]	[0.540]	[0.000]	[0.195]	[0.515]	[0.884]	[0.593]	[0.899]		
	TO	0.4902	0.7023	1.9041	0.2583	0.4304	0.7792	0.7809	1.2967		NA
		[0.784]	[0.622]	[0.091]	[0.936]	[0.828]	[0.565]	[0.563]	[0.263]		

Sub-sample: 1 January 1998 to 27 June 2002

	Shanghai A		Shanghai B		Shenzhen A		Shenzhen B		Hong Kong	
	TO	RET	TO	RET	TO	RET	TO	RET	TO	RET
Shanghai A RET	NA		1.6066 [0.156]	0.8470 [0.516]	0.3448 [0.886]	39.6241 [0.000]	4.6496 [0.000]	1.4137 [0.217]	1.4328 [0.210]	0.7906 [0.556]
Shanghai A TO		NA	2.8003 [0.016]	0.8110 [0.542]	6.4660 [0.000]	3.2484 [0.006]	2.8145 [0.016]	0.8706 [0.500]	0.5275 [0.756]	0.2174 [0.955]
Shanghai B RET	1.9935 [0.077]	8.5531 [0.000]	NA		1.6382 [0.147]	8.5689 [0.000]	0.6628 [0.652]	8.7804 [0.000]	0.4852 [0.788]	0.5304 [0.753]
Shanghai B TO	0.7468 [0.588]	0.5829 [0.713]		NA	0.6332 [0.674]	0.4813 [0.790]	2.0514 [0.069]	133.8858 [0.000]	0.1296 [0.986]	0.4897 [0.784]
Shenzhen A RET	0.6433 [0.667]	41.5247 [0.000]	1.3115 [0.257]	0.6623 [0.652]	NA		4.2060 [0.001]	1.1497 [0.332]	1.2631 [0.278]	0.8166 [0.538]
Shenzhen A TO	5.5854 [0.000]	12.4215 [0.000]	1.4211 [0.214]	0.8673 [0.502]		NA	1.5522 [0.171]	1.3036 [0.260]	0.3831 [0.861]	0.3900 [0.856]
Shenzhen B RET	2.2918 [0.044]	10.9379 [0.000]	0.7855 [0.560]	13.7428 [0.000]	2.1811 [0.054]	12.3701 [0.000]	NA		0.4772 [0.793]	0.1450 [0.982]
Shenzhen B TO	0.7092 [0.617]	0.5209 [0.761]	1.7614 [0.118]	7.6007 [0.000]	0.6402 [0.669]	0.2738 [0.928]		NA	0.3211 [0.900]	0.3842 [0.860]
Hong Kong RET	1.1308 [0.342]	1.4273 [0.212]	3.0074 [0.011]	0.8815 [0.493]	1.3072 [0.258]	1.6539 [0.143]	1.6237 [0.151]	1.3140 [0.256]	NA	
Hong Kong TO	0.4297 [0.828]	0.9123 [0.472]	1.4583 [0.201]	0.0481 [0.999]	0.4132 [0.840]	1.0078 [0.412]	1.3965 [0.223]	0.1082 [0.991]		NA

Notes:

1. Figures in the tables are *F*-statistics for the test that the variable in the row Granger-causes the variable in the column.
2. *P*-values are in square brackets.

Table 6.8   *Direct causal linkages between returns and turnover for Hong Kong and other Chinese markets: whole sample and sub-samples*

	Whole sample period 6/10/92 – 27/6/02	Sub-sample 1 6/10/92 – 31/12/97	Sub-sample 2 1/1/98 – 27/6/02
Shanghai A Shanghai B	No Links	No Links	$RET^{SHB} \to TO^{SHA}$
Shanghai A Shenzhen A	$RET^{SHA} \to TO^{SZA}$ $RET^{SHA} \leftrightarrow RET^{SZA}$ $RET^{SZA} \to TO^{SHA}$ $TO^{SHA} \to TO^{SZA}$	$RET^{SHA} \to TO^{SZA}$ $RET^{SZA} \to TO^{SHA}$	$RET^{SHA} \leftrightarrow TO^{SZA}$ $RET^{SZA} \leftrightarrow TO^{SHA}$ $TO^{SHA} \leftrightarrow TO^{SZA}$
Shanghai A Shenzhen B	$RET^{SZB} \to TO^{SHA}$	$TO^{SHA} \to RET^{SZB}$	$RET^{SHA} \to RET^{SZB}$ $RET^{SZB} \to TO^{SHA}$
Shanghai A Hong Kong	No Links	No Links	No Links
Shanghai B Shenzhen A	$RET^{SHB} \to TO^{SZA}$ $RET^{SZA} \to TO^{SHB}$	$RET^{SZA} \to TO^{SHB}$ $RET^{SHB} \to TO^{SZA}$	$RET^{SHB} \to TO^{SZA}$
Shanghai B Shenzhen B	$TO^{SHB} \leftrightarrow TO^{SZB}$ $RET^{SHB} \leftrightarrow TO^{SZB}$ $RET^{SZB} \to TO^{SHB}$	$TO^{SZB} \to TO^{SHB}$ $RET^{SHB} \leftrightarrow TO^{SZB}$ $RET^{SZB} \to TO^{SHB}$ $RET^{SZB} \to RET^{SHB}$	$TO^{SZB} \leftrightarrow TO^{SHB}$ $RET^{SHB} \to TO^{SZB}$ $RET^{SZB} \to TO^{SHB}$
Shanghai B Hong Kong	$RET^{HK} \to RET^{SHB}$	$RET^{HK} \to RET^{SHB}$	$RET^{HK} \to RET^{SHB}$
Shenzhen A Shenzhen B	$RET^{SZB} \to TO^{SZA}$	$TO^{SZA} \to TO^{SZB}$	$RET^{SZA} \to RET^{SZB}$ $RET^{SZB} \to TO^{SZA}$
Shenzhen A Hong Kong	No Links	No Links	No Links
Shenzhen B Hong Kong	No Links	No Links	No Links

Notes: RET and TO denote return and turnover, respectively. The superscripts HK, SHA, SHB, SZA and SZB denote respectively Hong Kong, Shanghai A, Shanghai B, Shenzhen A and Shenzhen B. The notation $x \to y$ stands for x Granger-causes y, and $x \leftrightarrow y$ for a feedback relationship between x and y. This table summarizes results contained in Table 6.7. All causal relationships listed above are significant at the 1 per cent level.

Our next focus is the Shanghai and Shenzhen markets for the whole sample period. From the second column of Table 6.8, we observe that Shanghai A returns Granger-cause Shenzhen A turnover and have a feedback relationship with Shenzhen A returns. Indirectly, returns on Shanghai A help predict turnover on all Chinese markets as well as returns on Shanghai B. Shanghai B returns help predict turnovers on all Chinese markets and have a feedback relationship with returns on Shenzhen B. For Shenzhen markets, returns on Shenzhen A and Shenzhen B help predict turnovers on all Chinese markets directly and indirectly. Shenzhen A returns help predict returns on Shanghai

A and Shanghai B, while returns on Shenzhen B help predict returns on Shanghai B.

All in all, we find Hong Kong turnover and returns are good predictors of turnover on all Chinese markets and of returns on Shanghai B and Shenzhen B. They do not, however, help predict returns on the Chinese A markets. For the Shanghai and Shenzhen markets, the following observations are made: 1) they do not exert any influences on the Hong Kong market; 2) a feedback relationship between returns on both A markets and between returns on both B markets; 3) returns on Shanghai A and Shenzhen A help predict returns on Shanghai B; and 4) returns on each market help predict turnovers on all Chinese markets.

Table 6.9   Causal linkages between returns and turnovers for Hong Kong and other Chinese markets: whole sample

Direct	$RET^{HK} \rightarrow RET^{SHB}$
Indirect 1	$RET^{HK} \rightarrow RET^{SHB} \rightarrow TO^{SZA} \leftrightarrow TO^{SHA}$
Indirect 2	$RET^{HK} \rightarrow RET^{SHB} \leftrightarrow TO^{SZB} \leftrightarrow TO^{SHB}$
Indirect 3	$RET^{HK} \rightarrow RET^{SHB} \leftrightarrow TO^{SZB} \leftrightarrow RET^{SZB} \rightarrow TO^{SZA}$
Indirect 4	$RET^{HK} \rightarrow RET^{SHB} \leftrightarrow TO^{SZB} \leftrightarrow RET^{SZB} \rightarrow TO^{SHA}$
Indirect 5	$RET^{HK} \rightarrow RET^{SHB} \leftrightarrow TO^{SZB} \leftrightarrow RET^{SZB} \rightarrow TO^{SHB}$

Notes: This table summarizes results contained in Table 6.7. All causal relationships listed above are significant at the 1 per cent level.

6.3.6   Sub-sample Analysis

We split the data series into two sub-samples in order to examine the sensitivity of our results. There are two major events which took place in the latter half of 1997. The first of these is the return of Hong Kong to Chinese rule, which saw the establishment of the Hong Kong SAR. The second event is the onset of the Asian financial crisis that devastated many rapidly growing Asian economies, including Hong Kong, in the second half of 1997. However, China's economy has largely escaped the adverse effects of the 1997 Asian financial crisis. We choose the end of 1997 as the dividing point, so that the first sub-sample runs from 6 October 1992 to 31 December 1997 and the second sub-sample from 1 January 1998 to 27 June 2002.

Are there any significant differences in the results of the sub-samples from those of the whole sample? The results of the sub-sample 1 and sub-sample 2 are shown in the third and fourth columns of Table 6.8, respectively. Considering first the Hong Kong market, we find that the indirect predictive power of the Hong Kong market increases substantially after 1997. This can be seen from the fact that Hong Kong turnover or returns can help predict turnover and returns on all Chinese markets after 1997, whereas they can only help predict returns on Chinese B markets and turnover on Shanghai B, Shenzhen A and B up until the end of 1997. Thus, the sub-sample results clearly give evidence of the increasing importance of the Hong Kong market after 1997 in leading movement of returns and turnover in Shanghai and Shenzhen markets, regardless of whether they are A or B share markets. However, neither Hong Kong returns nor turnover is affected at all by the Chinese markets.

We consider next the impacts of Shanghai A and B markets before and after 31 December 1997. Up until 1997, Shanghai A returns Granger-cause turnover on all other Chinese markets and help predict returns on Shanghai B and Shenzhen B. After 1997, Shanghai A returns help predict turnover and returns on all Chinese markets. Up until the end of 1997, returns on Shanghai B have a feedback relationship with turnover on Shenzhen B and Granger-cause turnover on Shenzhen A, but do not help predict returns on other Chinese markets. After 1997, we see that Shanghai B returns help predict returns on Shanghai A and Shenzhen B as well as turnover on all Chinese markets. Clearly, Shanghai A and Shanghai B have experienced a surge of influences on other Chinese markets after the end of 1997.

Next we look at the impacts of Shenzhen A and B markets before and after the end of 1997. Up until the end of 1997, Shenzhen A returns help predict returns on Shanghai B and Shenzhen B as well as turnover on all Chinese markets. After 1997, Shenzhen A returns help explain returns on Shanghai A and Shenzhen B as well as all turnover except Shanghai B. Up until the end of 1997, Shenzhen B returns help predict turnover on Shenzhen B and Shanghai B as well as returns on Shanghai B. After 1997, Shenzhen B returns directly or indirectly Granger-cause returns on Shanghai A and Shenzhen A as well as turnovers on all Chinese markets.

6.4   DISCUSSION AND CONCLUSION

One of the main questions posed in this chapter is: what are the contemporaneous and dynamic causal relationships between returns and turnover on Shanghai, Shenzhen and Hong Kong markets and across these markets? First, we find a significant positive contemporaneous relationship between the absolute value of returns and turnover for all markets under study (the V-shaped relationship). More importantly, turnover is found to respond more robustly to rising returns than to falling returns for all markets except Hong Kong, indicating an asymmetry of the V-shape. Our results are thus consistent with the theoretical and empirical literature, which supports a positive contemporaneous relationship between returns and turnover. Moreover, the results of asymmetry for the Chinese market are consistent with findings of earlier studies such as Ratner and Leal (2001) and Smirlock and Starks (1985) for other markets.

Second, we find, at the 1 per cent significance level, that turnover Granger-causes returns on Hong Kong, while returns Granger-cause turnover on Shanghai A, B and Shenzhen B. Shenzhen B has a feedback relationship between its returns and turnover. The finding that turnover on the Hong Kong market Granger-causes its returns is consistent with the consensus of trading volume leading market returns for the well-developed markets. Furthermore, our results for the Chinese markets are in some contrast to the findings of Lee and Rui (2000) who use a shorter sample period.

What explains the different dynamic causal relationships between returns and turnover in China's markets compared to those of the well-developed markets? Like many other emerging markets, the Chinese stock markets exhibit a high degree of asymmetric information due to the highly controlled state media, poor disclosure practices and underdevelopment of information channels. The problem of asymmetric information is said to be severe in China (Xu, 2000) and is possibly the cause of herding behaviour among the small individual investors who have little current information about the performance of the economy and firms. They thus make their trading decisions by following the large institutional investors who have better access to information.

Third, Hong Kong is an important source of (indirect) influence for turnover on all Chinese markets as well as returns on Shanghai B and Shenzhen B markets. Results for the whole sample show that Hong Kong returns do not appear to influence returns on Shanghai A or Shenzhen A markets. However, evidence from the sub-sample analysis suggests that Hong Kong's influence has increased after 1997. In particular, it helps predict returns on both A markets as well as returns on both B markets after 1997. In view of our present results, one must be careful with the conclusion reached by Lee and Rui (2000) that: "…China's financial market, as an emerging market, is independent of the world financial market" (p. 357). On the contrary, we find a one-way spillover running from Hong Kong to Chinese B shares markets. We believe that recent relaxation of rules governing foreign ownership rights facilitates an increasing inflow of foreign investments to China that significantly strengthens the integration of the Chinese stock market into the world scene.

For the Shanghai and Shenzhen markets, the following observations are made: 1) they do not exert any influences on the Hong Kong market; 2) there exists a feedback relationship between returns on both A markets and between returns on both B markets; 3) returns on Shanghai A and Shenzhen A help predict returns on Shanghai B; and 4) returns on each market help predict turnover on all Chinese markets. Two generalizations are warranted from the above results. First, spillovers are more prevalent between both A or both B markets than between A and B market. Second, returns on Shanghai A and

Shenzhen A have significant predictive power for returns on Shanghai B for the whole sample and for returns on Shenzhen B for the second sub-sample. Thus, there seems to be some support for the argument that foreign investors in China face greater difficulties in obtaining reliable information about domestic firms (Chakravarty, Sarkar and Wu, 1998).

NOTES

1. Market turnover or the turnover ratio rather than the raw volume is frequently used to measure trading volume in the literature.
2. See Karpoff (1987) for a review of the early literature on the stock price-volume relation.
3. Aggarwal, Leal and Hernandez (1993), Barry and Lockwood (1995), Divecha, Drach and Stefek (1992), Errunza (1994) and Harvey (1995) discuss recent research on emerging markets and some of the differences between emerging and developed markets.
4. We also experimented with monthly indices in the preliminary stage of our study but found that the results were similar to those obtained using daily data and thus we do not report these results separately.

7.   Greater China share markets

There has been a growing interest in the inter-relationships between national stock markets although research into the relationships between the two mainland Chinese markets and those in the rest of the world is in its infancy.

The interest in inter-relationships in general is many-faceted. First, there is an interest by international investors who are increasingly looking to emerging markets to diversify their portfolios and take advantage of the spectacularly high returns which have been reported for some new markets. This has led to a focus on the international integration of stock markets, a question which has turned out to be rather more complicated than simply tracking correlations over time – see Ayuso and Blanco (2001) for a recent empirical study of this question.

A second source of interest is domestic investors: if there is a predictable relationship between one stock market and another, can this be used to make excess returns over a buy-and-hold strategy in the domestic market? While investors no doubt look to variables in addition to foreign stock returns, it is common to attribute daily movements in domestic stock prices to fluctuations in other closely related markets.

Thirdly, finance researchers are interested in inter-relationships because they can throw light on the validity or otherwise of the semi-strong efficient markets hypothesis (EMH) which states that in an informationally-efficient market returns cannot be predicted on the basis of any publicly available information, including returns in other markets.

We contribute to the growing knowledge of the operation of the mainland Chinese stock market by reporting on the results of an investigation into the dynamic inter-relationships between the Shanghai and Shenzhen exchanges and between them and the two closely related exchanges in Taiwan and Hong Kong.

The structure of the chapter is as follows. In the next section we provide a brief review of existing work and outline our contribution to the literature. We then set out our research procedures in section 7.2. We discuss the data in section 7.3 and present our main results in section 7.4, in which we focus on the relationship between the mainland Chinese market as a whole and the Hong Kong and Taiwan markets. We then move to presentation of further results in section 7.5 when we examine the basis for the combination of the Shanghai and Shenzhen markets into a single entity and the effect of the Asian crisis of 1997-98 on the inter-relationships between the markets. Our conclusions are reported in the final section.

7.1 OVERVIEW OF THE LITERATURE

Given the various reasons for interest in dynamic relationships between returns in different markets, it is not surprising that there has been considerable research in this area in the last decade. Early papers such as the one by Eun and Shim (1989) are defective in that they have ignored the non-stationarity of stock price indexes when specifying their model. Somewhat later papers by Corhay, Tourani Rad and Urbain (1993), Blackman, Holden and Thomas (1994) and Arshanapalli, Doukas and Lang (1995) introduced the notion of cointegration into the analysis and analysed the relationships between models mainly in these terms. In these and subsequent papers such as the one by Soydemir (2000) the cointegration analysis has often been supplemented by the more explicitly dynamic analysis of vector-error-correction models (VECMs), vector-autoregressive models (VARs) and the related dynamic tools of impulse-response functions (IRFs) and forecast-error-variance decompositions (FEVDs).

There have been several studies which have included applications to Asian markets, often in conjunction with developed markets; they include those by Eun and Shim (1989), Masih and Masih (1999), Cha and Oh (2000), Huang, Yang and Hu (2000) and Masih and Masih (2001). Of these papers all but the early paper by Eun and Shim use the notion of cointegration, estimate a simultaneous VAR or VECM model and employ IRFs and/or FEVDs. Only the paper by Huang, Yang and Hu (2000) include China among the Asian markets in their sample (see Chapter 3 for a review). Their sample consists of daily data for the period 1/10/1992-30/6/1997 for Hong Kong, Japan, Taiwan and the US as well as indexes for A share prices on the Shanghai and Shenzhen exchanges. They test the log share prices for stationarity and find that they are unambiguously I(1), as is common in the literature, and go on to test for cointegration, but only in pairs of indexes rather than for the entire set of markets simultaneously. This seems a serious limitation since it is possible that there are cointegrating relationships between a number of variables without one existing between any two of them. Moreover, restricting the cointegration analysis to pairs precludes the possibility of finding more than one cointegrating relationship. Interestingly, they find that of all the possible pairs only Shanghai and Shenzhen are clearly cointegrated. Their bivariate focus is carried over to modelling – they estimate a series of bivariate VARs which they use for testing Granger-causality between pairs of returns. They do not use the VARs for the standard dynamic analysis based on IRFs and FEVDs.

Thus, while there has been some investigation of the inter-relationships between Asian share markets, only one of the papers cited has included mainland stock markets in their sample of countries but this paper has serious limitations in the extent of the analysis carried out. The aim of this chapter is to overcome these problems and extend the analysis and sample period in the existing studies.

Like Huang, Yang and Hu (2000), we include both Shanghai and Shenzhen in our sample and use indexes for A shares. Our main results are based on daily data for the period 5/10/1992 to 16/11/2001 for three markets: a value-weighted average of the Shanghai and Shenzhen markets (the "mainland" market), the Hong Kong market and the Taiwan market. We also report the results of additional analysis. First we provide a case for the combination of the two mainland markets by analysing them separately both alone and in combination with Hong Kong and we show that they are cointegrated and behave like a single market.

We then go on to analyse the effects of the Asian crisis of 1997-98 on our results. There has been considerable attention paid in recent research to possible changes in various relationships due to the Asian crisis. Thus, for example, there has been analysis of the effects of the crisis on the nature of trade flows and on exchange rate fluctuations (see Nieh, 2002, for a recent reference). There has, however, been very little reported on the effects of the crisis on stock market inter-relationships. We go some way to remedying this omission by repeating our analysis for two sub-periods: 5/10/1992-30/6/1997 and 1/7/1998-16/11/2001 which were chosen to highlight the possible effects of the Asian financial crisis. We compare the nature of equilibrium relationships as well as of dynamic responses before and after the crisis.

In each of these country combinations we test for cointegration and specify and estimate a VECM or VAR as appropriate. We then use the estimated model to address questions of long-run and short-run dynamic relationships among the stock price indexes. Before discussing our results we briefly describe our research procedures and data.

7.2   RESEARCH PROCEDURE

We begin by testing each of the log price series for a unit root using the augmented Dickey-Fuller (ADF) test based on the following equation.[1]

$$\Delta \ln P_t = \alpha_0 + \alpha_1 \ln P_{t-1} + \alpha_2 t + \sum_{j=1}^{N} \beta_j \Delta \ln P_{t-j} + \varepsilon_t \qquad (7.1)$$

where $\ln P$ represents the log of the share price index, Δ is the first-difference operator, t is a trend term and ε is a serially-uncorrelated random error term. We test the hypothesis $H_0{:}\alpha_1{=}0$ so that the log price process has a unit root under the null. We conduct the tests with and without the trend term and for various lag lengths. If the log price has a unit root we test the first difference in the log price (the continuously compounded return) for a unit root and if the null is rejected in this case we conclude that the log price is I(1). We note that Huang, Yang and Hu (2000) use the test devised by Zivot and Andrews (1992) which allows for an undetermined break in the data when testing for a unit root. However, they report that all series are non-stationary despite allowing for the break and we do not pursue this variant of the ADF test. Besides, we compute the test for sub-periods with a break coinciding with the Asian crisis which is the date most likely to result in a shift in the process generating the price indexes.

For those series which we find to be non-stationary we conduct cointegration tests since it is possible that even though the individual series are non-stationary a linear combination of them is stationary so that a long-run relationship can be identified between them. The test for cointegration which naturally follows from the ADF test above is the test due to Engle and Granger (1987) which tests the residuals from the regression of one I(1) variable on one or more others for stationarity and concludes that if the residuals are stationary, a stationary linear combination of the I(1) variables has been found so that they are cointegrated. This test, however, has several statistical weaknesses – see Campbell and Perron (1991). Besides, the technique cannot discover all possible cointegrating vectors. For these reasons, the simultaneous-equation ML procedure based on Johansen (1988) and Johansen and Juselius (1990) is preferred and is the one we implement. The Johansen test is based on the following simultaneous-equation model:

$$\Delta \ln P_t = \gamma + \sum_{i=1}^{N-1} \Gamma_i \Delta \ln P_{t-i} + \Pi \ln P_{t-i} + \varepsilon_t \qquad (7.2)$$

where $\ln P$ is an m-vector of log share prices and Γ and Π are (mxm) coefficient vectors. The number of cointegrating relationships depends on the rank of Π. If the rank of Π is r then there exist two matrices, α and β, both (mxr) such that $\Pi = \alpha\beta'$ where β contains the r cointegrating vectors such that $\beta'\ln P$ are stationary even though the individual $\ln P$ series are themselves I(1) and α contains the corresponding error-correction coefficients. Johansen (1988) proposes tests based on the trace and maximum eigenvalues statistics and we report the results of the use of both of these tests.

In the case where no cointegrating relationships are found (the most common case, to anticipate our results) we estimate a VAR in the first differences of the log prices (i.e., the returns). Denoting the vector of returns by x, the model can be written as:

$$x_t = \Phi(L)x_t + \varepsilon_t , \ t = 1,1,...,T \qquad (7.3)$$

where $\Phi(L)$ is a pth-order matrix polynomial in the lag operator, L, where $L^n x_t \equiv x_{t-n}$. We assume that x_t is stationary and that $E(\varepsilon_t\varepsilon_t') = \Sigma$ is a positive definite matrix. We have ignored a constant (and other deterministic terms) for ease of exposition.

The two main tools for the analysis of the dynamic properties of our VAR model are the impulse response function (IRF) and the forecast-error-variance decomposition (FEVD). The IRF is easily derived from the vector moving-average (VMA) form of the model which can be obtained from equation (7.3) as:

$$x_t = A(L)\varepsilon_t, \tag{7.4}$$

where $A(L) = (I-\Phi(L))^{-1}$, an infinite-order matrix polynomial in L. One way of generating IRFs from (7.4) is to set one of the elements of ε_t at a non-zero value and all the others at zero and then trace the effects through successive values of x_t. However, this ignores the fact that the elements of ε_t will generally be correlated so that historically a shock to one of the elements of ε_t will be associated with changes in other of its elements. A common method of overcoming this difficulty is to re-define the error terms to make them orthogonal so that they can be shocked independently. This is generally achieved by using the Choleski decomposition of the contemporaneous covariance matrix of the errors, Σ. Since Σ is positive definite there exists a lower-triangular matrix (not necessarily unique), Q, such that

$$QQ' = \Sigma \tag{7.5}$$

The model can then be written in terms of the transformed errors, $\xi_t = Q^{-1}\varepsilon_t$, which are orthogonal. In this case the value of the IRF for the ith element of x following a shock to the jth error term n periods after the shock is given by

$$IRF_{ij}(n) = e_i'A_nQe_j, \quad i,j = 1,2,\ldots,m; \ n = 0,1,2\ldots \tag{7.6}$$

where e_i is the ith unit vector and A_n is the nth matrix in the matrix polynominal $A(L)$.

While this is a popular procedure, it has the weakness that the orthogonalization is not unique and nor are the resulting IRFs. Rather, they depend on the order in which the variables enter the model. An alternative method, recently suggested by Pesaran and Shin (1998), is to shock a particular error and then to shock all other errors in a way which preserves the historical relationship between them (or some other assumed correlations). They show that this involves computing the counterpart to equation (7.6) as:

$$IRF_{ij}^{G}(n) = \sigma_{jj}^{-1}e_i'A_n\Sigma e_j \ \ i,j = 1,2,\ldots,m; \ n = 0,1,2\ldots \tag{7.7}$$

where σ_{jj} is the jth diagonal element of Σ. The advantage of the use of the generalized IRFs is that they are not affected by the ordering of the variables in the model. However, since the shocks in this case are not orthogonal, the

IRFs cannot simply be added as they can in the conventional Choleski case. This is not usually a serious weakness since they are generally inspected one at a time. A more serious drawback of using the generalized procedure of Pesaran and Shin is that the FEVDs associated with it do not sum to one as they do when the Choleski decomposition is used. This will become evident from the tables presented below but will not affect our ability to interpret the results.

FEVDs based on the standard Choleski diagonalization are defined as the proportion of the forecast error variance at a particular forecast horizon which is accounted for by the orthogonalized errors of each of the variables in turn. As in the case of the IRFs, the FEVDs are generally dependent on the order in which the variables appear in the model, a limitation which is overcome by generalized FEVDs which take account of the sample information on the contemporaneous correlations of the errors. Using the notation of the generalized IRFs, the generalized FEVD can be defined as:

$$\text{FEVD}_{ij}^{G}(n) = \sigma_{jj}^{-1} \sum_{k=0}^{n} (e_i{}'A_k \Sigma e_j)^2 / \sum_{k=0}^{n} (e_i{}'A_k \Sigma A_k{}' e_i) , \qquad (7.8)$$

$$i,j = 1,2,\ldots,m; \; n = 1,2,3,\ldots$$

7.3 DATA

With one exception, all the data were obtained from the Datastream International database. The exception is the capitalization data for the Shanghai and Shenzhen markets which were obtained from the *Taiwan Economic Journal* database since they were not available from Datastream. Daily data were obtained for price indexes for Shanghai, Shenzhen, Taiwan and Hong Kong as well as capitalization data for the two mainland exchanges. The data for Shanghai and Shenzhen were for the prices for A shares. The capitalization data were used to construct a value-weighted A share index for the mainland as a whole.

We follow Huang, Yang and Hu (2000) in our use of A share prices. While B shares are available for purchase by foreign investors and are therefore likely to be a closer substitute for foreign shares, the market for B shares is very thin and recent evidence suggests substantial spurious autocorrelation due to thin trading.[2] We therefore use the A share indexes as more closely capturing the dominant trends in the mainland stock exchanges.

Our sample period runs from 5 October, 1992 to 16 November, 2001, the starting date being determined by the earliest date for which data for the Shenzhen market are available. We conducted tests using both the full sample and sub-samples. The sub-samples were chosen to isolate the effects of the Asian financial crisis which started in early July 1997 and continued in various countries into 1998. We experimented with two alternative divisions, used and we report results only for the sub-samples omitting the entire 1997-98 financial year.

Summary statistics are reported for returns calculated as the first differences in the logs of the price indexes in Table 7.1. They are reported for the full sample as well as for the two sub-samples.

Over the full sample, the Shanghai portfolio has both the highest return and the highest standard deviation, with Taiwan having both the lowest return and the lowest risk. Not surprisingly, the returns were higher before the crisis than they were after, with the difference being more marked for the non-mainland markets, although it is interesting that even the relatively isolated markets of Shanghai and Shenzhen showed the same trends.

The skewness, excess kurtosis and normality statistics have several interesting features. First, the returns are skewed for the mainland series but generally not for the Taiwan and Hong Kong series. Secondly, judging by the size of the statistics, the departures from normality were less pronounced after the crisis than before, with dramatic reductions for the mainland markets in particular. Nevertheless, overall the returns showed persistent and significant deviations from normality over both sub-periods, this being a common feature of all financial data.

Tests of stationarity of the log prices indexes are reported in Table 7.2. With only one exception, all the evidence points to non-stationarity of the log price indexes. The results are not sensitive to lag length or presence of a trend in the testing equation. Table 7.3 reports similar statistics for the first difference in the log of the price indexes.

The results in Table 7.3 clearly show that all return series are stationary for all periods, at all lag lengths, whether a trend is included in the Dickey-Fuller equation or not. Thus we conclude that all the log share price series are I(1) and we turn next to an examination of cointegration. This analysis throws preliminary light on the question of the inter-relationships between the markets since if two or more I(1) variables are cointegrated, then there exists a long-run equilibrium relationship between them and, by virtue of the Granger Representation Theorem, at least one of the variables Granger-causes another.[3]

For reasons outlined in section 7.2, we use Johansen's test, the results for which are reported in Table 7.4. Again we report results for the full sample and for the two sub-samples. Given the unimportance of the trend in the tests of stationarity, we computed the Johansen statistics within a model without a trend. We chose the lag order in the model as the minimum lag consistent with the absence of autocorrelated residuals in all the model equations.

We began with a test involving just the two mainland series in order to examine the relationship between these two markets in isolation. There is clear evidence of a cointegrating relationship between them if data for the full sample are used; at the 5 per cent level of significance, the null hypothesis that the number of cointegrating vectors is zero is clearly rejected by both the

Table 7.1 Summary statistics

	Mean	St Dev	Skewness	Kurtosis	Normality
Full Sample: 5/10/1992 - 16/11/2001					
DLSH	0.0004	0.0289	32.91	204.73	42909.7 [.000]
DLSZ	0.0002	0.0261	19.67	163.26	26985.4 [.000]
DLML	0.0003	0.0269	27.42	186.84	35587.3 [.000]
DLHK	0.0003	0.0186	0.61	83.09	6889.1 [.000]
DLTW	0.0001	0.0167	-0.58	26.06	678.2 [.000]
Sub-Sample 1: 5/10/1992 - 30/6/1997					
DLSH	0.0005	0.0376	20.79	91.86	8835.8 [.000]
DLSZ	0.0004	0.0329	13.87	82.23	6927.3 [.000]
DLML	0.0004	0.0344	18.19	88.80	8184.0 [.000]
DLHK	0.0008	0.0143	-5.84	25.77	695.5 [.000]
DLTW	0.0007	0.0151	0.16	22.52	505.2 [.000]
Sub-Sample 2: 1/7/1998 - 16/11/2001					
DLSH	0.0002	0.0147	3.42	41.99	1767.2 [.000]
DLSZ	0.0002	0.0153	2.53	37.40	1399.4 [.000]

DLML	0.0002	0.0148	3.13	40.83	1669.6 [.000]
DLHK	0.0003	0.0192	0.55	13.60	184.4 [.000]
DLTW	-0.0006	0.0189	0.51	12.26	149.8 [.000]

Notes: DL = change in logs, SH = Shanghai, SZ = Shenzhen, CH = China (a value-weighted average of the Shanghai and Shenzhen data), HK = Hong Kong and TW = Taiwan. The skewness and kurtosis statistics are $N(0,1)$-distributed under the null hypothesis of normal returns and the Normality statistic is the Jarque-Bera statistic which is χ^2 – distributed with 2 degrees of freedom under the same null. Figures in square brackets after the Normality statistics are *p*-values.

Table 7.2 Stationarity tests: log price indexes

Test	Shanghai		Shenzhen		Mainland		Hong Kong		Taiwan	
	No Trend	Trend	No Trend	Trend	No Trend	Trend	No Trend	Trend	No Trend	Trend
Full Sample: 5/10/1992-16/11/2001										
DF	-1.63	-2.78	-1.01	-2.10	-1.44	-2.57	-2.42	-2.35	-1.94	-1.27
ADF(1)	-1.64	-2.80	-1.03	-2.11	-1.46	-2.61	-2.44	-2.41	-1.95	-1.29
ADF(2)	-1.69	-2.90	-1.08	-2.17	-1.50	-2.67	-2.41	-2.33	-2.01	-1.39
ADF(3)	-1.86	-3.20	-1.10	-2.20	-1.62	-2.87	-2.49	-2.57	-2.06	-1.47
ADF(4)	-1.96	-3.38	-1.22	-2.34	-1.72	-3.03	-2.46	-2.49	-1.98	-1.32
ADF(5)	-2.03	-3.52	-1.23	-2.36	-1.80	-3.18	-2.44	-2.42	-2.02	-1.40
ADF(6)	-1.91	-3.31	-1.14	-2.25	-1.67	-2.96	-2.42	-2.37	-1.97	-1.30
Sub-Sample 1: 5/10/1992-30/6/1997										
DF	-1.99	-2.02	-0.83	-0.94	-1.61	-1.69	-1.05	-2.10	-0.89	-1.54
ADF(1)	-1.98	-2.04	-0.84	-0.95	-1.64	-1.73	-1.11	-2.22	-0.85	-1.50
ADF(2)	-2.11	-2.17	-0.95	-1.05	-1.74	-1.82	-1.14	-2.30	-0.91	-1.57
ADF(3)	-2.39	-2.45	-0.97	-1.07	-1.93	-2.00	-1.17	-2.37	-0.98	-1.66
ADF(4)	-2.56	-2.62	-1.14	-1.22	-2.09	-2.16	-1.15	-2.32	-0.96	-1.64
ADF(5)	-2.71	-2.76	-1.18	-1.26	-2.25	-2.32	-1.13	-2.28	-1.01	-1.70

ADF(6)	-2.50	-2.55	-1.03	-1.12	-2.02	-2.10	-1.08	-2.17	-0.93	-1.61

Sub-Sample 2: 1/7/1998-16/11/2001

DF	-1.17	-1.05	-1.16	-0.77	-1.17	-1.05	-1.79	-1.18	-0.60	-1.40
ADF(1)	-1.20	-1.13	-1.19	-0.85	-1.19	-1.13	-1.81	-1.24	-0.65	-1.45
ADF(2)	-1.13	-0.92	-1.11	-0.63	-1.12	-0.92	-1.79	-1.19	-0.74	-1.52
ADF(3)	-1.19	-1.13	-1.18	-0.83	-1.18	-1.13	-1.82	-1.24	-0.79	-1.56
ADF(4)	-1.21	-1.20	-1.21	-0.93	-1.21	-1.20	-1.82	-1.26	-0.60	-1.39
ADF(5)	-1.20	-1.16	-1.19	-0.86	-1.19	-1.16	-1.77	-1.12	-0.70	-1.48
ADF(6)	-1.16	-1.03	-1.15	-0.74	-1.15	-1.03	-1.78	-1.15	-0.64	-1.43

Notes: DF = Dickey-Fuller test, and ADF = augmented Dickey-Fuller test; 5% critical value = -2.8633 for the test without trend and -3.4143 with trend.

Table 7.3 Stationarity tests: first differences of log price indexes

Test	Shanghai		Shenzhen		Mainland		Hong Kong		Taiwan	
	No Trend	Trend	No Trend	Trend	No Trend	Trend	No Trend	Trend	No Trend	Trend
Full Sample: 5/10/1992-16/11/2001										
DF	-48.36	-48.35	-48.18	-48.18	-48.06	-48.05	-47.62	-47.63	-48.27	-48.33
ADF(1)	-33.22	-33.21	-33.04	-33.03	-33.42	-33.42	-35.09	-35.11	-32.66	-32.72
ADF(2)	-24.96	-24.95	-26.73	-26.73	-25.67	-25.66	-25.93	-25.95	-26.21	-26.27
ADF(3)	-21.05	-21.05	-21.65	-21.65	-21.45	-21.45	23.63	-23.65	-24.52	-24.60
ADF(4)	-18.60	-18.59	-19.53	-19.53	-18.73	-18.72	-21.80	-21.83	-21.19	-21.27
ADF(5)	-18.52	-18.51	-19.33	-19.33	-18.85	-18.84	-20.34	-20.37	-20.15	-20.24
ADF(6)	-17.72	-17.71	-18.30	-18.30	-17.94	-17.94	-19.40	-19.43	-18.72	-18.82
Sub-Sample 1: 5/10/1992-30/6/1997										
DF	-34.81	-34.81	-34.76	-34.81	-34.59	-34.59	-33.14	-33.12	-35.94	-35.92
ADF(1)	-23.51	-23.51	-23.26	-23.31	-23.62	-23.62	-23.27	-23.26	-24.00	-23.99
ADF(2)	-17.68	-17.68	-19.15	-19.21	-18.23	-18.24	-18.86	-18.85	-18.88	-18.87
ADF(3)	-14.94	-14.94	-15.46	-15.52	-15.26	-15.26	-16.99	-16.99	-16.83	-16.82
ADF(4)	-13.16	-13.16	-13.85	-13.91	-13.22	-13.23	-15.58	-15.57	-14.67	-14.66
ADF(5)	-13.19	-13.19	-13.88	-13.95	-13.44	-13.45	-14.96	-14.96	-14.19	-14.19

ADF(6)	-12.68	-12.68	-13.14	-13.22	-12.85	-12.86	-13.80	-13.79	-13.56	-13.56
Sub-Sample 2: 1/7/1998-16/11/2001										
DF	-28.88	-28.88	-28.80	-28.81	-28.86	-28.86	-28.50	-28.56	-28.76	-28.77
ADF(1)	-22.41	-22.42	-22.41	-22.42	-22.44	-22.45	-21.14	-21.22	-19.68	-19.69
ADF(2)	-16.56	-16.57	-16.68	-16.69	-16.60	-16.61	-16.62	-16.70	-15.98	-15.99
ADF(3)	-14.13	-14.14	-14.06	-14.08	-14.12	-14.13	-14.34	-14.43	-15.53	-15.55
ADF(4)	-12.96	-12.97	-13.05	-13.08	-12.97	-12.99	-13.93	-14.04	-12.99	-13.01
ADF(5)	-12.44	-12.46	-12.45	-12.48	-12.46	-12.48	-12.35	-12.46	-12.25	-12.28
ADF(6)	-11.56	-11.58	-11.71	-11.75	-11.65	-11.67	-11.31	-11.44	-11.24	-11.27

Notes: DF = Dickey-Fuller test, and ADF = augmented Dickey-Fuller test; 5% critical value = -2.8633 for the test without trend and -3.4143 with trend.

Table 7.4 Cointegration tests

Variables	Lag Order	Test	H_o	H_A	Statistic	95% cv	90% cv	Cointegrating Vector
Full Sample: 5/10/1992-16/11/2001								
Shanghai, Shenzhen	8	Maximal Eigenvalue	r = 0 r ≤ 1	r = 1 r = 2	19.44 1.12	14.88 8.07	12.98 6.50	LSH: 0.1643 (-0.1000)
		Trace	r = 0 r ≤ 1	r = 1 r = 2	20.56 1.12	17.86 8.07	5.75 6.50	LSZ: -0.1201 (0.7308)
Shanghai, Shenzhen, Hong Kong	8	Maximal Eigenvalue	r = 0 r ≤ 1	r = 1 r = 2	19.53 9.34	21.12 14.88	19.02 12.98	LSH: 0.1663 (-1.0000)
		Trace	r = 0 r ≤ 1	r = 1 r = 2	30.38 10.86	31.54 17.86	28.78 15.75	LSZ: -0.1193 (0.7173) LHK: -0.0071 (0.0429)
Mainland, Hong Kong	7	Maximal Eigenvalue	r = 0 r ≤ 1	r = 1 r = 2	8.11 3.01	14.88 8.07	12.98 6.50	No Cointegrating Vector

Mainland, Hong Kong, Taiwan	6	Trace	$r = 0$	$r = 1$	11.12	17.86	15.75	No Cointegrating Vector
			$r \leq 1$	$r = 2$	3.01	8.07	6.50	
		Maximal Eigenvalue	$r = 0$	$r = 1$	9.79	21.12	19.02	
			$r \leq 1$	$r = 2$	5.65	14.88	12.98	
		Trace	$r = 0$	$r = 1$	17.76	31.54	28.78	
			$r \leq 1$	$r = 2$	7.98	17.86	15.75	
Sub-Sample 1: 5/10/1992-30/6/1997								
Shanghai, Shenzhen	5	Maximal Eigenvalue	$r = 0$	$r = 1$	18.75	14.88	12.98	LSH: 0.2009 (-1.0000)
			$r \leq 1$	$r = 2$	1.09	8.07	6.50	
		Trace	$r = 0$	$r = 1$	19.83	17.86	15.75	LSZ: -0.1082 (0.5388)
			$r \leq 1$	$r = 2$	1.09	8.07	6.50	
Shanghai, Shenzhen, Hong Kong	6	Maximal Eigenvalue	$r = 0$	$r = 1$	19.54	21.12	19.02	LSH: 0.1975 (-1.0000)
			$r \leq 1$	$r = 2$	6.20	14.88	12.98	LSZ: -0.0982 (0.4971)
		Trace	$r = 0$	$r = 1$	25.80	31.54	28.78	LHK: 0.0038 (-0.0191)
			$r \leq 1$	$r = 2$	6.26	17.86	15.75	

Table 7.4 (continued)

Variables	Lag Order	Test	H₀	Hₐ	Statistic	95% cv	90% cv	Cointegrating Vector
Mainland, Hong Kong	6	Maximal Eigenvalue	$r = 0$ $r \leq 1$	$r = 1$ $r = 2$	8.86 0.76	14.88 8.07	12.98 6.50	No Cointegrating Vector
		Trace	$r = 0$ $r \leq 1$	$r = 1$ $r = 2$	9.62 0.76	17.86 8.07	15.75 6.50	
Mainland, Hong Kong, Taiwan	6	Maximal Eigenvalue	$r = 0$ $r \leq 1$	$r = 1$ $r = 2$	10.19 5.73	21.12 14.88	19.02 12.98	No Cointegrating Vector
		Trace	$r = 0$ $r \leq 1$	$r = 1$ $r = 2$	16.68 6.50	31.54 17.86	28.78 15.75	
Sub-Sample 2: 1/7/1998-16/11/2001								
Shanghai, Shenzhen	5	Maximal Eigenvalue	$r = 0$ $r \leq 1$	$r = 1$ $r = 2$	3.90 1.59	14.88 8.07	12.98 6.50	No Cointegrating Vector
		Trace	$r = 0$ $r \leq 1$	$r = 1$ $r = 2$	5.49 1.59	17.86 8.07	15.75 6.50	

Variables	Test	H_0	H_A	Statistic	95% cv	90% cv	Coint. Vector
Shanghai, Shenzhen, Hong Kong 5	Maximal Eigenvalue	$r = 0$	$r = 1$	10.83	21.12	19.02	No Cointegrating Vector
		$r \leq 1$	$r = 2$	4.60	14.88	12.98	
	Trace	$r = 0$	$r = 1$	19.00	31.54	28.78	No Cointegrating Vector
		$r \leq 1$	$r = 2$	8.16	17.86	15.75	
Mainland, Hong Kong 5	Maximal Eigenvalue	$r = 0$	$r = 1$	9.07	14.88	12.98	No Cointegrating Vector
		$r \leq 1$	$r = 2$	4.36	8.07	6.50	
	Trace	$r = 0$	$r = 1$	13.43	17.86	15.75	No Cointegrating Vector
		$r \leq 1$	$r = 2$	4.36	8.07	6.50	
Mainland, Hong Kong, Taiwan 5	Maximal Eigenvalue	$r = 0$	$r = 1$	13.53	21.12	19.02	No Cointegrating Vector
		$r \leq 1$	$r = 2$	5.81	14.88	12.98	
	Trace	$r = 0$	$r = 1$	23.22	31.54	28.78	Coint. Vector
		$r \leq 1$	$r = 2$	9.69	17.86	15.75	

trace and eigenvalue tests. This points to a long-run equilibrium relationship between them, a relationship which is captured by the cointegrating vector reported in the last column of the table. Moreover, it makes for Granger causation between the price series in at least one direction, thus violating the semi-strong Efficient Markets Hypothesis (EMH).

A similar result is obtained for the two markets using data before the Asian crisis, reported in the second panel of the table; the null of no cointegrating relationship is clearly rejected at the 5 per cent level by both tests. However, the outcome of the test is dramatically reversed in the second sub-sample – both trace and eigenvalue statistics are well short even of the 10 per cent critical values. Interpreting this finding within the framework of the EMH, there is therefore evidence that the efficiency of the markets improved after the crisis although we would hesitate to attribute this improvement to the crisis itself – it may simply be the outcome of increasing maturity of the market in the second half of the decade.

We next combine the two mainland indexes with the price index for the Hong Kong market. For the sample period as a whole, there is weak evidence of cointegration – for both tests we can reject the null of no cointegration at the 10 per cent but not at the 5 per cent level. The estimated cointegrating vector reported in the last column of the table indicates that by far the strongest relationship is between the two mainland markets with little impact of a change in the Hong Kong index on the other two. The evidence for cointegration is weaker for the sub-periods – for the pre-crisis period there is evidence of cointegration at the 10 per cent level from only one of the two tests and for the post-crisis period the test statistics are again quite far from their critical values (although, interestingly, not as far as when the two mainland indexes are tested together for this sub-sample).

Thus, there is evidence, at least for the pre-crisis period, that the two mainland markets have cointegrated prices but that they are not cointegrated with the Hong Kong market. Given the strong relationship between Shanghai and Shenzhen as well as evidence to be presented below of their strong dynamic inter-relationship, we decided to experiment with a single mainland index constructed as the capitalization-weighted average of the Shanghai and Shenzhen indexes. The next results reported in Table 7.4 relate to the question of the cointegration of the mainland index and the Hong Kong index. Not surprisingly, in light of our previous findings, there is no evidence of cointegration between the Hong Kong and mainland index either for the full sample or for either of the sub-samples.

Finally, we add the index for Taiwan to the Hong Kong and mainland indexes and investigate the possibility of cointegration between the three indexes. The results show clearly that prices in the three markets are not cointegrated. This is true for the full sample as well as the two sub-samples and for both the trace and the eigenvalue tests.

We conclude on the basis of the cointegration analysis that prices for the three stock markets are not cointegrated so that there is no long-run equilibrium relationship between them. However, for the first part of the sample period there is strong evidence of cointegration between the two individual mainland markets of Shanghai and Shenzhen, evidence of inefficiency in the semi-strong sense which seems to have disappeared in the post-crisis period. Our evidence is consistent with but extends that of Huang, Yang and Hu (2000) who find cointegration (using the Gregory and Hansen, 1996, extension of the Engle-Granger test for cointegration) between the two mainland indexes for the period before the Asian crisis. Our results show that using the alternative and generally-preferred Johansen test there is evidence for cointegration before the crisis but none after the crisis. Their results are, therefore, sample-specific and reversed for a later sample period.

7.4 MAIN FINDINGS

While we have information for four markets, we concentrate our attention on the results obtained by combining the two mainland Chinese markets. The cointegration results reported above indicate that, at least for the first half of the sample period, the two markets were cointegrated. We report in more detail in the next section analyses based on considering the two markets separately which indicates that they behave very much like a single market relative to the other markets in the region.

Since the cointegration analysis shows that the prices in the three markets are not cointegrated, we estimate a VAR model in the first differences of the logs of the prices (i.e., the continuously-compounded returns). The lag length was chosen as the minimum lag length necessary for all three equations to be free of autocorrelation at the 5 per cent level. This required five lags. A similar lag length was used for each of the sub-periods to ensure comparability.

The estimated VAR models, one for the full sample and one for each of the sub-samples obtained by omitting the whole of 1997-98, are in Table 7.5. The explanatory power for the returns for all three markets is very low as is common for models of this type – daily returns are notoriously difficult to predict as they should be if the EMH holds. Of the three, the equation for the Hong Kong market has the least explanatory power, indicating that it is, in this sense, the most efficient. All three markets show autoregressive characteristics with at least one lag of the market's own return being significant in each case. In the case of the return for the mainland market, we found that the lagged return in each of the other two markets has weak predictive power. The Hong Kong market is relatively independent of the other two – only its own lagged returns have any significant predictive power. The market for Taiwan, on the other hand, is significantly influenced by the lagged returns on both of the other markets, particularly Hong Kong at

Table 7.5 VAR for mainland China, Hong Kong and Taiwan stock markets

Regressor	Mainland Equation		Hong Kong Equation		Taiwan Equation	
	Coefficient	t-stat	Coefficient	t-stat	Coefficient	t-stat
Full Sample: 5/10/1992-16/11/2001						
DLML(-1)	0.0025	0.12	-0.0181	-1.28	0.0020	0.16
DLML(-2)	0.0170	0.83	-0.0120	-0.84	-0.0261	-2.06
DLML(-3)	0.0692	3.38	-0.0142	-1.01	-0.0110	-0.87
DLML(-4)	0.0553	2.69	-0.0157	-1.11	0.0082	0.65
DLML(-5)	0.0452	2.20	-0.0068	-0.48	-0.0063	-0.50
DLHK(-1)	0.0128	0.42	0.0301	1.44	0.1075	5.73
DLHK(-2)	-0.0330	-1.08	-0.0337	-1.60	-0.0001	0.00
DLHK(-3)	0.0527	1.73	0.0855	4.07	0.0272	1.44
DLHK(-4)	0.0172	0.56	-0.0385	-1.82	0.0011	0.06
DLHK(-5)	0.0583	1.91	-0.0263	-1.24	0.0347	1.84
DLTW(-1)	0.0378	1.11	-0.0201	-0.86	-0.0139	-0.66
DLTW(-2)	-0.0255	-0.75	0.0229	0.98	0.0482	2.30
DLTW(-3)	-0.0018	-0.05	0.0286	1.22	0.0242	1.15
DLTW(-4)	0.0381	1.13	0.0274	1.17	-0.0698	-3.34
DLTW(-5)	0.0617	1.83	-0.0109	-0.47	0.0213	1.02
INT	0.0002	0.41	0.0003	0.79	0.0001	0.15
SC	2.8961 [0.089]		1.1199 [0.290]		0.3838 [0.536]	
$\bar{R}^2$	0.0117		0.0096		0.0200	

Granger:

	DLML	DLHK	DLTW
DLML	25.5118 [0.000]	5.4207 [0.367]	5.8532 [0.321]
DLHK	7.7836 [0.169]	25.7224 [0.000]	36.7946 [0.000]
DLTW	6.0939 [0.297]	4.6171 [0.464]	19.1096 [0.002]

Sub-Sample 1: 5/10/1992-30/6/1997

	DLML		DLHK		DLTW	
DLML(-1)	-0.0009	-0.03	0.0033	0.27	0.0069	0.55
DLML(-2)	0.0335	1.17	-0.0106	-0.89	-0.0272	-2.19
DLML(-3)	0.0714	2.51	-0.0092	-0.77	-0.0090	-0.72
DLML(-4)	0.0553	1.94	-0.0139	-1.16	0.0081	0.65
DLML(-5)	0.0535	1.87	0.0005	0.04	-0.0028	-0.23
DLHK(-1)	-0.0343	-0.50	0.0528	1.83	0.0749	2.49
DLHK(-2)	-0.0803	-1.17	0.0321	1.11	-0.0322	-1.07
DLHK(-3)	0.0984	1.43	0.0266	0.92	0.0043	0.14
DLHK(-4)	0.0540	0.78	-0.0269	-0.93	-0.0184	-0.61
DLHK(-5)	0.1077	1.56	-0.0228	-0.79	0.0737	2.45
DLTW(-1)	0.0439	0.66	-0.0153	-0.55	-0.0311	-1.08
DLTW(-2)	-0.0499	-0.76	0.0163	0.59	0.0473	1.64
DLTW(-3)	-0.0060	-0.09	0.0138	0.50	0.0457	1.59
DLTW(-4)	0.0621	0.94	0.0298	1.08	-0.0153	-0.53
DLTW(-5)	0.1317	2.01	0.0112	0.41	0.0216	0.76
INT	0.0001	0.08	0.0007	1.73	0.0006	1.46
SC	0.3541 [0.552]		0.7656 [0.382]		0.8858 [0.347]	
$\overline{R}^2$	0.0120		-0.0022		0.0090	

Table 7.5 *(continued)*

Granger:

	Mainland	Hong Kong	Taiwan
DLML	16.1756 [0.006]	2.8987 [0.716]	6.1472 [0.292]
DLHK	6.8761 [0.230]	7.1970 [0.206]	13.0117 [0.023]
DLTW	5.7364 [0.333]	2.2296 [0.817]	7.3901 [0.193]

Sub-Sample 2: 1/7/1998-16/11/2001

Regressor	Mainland Equation		Hong Kong Equation		Taiwan Equation	
	Coefficient	t-stat	Coefficient	t-stat	Coefficient	t-stat
DLML(-1)	0.0220	0.65	-0.0792	-1.78	-0.0299	-0.69
DLML(-2)	-0.0863	-2.53	-0.0492	-1.11	-0.0313	-0.72
DLML(-3)	0.0650	1.91	0.0183	0.41	-0.0061	-0.14
DLML(-4)	0.0238	0.70	-0.0358	-0.81	0.0063	0.15
DLML(-5)	-0.0215	-0.63	0.0006	0.01	-0.0283	-0.66
DLHK(-1)	0.0222	0.83	0.0422	1.21	0.1217	3.59
DLHK(-2)	0.0027	0.10	-0.0327	-0.93	0.0386	1.13
DLHK(-3)	0.0573	2.13	0.0179	0.51	-0.0058	-0.17
DLHK(-4)	0.0213	0.79	0.0106	0.30	0.0321	0.94
DLHK(-5)	0.0613	2.29	-0.0762	-2.18	0.0358	1.05
DLTW(-1)	0.0389	1.42	0.0192	0.54	0.0056	0.16
DLTW(-2)	-0.0107	-0.39	0.0389	1.09	0.0426	1.23
DLTW(-3)	0.0064	0.23	0.0232	0.65	0.0177	0.51

DLTW(-4)	0.0059	0.22	0.0186	0.52	-0.1163	-3.36
DLTW(-5)	0.0226	0.83	0.0097	0.27	0.0446	1.29
INT	0.0002	0.44	0.0004	0.65	-0.0007	-1.04
SC	0.0389 [0.844]		0.5105 [0.475]		0.7542 [0.385]	
$\bar{R}^2$	0.0162		0.0010		0.0200	
Granger:						
DLML	11.7471 [0.038]		5.5750 [0.350]		1.6193 [0.899]	
DLHK	10.6939 [0.058]		7.6106 [0.179]		16.4848 [0.006]	
DLTW	2.8015 [0.731]		2.3218 [0.803]		14.6076 [0.012]	

Notes: DLML = first difference in the log of the value-weighted average of the Shanghai and Shenzhen indexes (=mainland index), DLHK is the first difference in the log of the Hong Kong index and DLTW is the first difference in the log of the Taiwan index. SC is a test statistic for a test of first- to fourth-order autocorrelation in the equation residuals with prob values in brackets. Granger statistics are for an LM test of the hypothesis that all lags of the indicated variable are jointly zero. *P* values are in square brackets.

one lag. Thus it appears that Taiwan is influenced significantly by the other two markets (as well as its own lagged returns) but it, in turn, has little effect on either Hong Kong or China. These conclusions are borne out by the Granger-causality statistics which show that Hong Kong Granger-causes Taiwan but there is no other causality in this set of three markets.

Consider next the results of estimating the model over two separate sub-periods obtained by deleting all the observations for 1997-98. There is no clear improvement in explanatory power and the variables which are significant in each equation are similar to those which feature in the full-sample results, although for both sub-samples fewer variables are significant than is the case for the full sample. Granger causality tests also have the same outcome for the pre-crisis period – the only causality is that from Hong Kong to Taiwan – but there is additional causation after the crisis – from Hong Kong to mainland China, albeit only at the 10 per cent level of significance. There is some evidence therefore, that the mainland market became more closely linked to the Hong Kong market after the crisis but the regression results show that the link to Taiwan was weaker.

All in all, it appears that the mainland stock market is relatively isolated from the other two – it has little effect on either Hong Kong or Taiwan and is, in turn, little affected by them. On the other hand, the other two markets are related although the relationship is mainly one-way from Hong Kong to Taiwan. The isolation of the mainland market, however, was less marked after the Asian crisis than before, although it was influenced by Hong Kong and not Taiwan.

The discussion so far has been based on the estimated VAR and concentrated on the significance of the estimated coefficients. We consider now the IRFs which show the dynamic interaction between the two markets and reflect the size and sign of the coefficients rather than their significance. We present first the IRFs based on the model estimated from data for the full sample; they are given in Figure 7.1 where we can see the effects of a single shock on all markets.

The IRFs make it clear that the three markets are relatively isolated from each other over the sample as a whole. By far the greatest effect of a shock is on the market in which the shock occurs – the effects on the other two markets are relatively minor. There is some evidence to support the conclusion drawn from the regression results reported above; that the influence of Hong Kong on Taiwan is greater than in the opposite direction and that the influence of the mainland Chinese market on the other two is negligible.

It appears, therefore, that the mainland market is relatively isolated – shocks to it are felt mainly in its own market and it is, in turn relatively unaffected by shocks to the other markets. Taiwan and Hong Kong do show some inter-relationships even though their shocks are felt mainly in their own markets.

Response to Shock to Mainland China

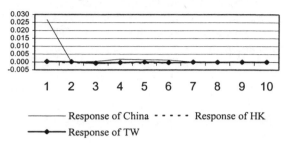

Response to Shock to Hong Kong

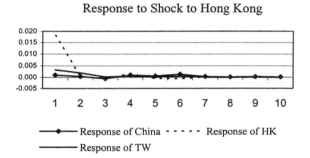

Response to Shock to Taiwan

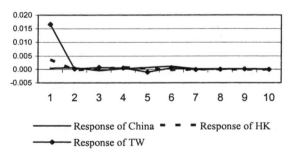

Figure 7.1   IRFs for mainland China, Hong Kong and Taiwan (full sample)

Consider now the question as to whether these dynamic inter-relationships changed as a result of the Asian crisis in 1997-98. We present IRFs for the two sub-samples in Figure 7.2 which contains nine graphs, one for the effects of each of the three shocks on each of the three markets separately, with each graph showing the effects before and after the crisis. The size of the effects is not strictly comparable to those in Figure 7.1 since we standardized the variables separately for each sub-sample before deriving the IRFs in Figure 7.2. All shocks are equal to one standard deviation of the equation error term and comparisons across sub-samples may simply reflect the differences in the size of these standard deviations and therefore the differences in the magnitude of the shock if the shocks are not standardized across the two halves of the sample.

It is clear that the own-effects are little different after the Asian crisis than before and that mainland China is relatively isolated after as well as before 1997. Interestingly, the inter-relationships between Taiwan and Hong Kong seem to have strengthened after the crisis – shocks which had effects on the other market of around 0.1 before the break and around 0.2 after the break, showing that contemporaneous effects between these two markets has strengthened. Further, the general volatility of the responses of one to the other has generally increased over the period. These conclusions are largely supported by the evidence provided by the FEVDs reported in Table 7.6.

As is common in FEVDs and as we saw in the IRFs, the own effects dominate so that most of the forecast error variance is accounted for by the errors in the market being analysed. The first sub-period results are quite similar to those for the sample as a whole but there is evidence of somewhat greater interdependence in the post-crisis period – in each case more of the forecast error variance is accounted for by shocks to the other two markets, this being particularly true of the relationships between Hong Kong and the mainland markets.

We can conclude this section by remarking that the mainland Chinese market has been relatively isolated from the other two markets considered. This was borne out by the regression results but particularly by the dynamics – both the IRFs and the FEVDs showed clearly that shocks to the mainland market were felt primarily in that market itself and that shocks in the other two markets had relatively little impact on the mainland Chinese markets. However, there is some evidence that the inter-relationships strengthened during the course of the 1990s, particularly between the mainland market and Hong Kong. It is unfortunate (from a statistical point of view) that the return of Hong Kong to the People's Republic of China and the Asian crisis occurred more or less simultaneously so that their effects are difficult to disentangle. Thus whether the modest growth in inter-relationships is due to the one or the other is difficult to discern at this level of aggregation.

Response of Mainland China to Mainland China

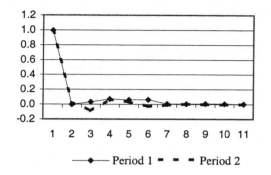

Response of Hong Kong to Mainland China

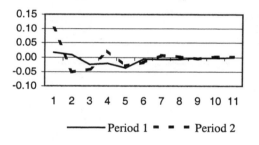

Response of Taiwan to Mainland China

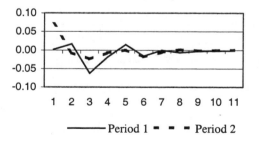

Figure 7.2 IRFs for mainland China, Hong Kong and Taiwan (sub-samples)

Response of Mainland China to Hong Kong

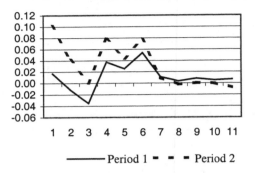

Response of Hong Kong to Hong Kong

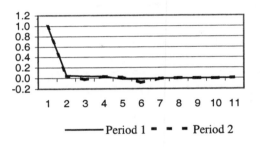

Response of Taiwan to Hong Kong

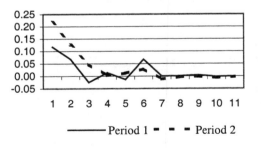

Figure 7.2   (continued)

Response of Mainland China to Taiwan

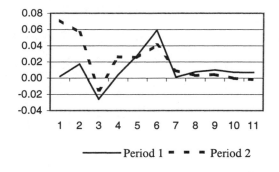

Response of Hong Kong to Taiwan

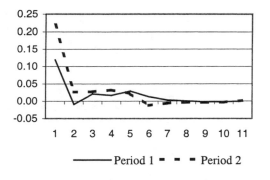

Response of Taiwan to Taiwan

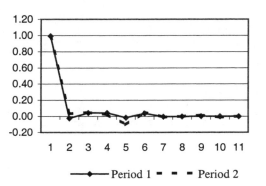

Figure 7.2 (continued)

Table 7.6 FEVDs for mainland China, Hong Kong and Taiwan

Horizon	Mainland			Hong Kong			Taiwan		
	DLML	DLHK	DLTW	DLML	DLHK	DLTW	DLML	DLHK	DLTW
Full Sample: 5/10/1992 – 16/11/2001									
0	1.00000	0.00134	0.00038	0.00134	1.00000	0.03866	0.00038	0.03866	1.00000
1	0.99930	0.00152	0.00101	0.00198	0.99899	0.03875	0.00042	0.05176	0.98626
2	0.99852	0.00201	0.00140	0.00235	0.99831	0.03884	0.00236	0.05164	0.98430
3	0.99739	0.00332	0.00147	0.00258	0.99732	0.04025	0.00266	0.05276	0.98307
4	0.99646	0.00379	0.00224	0.00336	0.99609	0.04044	0.00270	0.05256	0.98284
5	0.99310	0.00608	0.00421	0.00363	0.99583	0.04053	0.00300	0.05340	0.98190
6	0.99296	0.00622	0.00423	0.00365	0.99581	0.04053	0.00302	0.05340	0.98189
7	0.99292	0.00623	0.00427	0.00367	0.99579	0.04053	0.00304	0.05341	0.98185
8	0.99282	0.00632	0.00431	0.00368	0.99575	0.04057	0.00305	0.05341	0.98184
9	0.99279	0.00634	0.00432	0.00369	0.99575	0.04057	0.00306	0.05342	0.98183
10	0.99278	0.00635	0.00433	0.00369	0.99575	0.04057	0.00306	0.05342	0.98182
11	0.99277	0.00635	0.00433	0.00369	0.99575	0.04057	0.00306	0.05342	0.98182
12	0.99277	0.00635	0.00433	0.00369	0.99575	0.04057	0.00306	0.05343	0.98182
13	0.99277	0.00635	0.00433	0.00369	0.99575	0.04057	0.00306	0.05343	0.98182
14	0.99277	0.00635	0.00433	0.00369	0.99575	0.04057	0.00306	0.05343	0.98182
15	0.99277	0.00635	0.00433	0.00369	0.99575	0.04057	0.00306	0.05343	0.98182

Sub-Sample 1: 5/10/1992 – 30/6/1997

0	1.00000	0.00028	0.00000	1.00000	0.01405	0.00000	0.01405	1.00000
1	0.99949	0.00043	0.00031	0.99969	0.01410	0.00029	0.01865	0.99464
2	0.99774	0.00166	0.00098	0.99879	0.01450	0.00417	0.01915	0.98992
3	0.99644	0.00305	0.00099	0.99818	0.01475	0.00452	0.01930	0.98949
4	0.99518	0.00369	0.00181	0.99595	0.01555	0.00474	0.01946	0.98914
5	0.98965	0.00651	0.00530	0.99569	0.01570	0.00497	0.02384	0.98494
6	0.98954	0.00663	0.00530	0.99564	0.01571	0.00497	0.02384	0.98494
7	0.98947	0.00664	0.00535	0.99559	0.01571	0.00501	0.02384	0.98489
8	0.98932	0.00671	0.00545	0.99558	0.01571	0.00502	0.02386	0.98487
9	0.98926	0.00674	0.00550	0.99557	0.01572	0.00502	0.02387	0.98486
10	0.98918	0.00678	0.00555	0.99557	0.01572	0.00503	0.02387	0.98485
11	0.98917	0.00678	0.00555	0.99557	0.01572	0.00503	0.02387	0.98485
12	0.98917	0.00678	0.00555	0.99557	0.01572	0.00503	0.02387	0.98485
13	0.98917	0.00679	0.00555	0.99557	0.01572	0.00503	0.02387	0.98485
14	0.98917	0.00679	0.00555	0.99557	0.01572	0.00503	0.02387	0.98485
15	0.98917	0.00679	0.00556	0.99557	0.01572	0.00503	0.02387	0.98485

Sub-Sample 2: 1/7/1998 – 16/11/2001

0	1.00000	0.01087	0.00512	1.00000	0.04971	0.00512	0.04971	1.00000
1	0.99613	0.01261	0.00839	0.99616	0.05000	0.00515	0.06404	0.98533

Table 7.6 (continued)

Horizon	Mainland				Hong Kong				Taiwan		
	DLML	DLHK	DLTW	DLML	DLHK	DLTW	DLML	DLHK	DLTW		
2	0.99596	0.01251	0.00856	0.01556	0.99339	0.05050	0.00573	0.06628	0.98273		
3	0.99069	0.01863	0.00919	0.01597	0.99255	0.05124	0.00584	0.06624	0.98258		
4	0.98917	0.02018	0.00974	0.01658	0.99142	0.05165	0.00578	0.06563	0.98154		
5	0.98174	0.02633	0.01139	0.01679	0.99133	0.05145	0.00617	0.06641	0.98048		
6	0.98157	0.02643	0.01147	0.01683	0.99125	0.05148	0.00621	0.06655	0.98035		
7	0.98155	0.02643	0.01147	0.01684	0.99123	0.05149	0.00621	0.06656	0.98034		
8	0.98153	0.02643	0.01149	0.01686	0.99121	0.05150	0.00621	0.06655	0.98032		
9	0.98153	0.02643	0.01149	0.01686	0.99119	0.05151	0.00621	0.06658	0.98031		
10	0.98148	0.02649	0.01150	0.01686	0.99119	0.05151	0.00621	0.06658	0.98030		
11	0.98148	0.02649	0.01150	0.01686	0.99119	0.05151	0.00621	0.06658	0.98030		
12	0.98147	0.02649	0.01150	0.01686	0.99119	0.05151	0.00621	0.06658	0.98030		
13	0.98147	0.02649	0.01150	0.01686	0.99119	0.05151	0.00621	0.06658	0.98030		
14	0.98147	0.02649	0.01150	0.01686	0.99119	0.05151	0.00621	0.06658	0.98030		
15	0.98147	0.02649	0.01150	0.01686	0.99119	0.05151	0.00621	0.06658	0.98030		

Notes: DLML = first difference in the log of the value-weighted average of the Shanghai and Shenzhen indexes (=mainland index), DLHK is the first difference in the log of the Hong Kong index and DLTW is the first difference in the log of the Taiwan index.

7.5 FURTHER ANALYSIS

In the previous section we presented our main results based on the combination of the two markets of Shanghai and Shenzhen into a single market by using a value-weighted average of their prices to represent the mainland market. In this section we present a further analysis where the two mainland markets are treated separately. We begin by considering them in isolation from the other markets before adding the Hong Kong market to the model.

7.5.1 Shanghai and Shenzhen

We begin with the two mainland markets of Shanghai and Shenzhen in isolation and consider the estimated dynamic model. Recall from section 7.4 that the logs of the price indexes are cointegrated for the full sample and for the first of the two sub-samples but not for the second sub-sample. Thus we could estimate a VECM for the two samples for which the indexes are cointegrated. That, however, would have made the comparison of responses before and after the crisis difficult. Given our interest in the effect of the crisis on the inter-relationships, we decided to estimate an unrestricted VAR in the first differences of the logs for each period. Since the VECM is simply the VAR with an error-correction term added, it is possible to compare the two estimated models. A comparison for the whole sample shows that the coefficients of the VAR are almost identical to their counterparts in the VECM – the signs are all the same and the magnitudes are very similar. Thus, while strictly speaking the VARs for the full sample and the first sub-sample are mis-specified, there seems to be little effect on the estimated coefficients and we proceed with a consideration of the VARs only. The results for the full sample and the two sub-samples are reported in Table 7.7.

Consider the full sample results first. The explanatory power of the equations is low in both cases but consistent with previous results. Explanatory power is somewhat higher for the Shanghai equation than it is for the Shenzhen one and in both equations there are some significant lags of the dependent variable, indicating violation of the weak EMH, although this effect is stronger for Shanghai. For both equations at least one lag of the return in the other market is significant, indicating violation of the semi-strong EMH, and it is interesting that in the equation for Shenzhen lagged Shanghai returns seem to be more important than lagged returns for Shenzhen itself. The test for Granger causality indicates two-way causality in which each Granger-causes the other.

In the first of the two sub-samples (pre-crisis) the explanatory power of the Shanghai equation is marginally better than for the sample as a whole but identical for the Shenzhen equation. Lagged returns for both markets have a

Table 7.7 VAR for Shanghai and Shenzhen

| | Full Sample: 5/10/1992-16/11/2001 | | | | Sub-Sample1: 5/10/1992-30/6/1997 | | | | Sub-Sample2: 1/7/1998-16/11/2001 | | | |
| | Shanghai Eqn. | | Shenzhen Eqn. | | Shanghai Eqn. | | Shenzhen Eqn. | | Shanghai Eqn. | | Shenzhen Eqn. | |
Regressor	Coeff	t-stat	Coeff	t-stat	Coeff	t-stat	Coeff	t-stat	Coeff	t-stat	Coeff	t-stat
DLSH(-1)	-0.0499	-1.63	0.0329	1.18	-0.0505	-1.25	0.0313	0.88	0.1113	0.59	0.0702	0.36
DLSH(-2)	0.0774	2.52	0.0224	0.80	0.0812	2.01	0.0252	0.71	0.1141	0.61	0.1563	0.80
DLSH(-3)	0.1383	4.54	0.0676	2.44	0.1381	3.45	0.0665	1.88	0.1556	0.83	0.1108	0.57
DLSH(-4)	0.0487	1.59	0.0613	2.20	0.0504	1.25	0.0649	1.83	-0.2008	-1.07	-0.2374	-1.21
DLSH(-5)	-0.0435	-1.43	0.0594	2.14	-0.0448	-1.12	0.0585	1.65	0.1953	1.04	0.2581	1.32
DLSH(-6)	-0.0208	-0.68	-0.0015	-0.05	-0.0229	-0.57	-0.0030	-0.09	-0.2845	-1.52	-0.2975	-1.52
DLSH(-7)	0.0443	1.46	-0.0133	-0.48	0.0419	1.05	-0.0144	-0.41	0.0367	0.20	-0.0092	-0.05
DLSZ(-1)	0.0725	2.15	-0.0259	-0.84	0.0755	1.65	-0.0275	-0.68	-0.0733	-0.41	-0.0279	-0.15
DLSZ(-2)	-0.0602	-1.78	0.0151	0.49	-0.0432	-0.94	0.0348	0.86	-0.1865	-1.04	-0.2246	-1.19
DLSZ(-3)	-0.0550	-1.63	-0.0325	-1.06	-0.0545	-1.19	-0.0425	-1.05	-0.0741	-0.41	-0.0325	-0.17
DLSZ(-4)	0.0068	0.20	0.0275	0.90	0.0069	0.15	0.0301	0.75	0.2180	1.22	0.2595	1.39
DLSZ(-5)	0.1163	3.46	-0.0349	-1.14	0.1376	3.02	-0.0256	-0.64	-0.2052	-1.15	-0.2697	-1.44
DLSZ(-6)	-0.0627	-1.85	-0.0677	-2.20	-0.0731	-1.60	-0.0781	-1.93	0.2320	1.29	0.2399	1.28
DLSZ(-7)	-0.0971	-2.88	-0.0081	-0.26	-0.1092	-2.38	-0.0088	-0.22	-0.0438	-0.24	-0.0111	-0.06
INT	0.0003	0.55	0.0002	0.37	0.0004	0.39	0.0003	0.35	0.0002	0.42	0.0002	0.31
$\bar{R}^2$	0.0269		0.0141		0.0287		0.0141		0.0064		0.0074	
SC	0.0803 [0.777]		0.0003 [0.986]		0.1257 [0.723]		0.0026 [0.959]		0.4281 [0.513]		0.0197 [0.888]	
Granger:												
DLSH	32.4738 [0.000]		17.2187 [0.016]		19.2669 [0.007]		10.8217 [0.147]		5.5637 [0.592]		6.2797 [0.507]	
DLSZ	33.6070 [0.000]		8.9720 [0.255]		22.2636 [0.002]		7.1730 [0.411]		5.6463 [0.582]		6.8696 [0.443]	

Notes: DLSH = first difference in the log of the index for Shanghai; DLSZ = first difference in the log of the index for Shenzhen. SC is a test statistic for a test of first- to fourth-order autocorrelation in the equation residuals with prob values in brackets. The Granger statistics are for an LM test of the joint significance of the lags of the indicated variable.

significant effect on the Shanghai return but no lagged returns are significant at the 5 per cent level in the Shenzhen equation although several are significant at the 10 per cent level. These features are reflected in the Granger causality test results – Shenzhen Granger-causes Shanghai at the 1 per cent level but causation in the opposite direction fails evens at 10 per cent. In the post-crisis period the explanatory power of both equations is much weaker as evidenced by the adjusted R^2 figures and in neither equation is any lagged return significant even at the 10 per cent level. The Granger-causality tests now indicate that there is no causation in either direction. Thus the predictability that was evident before the crisis on the basis of lagged returns in both markets is altogether absent after the crisis, suggesting a marked improvement of the efficiency of the two markets if we view the results in the framework of the EMH. These results are, of course, consistent with the cointegration results reported in section 7.3.

Consider next the IRFs and FEVDs. We present first the IRFs based on the model estimated from data for the full sample; they are given in Figure 7.3. The first graph in Figure 7.3 shows the effects on both the Shanghai and Shenzhen markets of the shock to the error in the equation for the return in the Shanghai market. The second shows the effect on the two markets of a shock to Shenzhen. They are remarkably similar – a shock to one market has only a slightly larger effect on that market's own return and this is true for both markets. In both cases the effect of the shock dies out very quickly; in fact, there is little effect on either market after the initial shock is felt. These results point to a high degree of integration between the two markets – shocks are transmitted across markets very quickly and it is difficult to distinguish between the markets in terms of the effects of the shocks.

We also present IRFs for the two sub-samples in Figure 7.4 which contains four graphs, one for the effects of each of the two shocks on each of the two markets separately, with each graph showing the effects before and after the crisis. Recall that the size of the effects are not strictly comparable to those in Figure 7.3 since we standardized the variables separately for each sub-sample before deriving the IRFs in Figure 7.4.

The four graphs in Figure 7.4 show that the own-effects are almost identical over the two sub-periods – the initial effects are indistinguishable and all shocks die out quickly. The cross-market effects differ somewhat in magnitude but are similar in shape. In both cases the initial effect of the shock is bigger after the crisis, suggesting that the markets are more integrated after the crisis than before. This contrasts with the results described in Table 7.7 which show that causality between the two markets was weaker after the crisis than it was before. However, it should be recalled that the causality and predictability were based on significance and the IRFs reflect the size and sign of the estimated coefficients, whether significant or not. Moreover, the VAR does not capture contemporaneous effects while the IFRs do. Hence it is likely that the two markets were more integrated after the crisis than before in the sense of contemporaneous correlations because, e.g., they reacted to very similar shocks but there was weaker predictability so that shocks in one market were not transmitted to the other with a lag.

Response to Shock to Shanghai

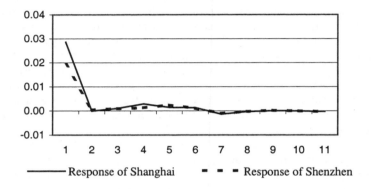

Response to Shock to Shenzhen

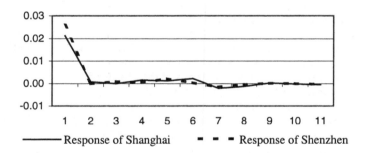

Figure 7.3   Impulse response functions: Shanghai and Shenzhen (full sample)

The conclusions drawn from the IRFs are confirmed by the information gained from the FEVDs reported in Table 7.8. Clearly, for the sample as a whole, the Shanghai error explains the major part of Shanghai's forecast error at all horizons and similarly for Shenzhen. However, the error in the other market also contributes substantially to each market's forecast error – over a third in each case, in contrast to the results reported in the previous section, for example, where the errors in the other markets contributed less than 5 per cent to the error variance. In all cases there is little variation across the forecast horizon. For the sub-periods, the results are broadly similar for the pre-crisis period but markedly different for the post-crisis period when the relative contributions of the two errors are approximately the same for each market, confirming the results we obtained above.

The implications of the IRFs and FEVDs are that the markets are closely integrated in that a shock in a particular market has a similar effect in each of the markets and that these features are more marked after the crisis than they were before. There is no evidence, however, that the cross-market predictability has become stronger – the effect is largely contemporaneous.

The above results suggest that we would be justified in treating the two markets as one, as we did in the previous section. Before coming to a firm conclusion of this nature, however, we add the Hong Kong market to the model, Hong Kong being the market which is likely to be the most closely related to the mainland markets. This will allow us to ascertain whether the results we have just reported survive the addition of a further market and whether either of the two mainland markets is more closely related to Hong Kong than the other, a feature which would undermine our combination of the two markets into a single market.

Response of Shanghai to Shanghai

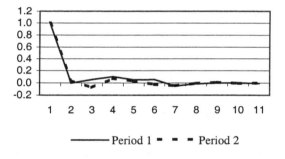

Response of Shenzhen to Shanghai

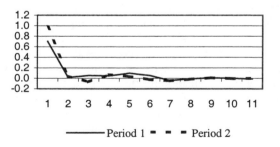

Figure 7.4   Impulse response functions: Shanghai and Shenzhen (sub-samples)

Response of Shenzhen to Shenzhen

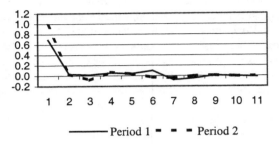

—— Period 1 ▪ ▪ ▪ Period 2

Response of Shenzhen to Shenzhen

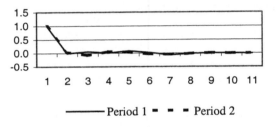

—— Period 1 ▪ ▪ ▪ Period 2

Figure 7.4   (continued)

7.5.2   Shanghai, Shenzhen and Hong Kong

The estimated VARs in the returns for these three markets are reported in Table 7.9 which has three panels, the first with the full-sample results, the second with the results for the first sub-sample and the third with the results for the post-crisis period.

Consider the full-sample results first. The explanatory power is somewhat higher than for the two-equation model indicating that the inclusion of the Hong Kong returns increases the ability of the VAR to explain the returns over the period. As in the case of the two-variable model, more of the Shanghai returns than the Shenzhen returns can be explained. The explanatory power of the equation for the Hong Kong return is lower than for either of the mainland exchanges. This result is not surprising if they are interpreted in terms of the EMH, since it is likely that the Hong Kong market, being more mature than either of the mainland markets would be more efficient.

Some lagged values of returns for both Shanghai and Shenzhen are significant in each of the Shanghai and Shenzhen equations and a lagged Shanghai return is significant in the Hong Kong equation. On the other hand, lagged Hong Kong returns have no predictive power (at the 5 per cent level) for either the Shanghai or Hong Kong returns but one lagged Hong Kong return is significant in the Shenzhen equation. Thus the two mainland markets seem to be more strongly interconnected with each other than they are with the Hong Kong market although the latter does have an effect on the Shenzhen market and is, in turn, influenced by the Shanghai market. Granger causation results confirm this conclusion: there is two-way causation between Shanghai and Shenzhen as there was in the two variable model but Hong Kong neither causes nor is caused by either of the mainland markets.

The results for the pre-crisis period are quite similar to those for the whole sample: Shanghai and Shenzhen both have some predictive power for each other while Hong Kong has predictive power only for Shenzhen but is predicted by Shanghai. The Granger results are not quite as clear-cut; there is again two-way causation between Shanghai and Shenzhen returns (but only at the 10 per cent level for the Shanghai to Shenzhen direction), Hong Kong causes neither Shanghai not Shenzhen but is, in this case, caused by Shanghai. So, there is some weak relationship between the mainland exchanges and Hong Kong but it seems that the relationship runs from Shanghai to Hong Kong to Shenzhen rather than being clearly stronger with its neighbouring market of Shenzhen.

In the second sub-sample the explanatory power of all the equations is higher than in the full sample, and for Shenzhen and Hong Kong they are also higher than in the pre-crisis period, suggesting an increase in predictability. However, the significance of the individual coefficients is quite different compared to the other two periods – only two lagged Hong Kong returns are significant at the 5 per cent level in each of the Shanghai and Shenzhen equations and no variables are significant in the equation explaining the returns in Hong Kong. This is strongly confirmed by the results of the Granger-causality tests: Shanghai and Shenzhen cause nothing (neither each other or Hong Kong) and Hong Kong Granger-causes both of the mainland exchanges.

We turn next to the dynamic interactions as portrayed by the IRFs and FEVDs. The IRFs are shown in Figures 7.5 and 7.6, the first showing IRFs based on the full sample and comparing the effects of shocks across markets and the second comparing shocks across the two sub-samples.

What stands out from these IRFs is the similarity of Shanghai and Shenzhen relative to Hong Kong. As indicated earlier on the basis of the results for Shanghai and Shenzhen on their own, these two mainland markets seem to behave as one and clearly the addition of the Hong Kong market to the model has done nothing to change this feature. Moreover, there is not a pronounced difference in the response of the two mainland Chinese markets to shocks originating in Hong Kong. This is also true when we compare effects before and after the Asian crisis as we do in Figure 7.6. The own

Table 7.8 Generalized forecast error variance decompositions: Shanghai and Shenzhen

| | Full Sample: 5/10/1992 - 16/11/2001 | | | | Sub-Sample 1: 5/10/1992 – 30/6/1997 | | | | Sub-Sample 2: 1/7/1998 - 16/11/2001 | | | |
| | Shanghai | | Shenzhen | | Shanghai | | Shenzhen | | Shanghai | | Shenzhen | |
Horizon	DLSH	DLSZ	DLSH	DLSZ	DLSH	DLSZ	DLSH	DLSZ	DLSH	DLSZ	DLSH	DLSZ
0	1.00000	0.55173	0.55173	1.00000	1.00000	0.49613	0.49613	1.00000	1.00000	0.96774	0.96774	1.00000
1	0.99805	0.55149	0.55169	0.99941	0.99776	0.49598	0.49607	0.99937	0.99981	0.96739	0.96776	0.99985
2	0.99647	0.54982	0.55217	0.99920	0.99683	0.49429	0.49710	0.99904	0.99852	0.96715	0.96630	0.99909
3	0.99582	0.54718	0.55304	0.99662	0.99619	0.49164	0.49768	0.99604	0.99829	0.96654	0.96639	0.99869
4	0.99578	0.54755	0.55645	0.99463	0.99615	0.49205	0.50225	0.99337	0.99657	0.96542	0.96421	0.99707
5	0.99143	0.55018	0.55695	0.99233	0.98944	0.49671	0.50346	0.99062	0.99512	0.96438	0.96204	0.99527
6	0.98885	0.55234	0.55668	0.99234	0.98605	0.49960	0.50313	0.99064	0.99408	0.96288	0.96121	0.99373
7	0.98635	0.55263	0.55668	0.99234	0.98286	0.50032	0.50312	0.99064	0.99404	0.96283	0.96105	0.99347
8	0.98618	0.55265	0.55671	0.99232	0.98271	0.50033	0.50315	0.99061	0.99402	0.96281	0.96105	0.99346
9	0.98615	0.55265	0.55671	0.99231	0.98269	0.50033	0.50314	0.99060	0.99402	0.96281	0.96104	0.99345
10	0.98596	0.55273	0.55676	0.99228	0.98246	0.50045	0.50321	0.99057	0.99401	0.96280	0.96102	0.99343

11	0.98594 0.55278 0.55678 0.99228	0.98241 0.50057 0.50324 0.99056	0.99401 0.96280 0.96102 0.99343
12	0.98587 0.55279 0.55678 0.99228	0.98232 0.50057 0.50324 0.99056	0.99400 0.96279 0.96101 0.99341
13	0.98587 0.55279 0.55678 0.99228	0.98232 0.50057 0.50324 0.99056	0.99400 0.96279 0.96101 0.99341
14	0.98587 0.55279 0.55678 0.99228	0.98231 0.50058 0.50324 0.99056	0.99400 0.96278 0.96101 0.99341
15	0.98587 0.55279 0.55678 0.99228	0.98231 0.50057 0.50324 0.99056	0.99400 0.96278 0.96101 0.99341

Notes: DLSH = first difference in the log of the index for Shanghai; DLSZ = first difference in the log of the index for Shenzhen.

Table 7.9 *VARs for Shanghai, Shenzhen and Hong Kong stock markets*

Regressor	Shanghai		Shenzhen		Hong Kong	
	Coefficient	t-stat	Coefficient	t-stat	Coefficient	t-stat
Full Sample: 5/10/1992-16/11/2001						
DLSH(-1)	-0.0483	-1.57	0.0338	1.21	-0.0027	-0.14
DLSH(-2)	0.0767	2.50	0.0215	0.77	-0.0019	-0.09
DLSH(-3)	0.1405	4.61	0.0713	2.57	-0.0295	-1.49
DLSH(-4)	0.0502	1.64	0.0623	2.24	-0.0214	-1.08
DLSH(-5)	-0.0426	-1.40	0.0617	2.22	0.0153	0.77
DLSH(-6)	-0.0196	-0.64	0.0002	0.01	-0.0382	-1.93
DLSH(-7)	0.0489	1.60	-0.0104	-0.38	0.0304	1.54
DLSZ(-1)	0.0695	2.05	-0.0280	-0.91	-0.0197	-0.90
DLSZ(-2)	-0.0592	-1.74	0.0148	0.48	-0.0095	-0.43
DLSZ(-3)	-0.0599	-1.77	-0.0369	-1.20	0.0223	1.02
DLSZ(-4)	0.0045	0.13	0.0263	0.86	0.0046	0.21
DLSZ(-5)	0.1156	3.43	-0.0383	-1.25	-0.0281	-1.29
DLSZ(-6)	-0.0625	-1.84	-0.0660	-2.14	0.0188	0.86
DLSZ(-7)	-0.0993	-2.93	-0.0077	-0.25	-0.0319	-1.46
DLHK(-1)	0.0300	0.94	0.0283	0.98	0.0281	1.36
DLHK(-2)	-0.0454	-1.42	-0.0082	-0.28	-0.0346	-1.68
DLHK(-3)	0.0509	1.59	0.0445	1.53	0.0906	4.39
DLHK(-4)	0.0201	0.63	0.0076	0.26	-0.0286	-1.38

DLHK(-5)	0.0524	1.64	0.0845	2.92	-0.0258	-1.25
DLHK(-6)	0.0054	0.17	-0.0097	-0.33	-0.0192	-0.93
DLHK(-7)	0.0039	0.12	-0.0056	-0.19	-0.0300	-1.45
INT	0.0003	0.49	0.0002	0.29	0.0003	0.82
SC		0.0037 [0.952]		0.0784 [0.779]		0.0005 [0.983]
$\overline{R}^2$		0.0274		0.0160		0.0123
Granger:						
DLSH		33.3635 [0.000]		18.3765 [0.010]		11.4569 [0.120]
DLSZ		33.5973 [0.000]		9.4360 [0.223]		7.1099 [0.418]
DLHK		8.1411 [0.320]		11.6253 [0.114]		7.0129 [0.220]
Sub-Sample 1: 5/10/1992-30/6/1997						
DLSH(-1)	-0.0485	-1.20	0.0326	0.91	0.0068	0.43
DLSH(-2)	0.0804	1.98	0.0243	0.68	-0.0132	-0.84
DLSH(-3)	0.1431	3.56	0.0733	2.07	-0.0280	-1.81
DLSH(-4)	0.0521	1.29	0.0682	1.91	-0.0267	-1.71
DLSH(-5)	-0.0438	-1.09	0.0650	1.83	0.0080	0.51
DLSH(-6)	-0.0205	-0.51	0.0003	0.01	-0.0382	-2.45
DLSH(-7)	0.0495	1.23	-0.0089	-0.25	0.0241	1.55
DLSZ(-1)	0.0700	1.52	-0.0317	-0.78	-0.0065	-0.37
DLSZ(-2)	-0.0431	-0.93	0.0318	0.78	0.0056	0.31
DLSZ(-3)	-0.0619	-1.35	-0.0503	-1.24	0.0276	1.56
DLSZ(-4)	0.0030	0.06	0.0269	0.67	0.0122	0.69

Table 7.9 (continued)

Regressor	Shanghai		Shenzhen		Hong Kong	
	Coefficient	t-stat	Coefficient	t-stat	Coefficient	t-stat
DLSZ(-5)	0.1369	3.00	-0.0327	-0.81	-0.0100	-0.57
DLSZ(-6)	-0.0770	-1.67	-0.0807	-1.99	0.0220	1.24
DLSZ(-7)	-0.1140	-2.48	-0.0106	-0.26	-0.0313	-1.76
DLHK(-1)	0.0079	0.11	0.0188	0.29	0.0537	1.86
DLHK(-2)	-0.1233	-1.66	0.0154	0.23	0.0262	0.91
DLHK(-3)	0.0900	1.21	0.0656	1.00	0.0276	0.96
DLHK(-4)	0.0606	0.81	0.0101	0.15	-0.0235	-0.82
DLHK(-5)	0.0874	1.18	0.1670	2.55	-0.0169	-0.59
DLHK(-6)	0.0682	0.92	0.0392	0.60	-0.0540	-1.88
DLHK(-7)	0.0201	0.27	0.0106	0.16	0.0023	0.08
INT	0.0002	0.23	0.0001	0.06	0.0008	1.94
SC	0.0250 [0.874]		0.0347 [0.852]		0.0740 [0.786]	
$\bar{R}^2$	0.0291		0.0154		0.0082	
Granger:						
DLSH	20.2677 [0.005]		12.3946 [0.088]		17.5465 [0.014]	
DLSZ	22.8635 [0.002]		8.0606 [0.327]		8.8513 [0.264]	
DLHK	7.5712 [0.372]		8.6856 [0.276]		10.5112 [0.161]	

Sub-Sample 2: 1/7/1998 – 16/11/2001

DLSH(-1)	0.1015	0.54	0.0618	0.31	0.1917	0.77
DLSH(-2)	0.1063	0.56	0.1393	0.71	0.0248	0.10
DLSH(-3)	0.1301	0.69	0.0822	0.42	-0.3262	-1.32
DLSH(-4)	-0.1597	-0.85	-0.1845	-0.94	0.3748	1.51
DLSH(-5)	0.2000	1.06	0.2570	1.31	-0.2097	-0.85
DLSH(-6)	-0.2890	-1.54	-0.2990	-1.52	-0.2471	-1.00
DLSH(-7)	0.0230	0.12	-0.0225	-0.12	0.3661	1.48
DLSZ(-1)	-0.0709	-0.39	-0.0295	-0.16	-0.2571	-1.07
DLSZ(-2)	-0.1834	-1.01	-0.2117	-1.12	-0.0727	-0.30
DLSZ(-3)	-0.0544	-0.30	-0.0110	-0.06	0.3402	1.44
DLSZ(-4)	0.1809	1.01	0.2093	1.12	-0.4048	-1.71
DLSZ(-5)	-0.2106	-1.17	-0.2706	-1.44	0.2042	0.86
DLSZ(-6)	0.2460	1.37	0.2520	1.34	0.1889	0.80
DLSZ(-7)	-0.0231	-0.13	0.0107	0.06	-0.3140	-1.33
DLHK(-1)	0.0210	0.81	0.0321	1.18	0.0566	1.65
DLHK(-2)	0.0106	0.40	0.0016	0.06	-0.0162	-0.47
DLHK(-3)	0.0611	2.34	0.0645	2.37	0.0196	0.57
DLHK(-4)	0.0157	0.61	0.0233	0.86	0.0185	0.54
DLHK(-5)	0.0609	2.34	0.0761	2.81	-0.0639	-1.87
DLHK(-6)	-0.0195	-0.74	-0.0187	-0.68	0.0260	0.75
DLHK(-7)	-0.0296	-1.13	-0.0346	-1.27	0.0058	0.17

Table 7.9 *(continued)*

INT	0.0002	0.36	0.0001	0.23	0.0003	0.47
	$\overline{R}^2$: 0.0148	SC: 3.3828 [0.066]	$\overline{R}^2$: 0.0200	SC: 2.0822 [0.149]	$\overline{R}^2$: 0.0055	SC: 2.7405 [0.098]
Granger:						
DLSH	5.0260 [0.657]		5.5182 [0.597]		8.8315 [0.265]	
DLSZ	5.3278 [0.620]		6.2395 [0.512]		9.4333 [0.223]	
DLHK	14.4903 [0.043]		18.2042 [0.011]		7.4307 [0.385]	

Notes: DLSH = first difference in the log of the index for Shanghai; DLSZ = first difference in the log of the index for Shenzhen; DLHK = first difference in the log of the index for Hong Kong. SC is a test statistic for a test of first- to fourth-order autocorrelation in the equation residuals with *p*-values in square brackets.

Granger is the LM statistic for a test that all the lags of the indicated variables are jointly zero with prob values in brackets.

Response to Shock to Shanghai

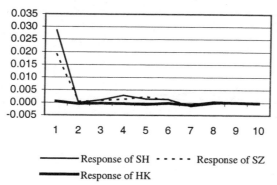

Response to Shock to Shenzhen

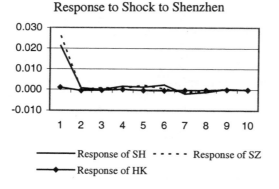

Response to Shock to Hong Kong

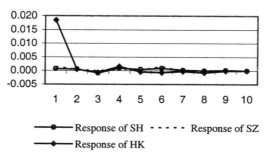

Figure 7.5   IRFs for Shanghai, Shenzhen and Hong Kong (full sample)

Response of Shanghai to Shanghai

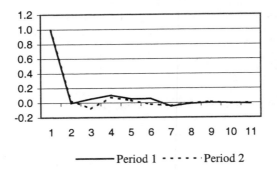

Response of Shenzhen to Shanghai

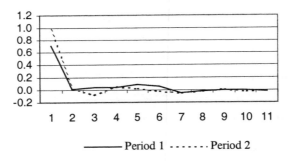

Response of Hong Kong to Shanghai

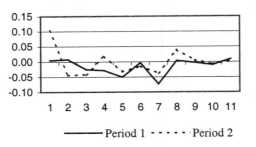

Figure 7.6   IRFs for Shanghai, Shenzhen and Hong Kong (sub-samples)

Response of Shanghai to Shenzhen

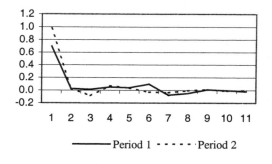

Response of Shenzhen to Shenzhen

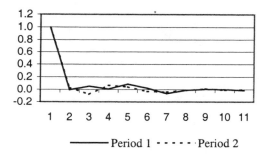

Response of Hong Kong to Shenzhen

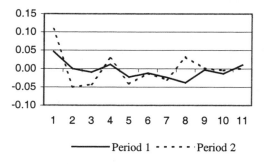

Figure 7.6   (continued)

Response of Shanghai to Hong Kong

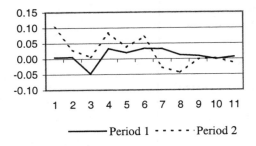

————— Period 1 - - - - - Period 2

Response of Shenzhen to Hong Kong

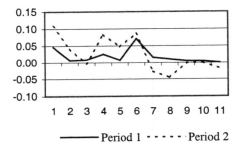

————— Period 1 - - - - - Period 2

Response of Hong Kong to Hong Kong

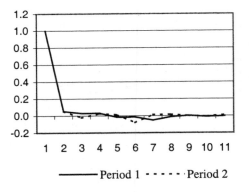

————— Period 1 - - - - - Period 2

Figure 7.6   (continued)

effects are almost identical across the periods for each of the three markets and, as for the cross-market effects, a Hong Kong shock has very similar effects on Shanghai and Shenzhen and, vice versa, the effects on Hong Kong of Shanghai and Shenzhen shocks is very similar. The cross-market effects, though, all appear to be more volatile after the crisis.

These conclusions are confirmed when we inspect the FEVDs, which are reported in Table 7.10. On the whole Hong Kong seems only very loosely connected to the mainland markets compared to their connections to each other, although the interconnection seems to be a little more substantial after the crisis. Thus it is clear that the relationship between the two mainland stock markets is very much stronger than either market's relationship to Hong Kong and we were quite justified in treating them as a single market for the purposes of our main results presented in section 7.5.

7.6   CONCLUSION

This chapter has examined the inter-relationships between the stock markets of the Chinese mainland – Shanghai and Shenzhen – and Hong Kong and Taiwan. We examined them both before and after the Asian crisis of 1997-98 using VAR models which we used for the analysis of individual coefficients, tests of Granger causality as well as a basis for impulse response functions (IRFs) and forecast-error-variance decompositions (FEVDs).

Our main results focused on the relationship between a single mainland index, calculated as a value-weighted average of the Shanghai and Shenzhen indexes, and the indexes for Hong Kong and Taiwan. We found that the mainland Chinese market had been relatively isolated from the other two markets considered. This was borne out by the regression results but particularly by the dynamics – both the IRFs and the FEVDs showed clearly that shocks to the mainland market were felt primarily in that market itself and that shocks in the other two markets had relatively little impact on the mainland Chinese markets. However, we found some evidence that the inter-relationships strengthened during the course of the 1990s, particularly between the mainland markets and Hong Kong. Whether the modest growth in inter-relationships is due to the occurrence of the Asian crisis in 1997-98 or the greater integration of the Chinese economy into the world economy (one aspect of which was the return of Hong Kong to the People's Republic) will require more detailed and disaggregated structural modelling.

We then explored the effects of treating the two mainland markets separately, both to test the assumption underlying their combination in the main results and to assess whether the other two markets had differential impacts on these two markets. We found that our assumption that they could be treated as a single market was vindicated: in all cases a shock to Shanghai

Table 7.10 FEVDs for Shanghai, Shenzhen and Hong Kong

Horizon	Shanghai			Shenzhen			Hong Kong		
	DLSH	DLSZ	DLHK	DLSH	DLSZ	DLHK	DLSH	DLSZ	DLHK
Full Sample: 5/10/1992 – 16/11/2001									
0	1.00000	0.55133	0.00065	0.55133	1.00000	0.00313	0.00065	0.00313	1.00000
1	0.99774	0.55090	0.00112	0.55107	0.99900	0.00351	0.00122	0.00398	0.99905
2	0.99526	0.54879	0.00199	0.55148	0.99878	0.00352	0.00144	0.00431	0.99878
3	0.99352	0.54546	0.00309	0.55187	0.99507	0.00443	0.00186	0.00427	0.99781
4	0.99322	0.54567	0.00341	0.55517	0.99306	0.00453	0.00293	0.00484	0.99677
5	0.98817	0.54788	0.00444	0.55375	0.98732	0.00793	0.00305	0.00559	0.99596
6	0.98545	0.54993	0.00449	0.55348	0.98733	0.00795	0.00524	0.00596	0.99326
7	0.98293	0.55021	0.00448	0.55346	0.98732	0.00796	0.00530	0.00618	0.99231
8	0.98276	0.55021	0.00451	0.55346	0.98726	0.00801	0.00530	0.00618	0.99231
9	0.98275	0.55022	0.00451	0.55347	0.98723	0.00801	0.00539	0.00622	0.99222
10	0.98251	0.55032	0.00451	0.55350	0.98721	0.00803	0.00543	0.00626	0.99218
11	0.98246	0.55036	0.00455	0.55353	0.98718	0.00804	0.00543	0.00626	0.99217
12	0.98237	0.55034	0.00457	0.55352	0.98716	0.00804	0.00543	0.00630	0.99212
13	0.98237	0.55034	0.00457	0.55352	0.98716	0.00804	0.00544	0.00631	0.99211
14	0.98236	0.55034	0.00458	0.55352	0.98716	0.00804	0.00544	0.00631	0.99210
15	0.98236	0.55034	0.00458	0.55352	0.98716	0.00805	0.00544	0.00631	0.99210

Sub-Sample 1: 5/10/1992 – 30/6/1997

0	1.00000	0.49691	0.00002	0.49691	1.00000	0.00218	0.00002	0.00218	1.00000
1	0.99806	0.49670	0.00006	0.49674	0.99926	0.00222	0.00008	0.00217	0.99984
2	0.99478	0.49382	0.00240	0.49763	0.99892	0.00229	0.00069	0.00226	0.99913
3	0.99284	0.49035	0.00348	0.49780	0.99469	0.00294	0.00149	0.00238	0.99655
4	0.99245	0.49048	0.00387	0.50245	0.99186	0.00296	0.00399	0.00289	0.99371
5	0.98519	0.49473	0.00495	0.50111	0.98393	0.00790	0.00400	0.00304	0.99353
6	0.98051	0.49694	0.00595	0.50057	0.98361	0.00811	0.00922	0.00356	0.98660
7	0.97710	0.49749	0.00609	0.50050	0.98349	0.00821	0.00920	0.00496	0.98351
8	0.97688	0.49747	0.00617	0.50049	0.98347	0.00824	0.00921	0.00497	0.98350
9	0.97688	0.49747	0.00617	0.50048	0.98335	0.00826	0.00930	0.00515	0.98333
10	0.97658	0.49761	0.00621	0.50055	0.98333	0.00826	0.00938	0.00526	0.98322
11	0.97652	0.49772	0.00624	0.50065	0.98322	0.00830	0.00940	0.00532	0.98316
12	0.97636	0.49766	0.00630	0.50063	0.98320	0.00831	0.00943	0.00541	0.98307
13	0.97636	0.49766	0.00630	0.50063	0.98320	0.00831	0.00943	0.00547	0.98296
14	0.97634	0.49767	0.00631	0.50063	0.98320	0.00831	0.00944	0.00547	0.98295
15	0.97634	0.49766	0.00631	0.50063	0.98320	0.00831	0.00944	0.00548	0.98295

Sub-Sample 2: 1/7/1998 – 16/11/2001

0	1.00000	0.96777	0.01107	0.96777	1.00000	0.01244	0.01107	0.01244	1.00000
1	0.99910	0.96677	0.01195	0.96623	0.99829	0.01429	0.01335	0.01526	0.99576

Table 7.10 (continued)

Horizon	Shanghai			Shenzhen			Hong Kong		
	DLSH	DLSZ	DLHK	DLSH	DLSZ	DLHK	DLSH	DLSZ	DLHK
2	0.99763	0.96640	0.01188	0.96488	0.99763	0.01421	0.01529	0.01736	0.99380
3	0.99183	0.96055	0.01859	0.95954	0.99178	0.02082	0.01563	0.01812	0.99094
4	0.98982	0.95905	0.01969	0.95660	0.98924	0.02271	0.01628	0.01930	0.98746
5	0.98237	0.95219	0.02485	0.94587	0.97857	0.03038	0.01651	0.01942	0.98714
6	0.98055	0.94991	0.02549	0.94434	0.97629	0.03094	0.01759	0.02003	0.98434
7	0.97878	0.94818	0.02721	0.94235	0.97414	0.03292	0.01901	0.02089	0.98131
8	0.97878	0.94818	0.02721	0.94235	0.97413	0.03292	0.01902	0.02089	0.98099
9	0.97875	0.94817	0.02721	0.94233	0.97412	0.03292	0.01907	0.02091	0.98081
10	0.97857	0.94800	0.02738	0.94206	0.97384	0.03318	0.01907	0.02091	0.98079
11	0.97856	0.94799	0.02739	0.94205	0.97382	0.03319	0.01913	0.02095	0.98068
12	0.97846	0.94786	0.02744	0.94192	0.97366	0.03324	0.01916	0.02097	0.98064
13	0.97845	0.94786	0.02744	0.94192	0.97366	0.03324	0.01917	0.02097	0.98062
14	0.97843	0.94784	0.02744	0.94190	0.97363	0.03324	0.01918	0.02098	0.98059
15	0.97843	0.94784	0.02744	0.94189	0.97363	0.03325	0.01918	0.02098	0.98059

Notes: DLSH = first difference in the log of the index for Shanghai; DLSZ = first difference in the log of the index for Shenzhen; DLHK = first difference in the log of the index for Hong Kong.

was felt mainly in Shenzhen and vice versa with little spillover to Taiwan or Hong Kong and, in addition, the two mainland markets responded in a very similar manner to outside shocks.

NOTES

1. See Dickey and Fuller (1981).
2. See, e.g., Groenewold, Tang and Wu (2001).
3. See Engle and Granger (1987).

8. The stock return-volume relation and policy changes: the case of the Chinese energy sector

In Chapter 6, we examined the relation between trading volume and return at the aggregate level. This chapter explores the issue further. We employ data of individual stocks (as well as aggregate indices) to assess the effect on the return-volume relationship of policy changes. The Chinese market is a rapidly developing one and the government often intervenes in its domestic markets in an unpredictable way. We investigate the effects on the return-volume relationship of such intervention, both in the energy market as well as in the stock market itself.

The rest of the chapter proceeds as follows. In section 8.1 we briefly review the literature on the stock return-volume relation. In section 8.2 we present summary statistics for the data, test the stationarity of the stock return and volume series, and detail the adjustment procedure to remove long-run trend from the volume data. In section 8.3 we examine the contemporaneous correlation as well as the causal relation between stock returns and trading volume, employing simple linear regressions and Granger causality tests. In section 8.4 we use a GARCH (1,1) model to estimate volatility spikes, which we associate with major changes in policies, and define the policy dummy variables on the basis of the spikes. We then go on to test the effects of exogenous policy changes on the relationship between trading volume and stock returns by observing whether the coefficients of the dummy variables are significant; we allow for both intercept and slope effects. Finally we summarize the findings of this chapter in section 8.5.

8.1 LITERATURE REVIEW

The stock return-volume relation in both developed and emerging financial markets has been subject to extensive research. This section presents a brief review of the literature relating to developed financial markets, emerging stock markets and the Chinese stock market, respectively (see a more detailed survey in Chapter 3).

Empirical studies on the return-volume relation in developed financial markets began in the 1960s. For example, Granger and Morgenstern (1963) and Godfrey, Granger and Morgenstern (1964) use weekly data to examine the relation between price changes and volume and find price changes follow a random walk. In the 1970s, Crouch (1970b) finds a positive correlation between daily volume and absolute values of daily price changes for both market indexes and individual stocks. Morgan (1976), Epps and Epps (1976), Westerfield (1977) and Rogalski (1978) find a positive correlation between volume and price changes for individual stocks by employing daily or monthly data. Up to the mid-1980s Smirlock and Starks (1985) find that the return-volume relation is asymmetric and later, in Smirlock and Starks (1988), they find a strong positive lagged relationship between volume and absolute price changes using individual stock data. Hiemstra and Jones (1994) use non-linear Granger causality tests to examine the non-linear causal relation between volume and return and find there is a positive bi-directional relation between them. Bhagat and Bhatia (1996) also employ daily data to test the causal relationship between volume and return, finding return causes volume but not vice versa.

Recently a number of studies have focused on investigating the return-volume relation in emerging financial markets. Basci, Suheyla and Kursat (1996) use weekly data on 29 individual stocks in Turkey and find that the price level and volume are cointegrated. Saatcioglu and Starks (1998) use monthly data from six Latin American stock markets to test the relation between price changes and volume, finding a positive price-volume relation and a causal relationship from volume to stock price changes but not vice versa. Silvapulle and Choi (1999) use daily Korean Composite Stock Index data to study the linear and non-linear Granger causality between stock price and trading volume, finding that there is a significant bi-directional linear and non-linear causality between the two series. Ratner and Leal (2001) examine the Latin American and Asian financial markets and find a positive contemporaneous relation between return and volume in these countries except India. At the same time they observed that there exists a bi-directional causal relation between return and volume.

There have been an increasing number of studies on the Chinese stock market in recent years (see Chapter 3 for a review). Many issues have been investigated but few studies have directly examined the relationship between return and volume in Chinese domestic stock markets. We extend the existing literature by updating the data, extending the analysis to individual stock data and examining the effects of policy-driven changes to market structure, both that of the energy market and that of the stock market as a whole.

8.2   DATA AND PRELIMINARY ANALYSIS

The data set comprises daily data on Shanghai A and Shenzhen A share price indexes and volume (turnover) as well as prices and volume data for ten individual energy stocks. We focus our attention on the energy sector because it is clearly impossible to include all individual stocks in a study which requires a detailed examination of the policy changes in the individual industries and because the energy sector is of central importance to the Chinese economy and has been undergoing continuing and rapid development (see, e.g., Wu, 2003 for a recent description). We include an analysis of the Shanghai and Shenzhen aggregate data to provide a basis for comparison for the ten individual companies selected from the energy sector, all of which issue A shares to domestic investors, some on the Shanghai exchange and some on the Shenzhen exchange.

   We chose our ten energy stocks as relatively representative on the following basis. Overall, there were 66 listed companies in the Chinese energy sector by the end of 2002. But half of them were listed after 1998, including some large and important companies such as China Petroleum & Chemical Corporation and SP Power Development, and to include them would unduly shorten the sample period. We use a sample period of 1 January 1997 to 31 December 2002 which leaves about 30 individual stocks from which to make our selection. To ensure that the selected individual stocks are representative of the entire energy industry, we selected ten individual stocks so that each energy sub-sector was represented according to their capitalization and performance as follows: three listed companies from the oil and gas sub-sector (Shandong Taishan Petroleum, Shanghai Petrochemical, and Shengli Oil Field Dynamic), three from the Electricity sub-sector (Guangdong Electric Power, Heilongjiang Electric Power, and Mengdian Huaneng Thermal Power), two from the coal sub-sector (Shanxi Cooking and Top Energy Company Limited) and two composite service companies (Shenergy Company Limited and Shenzhen Energy Investment). We obtained the stock closing price and trading volume (turnover by volume) for all stocks as well as for the A indexes from Datastream. Observations for non-trading days were deleted, leaving a number of observations which range from 1424 to 1445 (Table 8.1).

8.2.1   Summary Statistics

In this chapter, the stock return is calculated as the continuously-compounded return using the closing price:

$$R_t = [\ln(P_t) - \ln(P_{t-1})] \tag{8.1}$$

where ln(P_t) denotes the natural logarithm of the closing price at time t. We use daily turnover by volume as the raw trading volume series (Vol$_t$). Table 8.1 presents summary statistics for the return and trading volume series for Shanghai and Shenzhen A share markets and the ten individual energy stocks. The statistics show that mean return and standard deviation for the Shanghai A return have been higher than those for Shenzhen A. The mean returns for the ten individual stocks are mostly positive except for Shanghai Petrochemical and Shanxi Cooking. The returns for Shanghai A and Shenzhen A are skewed to the left, though the skewness is not large. For all the individual stocks skewness is positive and most are significantly different from normality at the 1 per cent level. All return series display significant excess kurtosis, indicating a further source of the non-normality in returns. In Table 8.1 we also report the Ljung-Box Q statistic for autocorrelation, Q(7), for the returns.[1] All results except for Shenergy Company are insignificant at the 1 per cent level, although for Mengdian Thermal, Shanxi Cooking and Top Energy they are significant at the 10 per cent level. There is some sensitivity to lag length however, since, as the footnote to the table shows, the Q(6) p-values for Shenergy and Top Energy are well in excess of 10 per cent. Moreover, we report ARCH (3) tests, indicating that ARCH effect exists up to the lagged order 3 in the log return series.

For the raw trading volume series, we observe the average trading volume for Shanghai A is slightly larger than that for Shenzhen A. The standard deviations for all series are quite large. The skewness and the excess kurtosis statistics show significant deviations from normality for all series.

8.2.2   The Stationarity Tests for Stock Return and Trading Volume Series

In order to correctly specify the empirical models and avoid spurious correlation in our results, we test the stationarity of the return and volume series. Table 8.2 reports Augmented Dickey-Fuller statistics with and without a trend for the log stock price, return and raw trading volume series. Clearly, prices are non-stationary while returns are stationary in all cases. This is so whether or not a trend is included in the test, and is consistent with evidence for other markets. We also see that all the raw trading volume series are stationary, irrespective of whether a trend is included in the testing equation. Previous studies (Su, 2003; Chen, Firth and Rui, 2001) reported strong evidence of time trends in raw trading volume series on the Chinese stock market. We assess the importance of this by reporting β_1, the coefficient of the time trend in the Dickey-Fuller equation. We find it to be significant in most cases. In addition, we find that the time-series plots of raw trading volume clearly indicate an upward trend for all series, especially for Shanghai A and Shenzhen A. We therefore follow the lead of earlier literature and work with detrended volume data.

Table 8.1   Summary statistics for return and trading volume series for Shanghai and Shenzhen A share market and ten individual energy stocks

Listed company	No. of observations	Return						Raw Trading Volume			
		Mean (%)	Standard deviation	Skewness	Excess Kurtosis	Q(7)	ARCH (3)	Mean ('000)	Standard deviation ('000)	Skewness	Excess Kurtosis
Shanghai A	1445	0.0300	0.1643	-0.1522* (0.0644)	6.1155* (0.1287)	8.3711 [0.301]	28.6104 [0.000]	5822.9	3817.2	2.8052* (0.0644)	17.0028* (0.1287)
Shenzhen A	1445	0.0111	0.0178	-0.0414* (0.0644)	5.7513* (0.1287)	9.4425 [0.222]	31.6537 [0.000]	5598.95	3681.3	2.1727* (0.0644)	7.1290* (0.1287)
Guangdong Electric	1428	0.0608	0.0242	0.3227* (0.0648)	3.9500* (0.1294)	5.4046 [0.610]	59.6330 [0.000]	3.3692	4.8402	3.4787* (0.0648)	15.4034* (0.1294)
Heilongjiang Electric	1424	0.0251	0.0235	0.3298* (0.0648)	2.9106* (0.1296)	8.5046 [0.290]	17.7573 [0.000]	1.5479	2.3254	3.9626* (0.0648)	22.8511* (0.1296)
Mengdian Thermal	1428	0.0446	0.0256	0.0407 (0.0648)	4.1662* (0.1291)	12.846 [0.076]	25.9592 [0.000]	1.8956	2.7210	4.7598* (0.0648)	36.4939* (0.1294)
Shandong Taishan	1434	0.0790	0.0262	0.0354 (0.0646)	3.3423* (0.1292)	5.0238 [0.657]	708.377 [0.000]	4.6731	5.8063	2.9475* (0.0646)	11.9355* (0.1292)
Shanghai Petrochemal	1432	-0.0453	0.0229	0.4556* (0.0647)	4.1487* (0.1292)	8.7479 [0.271]	25.0998 [0.000]	7.2366	11.341	5.5029* (0.0647)	49.8959* (0.1292)
Shanxi Cooking	1426	-0.0553	0.0254	0.0985 (0.0648)	2.0629* (0.1295)	17.364 [0.015]	31.7901 [0.000]	0.8993	1.1506	3.2021* (0.0648)	13.3950* (0.1295)
Shenergy Company	1427	0.0172	0.0259	0.4081* (0.0648)	2.8176* (0.1295)	23.3411 [0.001]	37.2229 [0.000]	3.3745	4.4955	3.5211* (0.0647)	16.7667* (0.1295)

Shengli Oil Field	1435	0.0483	0.0252	0.2707* (0.0646)	3.1820* (0.1291)	9.677 [0.208]	71.7799 [0.000]	3.5191	4.1314	5.5029* (0.0646)	49.8959* (0.1291)
Shenzhen Energy	1437	0.0468	0.0263	0.4852* (0.0646)	3.1622* (0.1290)	10.201 [0.177]	41.1959 [0.000]	5.1569	8.1902	4.0705* (0.0646)	22.0271* (0.1290)
Top Energy	1432	0.0297	0.0265	0.0272 (0.0647)	3.0467* (0.1292)	13.778 [0.055]	59.1562 [0.000]	1.0847	1.3468	4.6562* (0.0647)	34.8518* (0.1292)

Notes:

1. Figures in parentheses are heteroscedasticity-consistent standard errors and figures in square brackets are p-values.
2. "Return" denotes the continuously compounded return, $\ln(p_t)-\ln(p_{t-1})$. "Volume" denotes raw trading volume (thousands of shares).
3. Q(7) Denotes the Ljung-Box Q statistic for serial correlation with 7 lags. The Q(6) statistics for Shenergy Company and Top Energy are 9.7833 [0.134] and 6.2641[0.394], respectively.
4. ARCH (3) is the ARCH test statistic of order 3 for the autocorrelation return series.
5. * indicates significant at the 1% level.

Table 8.2 Stationarity tests for stock price, return and raw trading volume series

Listed Company	Log Stock Price		Return		Raw Trading Volume		
	ADF(1) without trend	ADF(1) with trend	ADF(1) without trend	ADF(1) with trend	ADF(1) without trend	ADF(1) with trend	β_1
Shanghai A	-2.4009	-1.6140	-22.9759	-28.0671	-10.0712	-10.4992	431.7237* (2.8802)
Shenzhen A	-2.0214	-1.5322	-27.7462	-27.8021	-7.6281	-7.6274	-16.7321 (-0.1738)
Guangdong Electric	-1.4435	-1.8700	-27.9870	-27.9829	-9.6455	-10.1866	-0.6193* (-3.1965)
Heilongjiang Electric	-2.8640	-2.4366	-27.7522	-27.8111	-12.1681	-13.0522	-0.4908* (-4.5044)
Mengdian Thermal	-3.9147	-3.6833	-28.1662	-28.2175	-14.3836	-14.7028	-0.3872* (-2.8700)
Shangdong Taishan	-0.6975	-1.5052	-27.6130	-27.6030	-27.6130	-27.6030	-0.5740** (-2.1736)
Shanghai Petrochemical	-2.1161	-2.1354	-28.1794	-28.1700	-14.8364	-15.2788	-1.7035* (-3.4171)

Shanxi Cooking	-1.6184	-1.6477	-29.6492	-29.6507	-11.0903	-11.2419	-0.0827*** (-1.7881)
Shenergy Company	-1.9815	-1.6069	-27.5423	-27.5765	-13.2549	-13.3042	-0.2022 (-1.1334)
Shengli Oil Field	-1.6711	-1.4148	-26.9700	-27.0046	-12.4427	-13.0650	-0.7109* (-3.8040)
Shenzhen Energy	-3.6594	-3.3085	-26.6959	-26.7634	-10.9168	-11.6139	-1.2750* (-3.8178)
Top Energy	-1.5235	-2.1483	-27.3039	-27.2948	-12.7723	-12.8456	-0.0863 (-1.3385)

Notes:
1. The ADF(1) test denotes the augmented Dickey-Fuller test statistic. The 95% critical value with a linear trend = -3.4154, and the 95% critical value without a trend = -2.8640.
2. * indicates significant at the 1% level, ** indicates significant at the 5% level and *** indicates significant at the 10% level.
3. Figures in parentheses are t-ratios for β_1 in the equation $\Delta Vol_t = \beta_0 + \beta_1 t + \gamma Vol_{t-1} + \delta \Delta Vol_{t-1} + \varepsilon_t$.

8.3.3   Detrending Raw Trading Volume

In order to detrend the trading volume time series, we regress the series on a deterministic function of time. To allow for a non-linear time trend and a linear time trend, we use a quadratic time trend equation:

$$Vol_t = \alpha + \beta_1 t + \beta_2 t^2 + \epsilon_t \qquad (8.2)$$

where Vol_t represents raw daily trading volume and t is time. Table 8.3a presents the estimated coefficients (with t-statistics in parentheses) of equation (8.2). In general, the coefficients for both the linear and quadratic terms are statistically significant, although the degree of explanation is low, judging by the adjusted R^2 values. In the following analysis we will employ trading volume with linear and quadratic trends removed for the two A-share indices and ten individual stocks. The detrended trading volumes are the residuals from equation (8.2).

Table 8.3b reports the summary and ADF statistics for the detrended volume series, V_t, for Shanghai A, Shenzhen A and ten individual stocks. Not surprisingly, apart from the mean which is near zero, the summary statistics are similar to those for the raw data. Given the removal of a quadratic trend term, it is not surprising that the trend term in the Dickey-Fuller equation, reported as α_1 in Table 8.3b, is insignificant in all cases. The ADF(1) tests with and without a trend show that the detrended volume data are clearly stationary so that we may confidently proceed to the modelling of returns and volume data without risk of spurious correlation. We turn to this task now.

8.3   EMPIRICAL INVESTIGATION OF THE STOCK RETURN-VOLUME RELATION

8.3.1   Contemporaneous Relation

Previous studies of the contemporaneous relation between stock returns and trading volume have estimated three forms of the empirical relationship: a positive relationship between volume and stock returns (Epps, 1975; Rogalski, 1978), a positive relationship between volume and absolute returns (Smirlock and Starks, 1988) and an unrestricted V-shaped relationship between volume and return (Karpoff, 1987; Gallant, Rossi and Tauchen, 1992; Blume, Easley and O'Hara, 1994).

We begin by showing the scatter plots of detrended trading volume against stock returns for Shanghai A, Shenzhen A and ten individual stocks in Figure 8.1. Although it is difficult to make any definitive statement about the relationship between trading volume and return just by observing the scatter plots, Figure 8.1 suggests a V-shaped relation by and large, consistent with previous work cited above.

To examine the data more formally, we estimate two alternative forms of the equation as follows:

$$V_t = \alpha_0 + \alpha_1 R_t + \varepsilon_t \qquad (8.3)$$

$$V_t = \beta_0 + \beta_1 |R_t| + \varepsilon_t \qquad (8.4)$$

where the dependent variable V_t is detrended daily trading volume, the independent variable in equation (8.3) is the natural logarithm of the price relative and, in equation (8.4), its absolute value, and ϵ_t is a random error term.

Table 8.4 reports the estimation results for these two equations. The results of equation (8.3) on the left in the table indicate that when signed price change is used as the measure of return, the slope coefficients are all significantly positive at the 1 per cent level but the estimated intercepts are not significant. This positive relation also holds for the equation with absolute return as the explanatory variable. With the exception of the case of Shanghai A, adjusted R^2 figures show that the relationship of volume to absolute return is considerably stronger, with all slope coefficients significantly positive and all intercepts significantly negative. These results provide strong evidence that the contemporaneous relationship between trading volume and return is V-shaped rather than positively linear. However, the values of adjusted R^2 are low in both regressions. This indicates that contemporaneous return explains a relatively small portion of trading volume. The use of the absolute return imposes a symmetric V-shaped relationship which can be relaxed and tested by estimating a more general form:

$$Vol_t = \beta_0 + \beta_1 R_t^{(+)} + \beta_2 R_t^{(-)} + \varepsilon_t \qquad (8.5)$$

where $R_t^{(+)} = \begin{cases} R_t, & \text{if } R_t > 0 \\ 0, & \text{otherwise;} \end{cases}$ and $R_t^{(-)} = \begin{cases} R_t, & \text{if } R_t < 0 \\ 0, & \text{otherwise.} \end{cases}$

Table 8.5 reports the results of the asymmetry tests. All coefficients (except β_2 in Shanghai A) are statistically significant at the 1 per cent level and the estimated β_1 are positive while estimated β_2 are negative. Most importantly, β_1 are larger in absolute value than β_2, suggesting asymmetry, consistent with previous findings (Ratner and Leal, 2001) that the response of trading volume to an upward return is stronger than that to a downward return. In addition, we also present the results of a Wald test for the null

Table 8.3a Linear and non-linear trend in trading volume ($Vol_t = \alpha + \beta_1 t + \beta_2 t^2 + \epsilon_t$)

Listed Company	α	β_1	β_2	$\overline{R}^2$
Shanghai A	3284.0* (11.3358)	5661.6* (6.1185)	-2.2344* (-3.6061)	0.07764
Shenzhen A	4035.6* (14.1600)	6796.0* (7.4656)	-4.8084* (-7.8882)	0.04034
Guangdong Electric	8.3640* (23.5361)	-13.4192* (-11.683)	0.0068* (8.6738)	0.14709
Heilongjiang Electric	3.7503* (21.7624)	-5.6051* (-10.035)	0.0026* (6.9752)	0.13345
Mengdian Thermal	3.1147* (14.6633)	-2.7886* (-4.0703)	0.0011** (2.4563)	0.03372
Shangdong Taishan	6.2690* (13.7830)	-2.7886* (-4.0703)	0.0011** (2.4563)	0.03372
Shanghai Petrochemical	11.2982* (12.8169)	-5.6715* (-1.9962)	0.0000 (0.0015)	0.04136
Shanxi Cooking	1.0298* (11.4323)	0.3158 (1.0878)	-0.0005* (-2.6577)	0.02747
Shenergy Company	3.2353* (9.9350)	1.1411 (0.9929)	-0.0014*** (-1.842)	0.00626
Shengli Oil Field	5.0680* (16.1688)	-0.72885 (-0.7230)	-0.0015** (-2.196)	0.08480

Shenzhen Energy	13.444*	-22.4761*	0.0114*	0.14221
	(22.6392)	(-11.7850)	(8.8979)	
	0.9265*	1.3042*	-0.0011*	
Top Energy	(8.7623)	(3.8163)	(-4.9100)	0.02474

Notes:
1. t-statistics are reported in parentheses.
2. * denotes significant at the 1% level, ** significant at the 5% level and ***significant at the 10% level.

Table 8.3b Summary statistics of the detrended trading volume for Shanghai A, Shenzhen A and ten individual stocks

Listed company	Mean (%)	Standard Deviation ('000)	Skewness	Kurtosis-3	ADF (1) without trend	ADF (1) with trend	α_1
Shanghai A	-0.0000	3663.2	2.8174* (0.0644)	17.7236* (0.1287)	-10.5590	-10.5553	-3.7391 (-0.0260)
Shenzhen A	-0.0000	3603.8	2.0612* (0.0644)	7.2502* (0.1287)	-7.8260	-7.8234	6.7257 (0.0699)
Guangdong Electric	-0.0000	4.4669	2.9070* (0.0648)	12.6624* (0.1294)	-10.4734	-10.4694	0.0327 (0.1800)
Heilongjiang Electric	-0.0000	2.1998	3.7313* (0.0648)	22.5141* (0.1296)	-13.0569	-13.0522	0.0047 (0.0464)
Mengtian Thermal	0.0000	2.6728	4.9145* (0.0648)	39.9789* (0.1294)	-14.7553	-14.7501	-0.0056 (-0.0423)
Shandong Taishan	0.0000	5.7335	2.8801* (0.0646)	11.7198* (0.1292)	-12.4273	-12.4234	-0.0278 (-0.1068)
Shanghai Petrochemical	0.0000	11.096	5.7913* (0.0647)	55.1241* (0.1292)	-15.2841	-15.2788	-0.0190 (-0.0391)
Shanxi Cooking	0.0000	1.1338	3.1518* (0.0648)	13.2966* (0.1295)	-11.2903	-11.2864	0.0037 (0.0811)
Shenergy Company	-0.0000	4.4745	3.5685* (0.0648)	17.4900* (0.1295)	-13.3195	-13.3145	0.0158 (0.0784)

Shengli Oil Field	0.0000	3.9496	3.2423* (0.0646)	15.5463* (0.1291)	-13.1233	-13.1201	0.0535 (0.3008)
Shenzhen Energy	0.0000	7.4877	3.9758* (0.0646)	23.6236* (0.1290)	-12.0295	-12.0253	-0.0303 (-0.0964)
Top Energy	-0.0000	1.3291	4.6733* (0.0647)	35.2653* (0.1292)	-12.9876	-12.9829	0.0055 (0.0865)

Notes:

1. Figures in parentheses are heteroscedasticity-consistent standard errors for skewness and kurtosis and t-ratios for α_1 in the equation $\Delta V_t = \alpha_0 + \alpha_1 t + \gamma V_{t-1} + \delta \Delta V_{t-1} + \varepsilon_t$.

2. ADF(1) test denotes the augmented Dicky-Fuller test statistic. The 95% critical value with a linear trend = -3.4154, the 95% critical value without a trend = -2.8640.

3. * denotes significant at the 1% level.

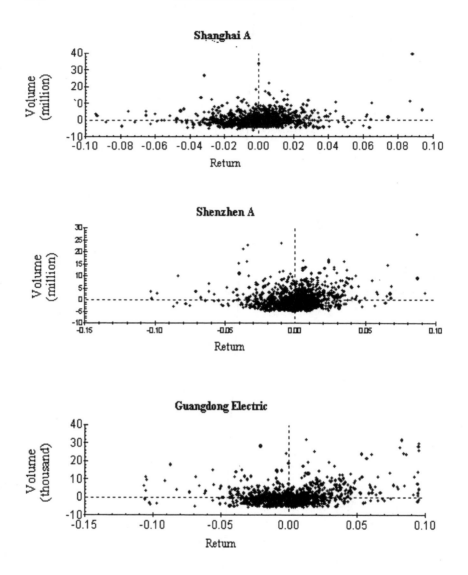

Figure 8.1   Scatter plots of stock return-volume

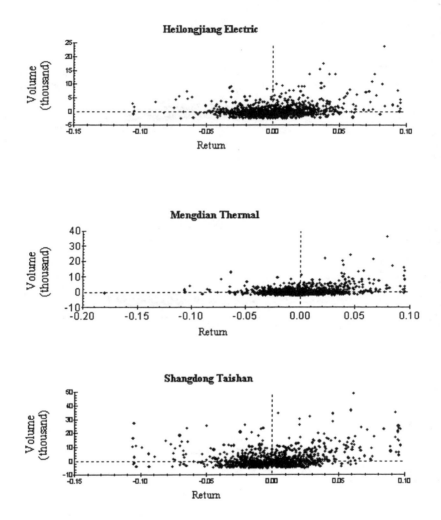

Figure 8.1 (continued)

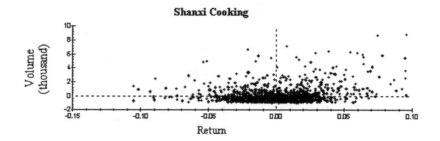

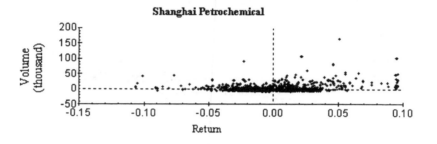

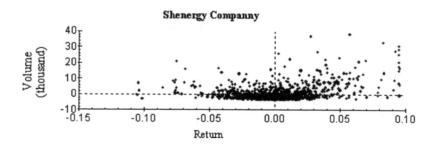

Figure 8.1   (continued)

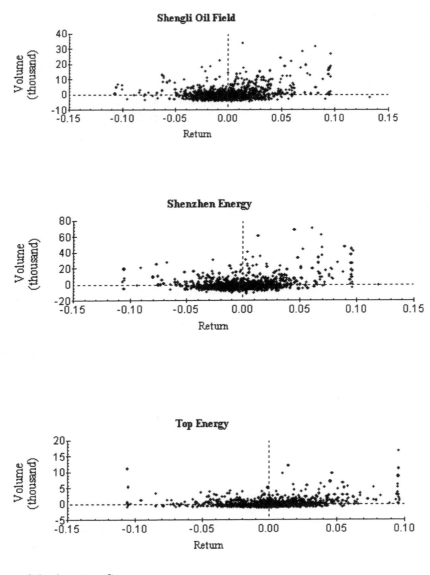

Figure 8.1   (continued)

Notes: These plots show the stock-price-volume relation for Shanghai A, Shenzhen A and ten individual stocks over the period 1 January 1997 to 31 December 2002. Return is calculated as the natural logarithm of the price relative and is plotted on the horizontal axis. The detrended volume is plotted on the vertical axis.

Table 8.4 Regression results

Listed company	$V_t = \alpha_0 + \alpha_1 R_t + \epsilon_t$				$V_t = \beta_0 + \beta_1 |R_t| + \epsilon_t$			
	α_0	α	F-Statistic	Adjusted R^2	β_0	β_1	F-Statistic	Adjusted R^2
Shanghai A share	-7.5584 (-0.0354)	30000* (2.6669)	26.3803* [0.000]	0.017285	-418.51*** (-1.8484)	37900* (2.3689)	22.6693* [0.000]	0.01480
Shenzhen A share	-4.8225 (-0.0516)	33600* (3.9091)	40.7120* [0.000]	0.026783	-823.467* (-6.1066)	68200* (6.1316)	93.5844 * [0.000]	0.06029
Guangdong Electric	-0.0286 (-0.1014)	49.616* (4.7733)	110.9933* [0.000]	0.071611	-1.7091* (-6.6538)	102.919* (5.3341)	280.4374* [0.000]	0.16385
Heilongjiang Electric	-5.6462 (-0.0541)	22.771* (4.8342)	89.2791* [0.000]	0.058452	-0.7338* (-7.2677)	0.7946* (5.9488)	165.0905* [0.000]	0.10346
Mengdian Thermal	-0.1213 (-0.0920)	30.166* (5.3423)	129.7257* [0.000]	0.082637	-0.9645* (-7.2198)	53.487* (5.3987)	215.8161* [0.000]	0.13068
Shangdong Taishan	-0.0430 (-0.1233)	53.374* (5.1103)	90.4418* [0.000]	0.058788	-2.4769* (-9.7994)	138.784* (9.7154)	393.7091* [0.000]	0.21522
Shanghai Petrochemical	63.5481 (0.0998)	1 32.19* (4.3144)	114.4192* [0.000]	0.073486	-4.3701* (-8.8635)	280.26* (6.0494)	309.3385* [0.000]	0.17738

Shanxi Cooking	-0.0001 (0.0247)	10.560* (5.1040)	84.3847* [0.000]	0.055098	-0.4264* (-8.8351)	22.931* (7.3941)	198.1118* [0.000]	0.13257
Shenergy Company	-0.0009 (-0.0230)	56.176* (5.7650)	168.2221* [0.000]	0.10489	-2.1166* (-8.8351)	116.93* (7.3941)	433.7041* [0.000]	0.23267
Shengli Oil Field	-0.0345 (-0.3456)	40.267* (10.1591)	103.2081* [0.000]	0.066576	-1.4635* (-8.3950)	81.578* (6.5819)	230.5452* [0.000]	0.13807
Shenzhen Energy	-34.323 (-0.0852)	82317* (4.5412)	130.8625* [0.000]	0.082987	-2.9392* (-7.8817)	160.75* (6.0583)	282.1187* [0.000]	0.16381
Top Energy	-0.00037 (-0.0527)	11.972* (6.3526)	86.2446* [0.000]	0.056407	-0.4946* (-4.9569)	26.552* (3.9770)	236.4911* [0.000]	0.14173

Notes:
1. t-statistics are in parentheses and the figures in square brackets are *p*-values.
2. * indicates significant at the 1% level, ** significant at the 5% level and *** significant at the 10% level.

hypotheses $\beta_1 = \beta_2$ and $\beta_1 = -\beta_2$ in Table 8.5. The first of these restrictions produces equation (8.3) while the second produces equation (8.4). The results show that both of them are statistically significant, thus rejecting both restrictions so that the relationship between trading volume and return is asymmetrically V-shaped for A share markets and ten individual stocks in the energy sector.

Table 8.5   Regression results of the asymmetry tests

Listed companies	β_0	β_1	β_2	$\overline{R}^2$	Wald test $(\beta_1 = \beta_2)$	$(\beta_1 = -\beta_2)$
Shanghai	-438.199**	69600*	-8153.7	0.0329	6.4906*	8.3663*
A	(-1.9622)	(2.9705)	(-0.6832)		[0.000]	[0.000]
Shenzhen	-885.16*	111000*	-34500*	0.0954	48.5191*	25.7515*
A	(-6.8047)	(7.3245)	(-3.3982)		[0.000]	[0.000]
Guangdong	-1.5891*	132.72*	-55.872*	0.2055	29.0477*	27.4349*
Electric	(-6.4199)	(3.7607)	(-5.0907)		[0.000]	[0.000]
Heilongjiang	-0.6742*	58.553*	-20.743*	0.1428	36.3198*	26.9579*
Electric	(-6.8870)	(6.4658)	(-3.7215)		[0.000]	[0.000]
Mengdian	-0.9045*	25.948*	-23.080*	0.1934	39.1129*	112.0042
Thermal	(-7.8576)	(6.7202)	(-4.1345)		[0.000]	*
						[0.000]
Shandong	-2.4322*	180.504	-87.948*	0.2592	65.8652*	35.8739*
Taishan	(-8.8929)	(1.0721)	(-5.8210)		[0.000]	[0.000]
Shanghai	-4.0423*	371.751*	-153.096*	0.2269	43.9171*	27.7637*
Petrochemal	(-9.1180)	(6.4614)	(-5.8410)		[0.000]	[0.000]
Shanxi	-0.4132*	32.095*	-12.402*	0.1689	68.8993*	32.4807*
Cooking	(-9.2186)	(8.2016)	(-5.5325)		[0.000]	[0.000]
Shenergy	-1.9489*	151.443*	-63.054*	0.2959	73.8486*	44.9270*
Company	(-11.179)	(9.3807)	(-5.3709)		[0.000]	[0.000]
Shengli	-1.3850*	110.515*	-41.938*	0.1857	43.1578*	43.1154*
Oil Field	(-7.8135)	(7.1213)	(-4.6042)		[0.000]	[0.000]
Shenzhen	2.6535*	205.28*	-81.955*	0.2084	43.7529*	29.5204*
Energy	(-7.7754)	(6.7069)	(-5.0436)		[0.000]	[0.000]
Top	-0.48577*	37.107*	-14.692**	0.1911	16.5411*	65.6948*
Energy	(-4.9761)	(5.2440)	(-2.4885)		[0.000]	[0.000]

Notes: t-statistics are in parentheses and *p*-values are in square brackets. * denotes significant at the 1% level, ** significant at the 5% level and *** significant at the 10% level.

8.3.2   Causal Relation between Trading Volume and Stock Return

So far we have restricted our analysis to the estimation of contemporaneous correlation between return and volume. We now turn to an examination of the dynamics, using the commonly applied tests of Granger causality.

The Granger causality test has been widely used to test the causal relation between two series, that is, to test whether variable X precedes variable Y after controlling for past values of Y, or vice versa. In this section we test whether trading volume causes return or return causes trading volume by employing Granger causality tests. We use the following bivariate vector autoregressions to test for causality between trading volume and stock returns:

$$V_t = \lambda_0 + \sum_{i=1}^{m} \lambda_i R_{t-i} + \sum_{j=1}^{n} \delta_j V_{t-j} + \varepsilon_{1t} \tag{8.6}$$

$$R_t = \gamma_0 + \sum_{i=1}^{m} \gamma_i R_{t-i} + \sum_{j=1}^{n} \beta_j V_{t-j} + \varepsilon_{2t} \tag{8.7}$$

We use five lags of the volume and return variables ($m=n=5$ in equations (8.6) and (8.7)) which amounts to allowing for week-long information in the regressions. Given the speed with which information is transmitted in securities markets, even emerging ones, a week seems ample. Granger causality from R to V is then tested by testing the hypothesis that $\lambda_i=0$, all i in (8.6) and Granger causality from V to R is tested by testing the hypothesis that $\beta_j=0$, all j in equation (8.7).

Table 8.6 presents the results for equations (8.6) and (8.7). In the test of the null hypothesis that return does not cause trading volume ($\lambda_i=0$ in equation (8.6)), the F-statistic is significant at the 1 per cent level in all cases – for both A share markets and all ten individual stocks. Thus we reject the null hypothesis and find strong evidence for stock return causing trading volume. Moreover, in all cases the higher value of adjusted R^2 indicates there is a higher explanatory power so that a large proportion of movement of trading volume can be predicted by past return and past trading volume. Inspection of individual coefficients for equation (8.6) (not reported) shows that much of the extra explanatory power comes from past volume terms indicating that volume has strong autoregressive properties. In the test of the null hypothesis that trading volume does not cause return based on equation (8.7), the F-statistic is significant for Shanghai A and Heilongjiang Electric Power at the 10 per cent level while for Shenzhen A share, Mengdian Thermal Power, Shanxi Cooking and Shenergy Company it is significant at the 5 per cent level. For the other six individual stocks the F-statistic is insignificant. Therefore, for A share indices we find some evidence supporting trading volume causing returns, yet for most individual stocks trading volume does not lead return. In addition, all adjusted R^2 values are very low, which indicates that there is little explanatory power for future returns predicted by publicly available information (i.e. past trading volume and past return). These findings are consistent with previous evidence from developed markets which has shown that return causes volume but not vice versa (Chen, Firth, and Rui, 2001).

In the third and fourth panels of Table 8.6 we report Granger causality tests using the absolute value of the return. Since we found in the previous section

Table 8.6 Granger causality test results

Listed company	Shanghai A	Shenzhen A	Guangdong Electric	Heilongjiang Electric	Mengtian Thermal	Shandong Taishan	Shanghai Petrochemical	Shanxi Cooking	Shenergy Company	Shengli Oil Field	Shenzhen Energy	Top Energy
Tests of causality from returns to volume; $\lambda_i=0$ in $V_t = \lambda_0 + \sum_{i=1}^{5} \lambda_i R_{t-i} + \sum_{j=1}^{5} \delta_j V_{t-j} + \varepsilon_{1t}$												
F-statistic	405.41 [0.000]	1112.5 [0.000]	361.67 [0.000]	257.58 [0.000]	140.44 [0.000]	268.35 [0.000]	246.36 [0.000]	360.34 [0.000]	233.60 [0.000]	197.87 [0.000]	259.19 [0.000]	171.10 [0.000]
$\bar{R}^2$	0.6312	0.8460	0.6345	0.5178	0.4437	0.5370	0.5624	0.6184	0.5328	0.5143	0.5937	0.4669
Tests of causality from volume to return; $\beta_j=0$ in $R_t = \gamma_0 + \sum_{i=1}^{5} \gamma_i R_{t-i} + \sum_{j=1}^{5} \beta_j V_{t-j} + \varepsilon_{2t}$												
F-statistic	1.877 [0.095]	2.586 [0.024]	1.129 [0.343]	2.181 [0.054]	2.913 [0.013]	0.716 [0.612]	1.705 [0.130]	4.033 [0.001]	2.365 [0.038]	0.894 [0.484]	0.708 [0.617]	1.228 [0.293]
$\bar{R}^2$	0.0049	0.0173	0.0053	0.0104	0.0039	0.0014	0.0035	0.0093	0.0062	0.0004	0.0040	0.0007

Tests of causality from absolute returns to volume; $\lambda = 0$ in $V_t = \lambda + \sum_{i=1}^{5} \lambda_i |R_{t-i}| + \sum_{j=1}^{5} \delta_j V_{t-j} + \epsilon_{1t}$

F-statistic	462.99	1224.6	369.14	239.46	23.129	239.20	242.42	382.84	216.56	225.32	273.92	180.74
	[0.000]	[0.000]	[0.000]	[0.000]	[0.000]	[0.000]	[0.000]	[0.000]	[0.000]	[0.000]	[0.000]	[0.000]
$\overline{R}^2$	0.6237	0.8255	0.6387	0.4965	0.4277	0.5338	0.5601	0.6127	0.5302	0.4993	0.0585	0.4542

Tests of causality from volume to absolute return; $\beta_j = 0$ in $|R_t| = \gamma_0 + \sum_{i=1}^{5} \gamma_i |R_{t-i}| + \sum_{j=1}^{5} \beta_j V_{t-j} + \epsilon_{2t}$

F-statistic	38.014	41.484	25.533	10.463	23.129	21.228	17.827	12.615	38.066	19.207	26.122	21.603
	[0.000]	[0.000]	[0.000]	[0.000]	[0.000]	[0.000]	[0.000]	[0.000]	[0.000]	[0.000]	[0.000]	[0.000]
$\overline{R}^2$	0.1118	0.1424	0.1460	0.0510	0.0963	0.1356	0.1035	0.0595	0.1043	0.0883	0.1533	0.1081

Notes:
1. t-statistics are in parentheses and p-values are in square brackets.
2. * denotes significant at the 1% level, ** significant at the 5% level and *** significant at the 10% level.
3. $\overline{R}^2$ =adjusted R^2.

that the dependence of volume on contemporaneous returns was clearly a non-linear one, we wish to gauge the possible effect of mis-specification of the form of the return variable on the outcome of the Granger tests by repeating the analysis using absolute returns. The tests can also be interpreted as tests of non-linear causality between returns and volume. In the third panel in which causality from returns to volume is tested, clearly not much changes by using absolute returns. This provides strong evidence that the outcome is robust to this change in specification, despite the superior performance of the absolute return in the contemporaneous regression. The fourth panel in comparison to the second shows a marked improvement in the explanatory power of the equation when the absolute return is used and, moreover, implies clear causality from volume to returns which is evidently masked by the form of the test in the second panel. This provides strong evidence that while volume has little predictive power for returns, it is able to significantly predict the magnitude of returns but not the sign.

Overall, the results indicate stronger evidence of return causing trading volume rather than volume causing return although at a 10 per cent significance level we find feedback relationships between trading volume and return for Shanghai A, Shenzhen A and four individual stocks. More interestingly, we find strong evidence that volume can contribute significantly to the prediction of absolute return. These findings extend those in the existing literature in which volume was found to fail to cause return during an earlier period for Shanghai A and Shenzhen A even at the 10 per cent significance level (Lee and Rui, 2000).

8.4   POLICY EFFECTS

It is well known that Chinese domestic stock markets are very sensitive to government regulations. Fan, Wu and Groenewold (2003) and Walter and Howie (2001) reported that important events and market regulations during 1997-2002 had a significant impact on the Chinese stock market. We now extend our analysis of the contemporaneous relationship between return and volume by investigating the effect on this relationship of exogenous policy changes, both changes which can be expected to affect the stock market as a whole and those which are specific to all or part of the energy sector.

In order to proceed we need to identify the changes and we carry this out using a combination of data-based and policy-based analysis. In particular, we begin by analysing abnormal return and return volatility using a GARCH (1,1) model and single out obvious volatility spikes. Then we examine policy history in order to identify the policies and events associated with each spike and define the dummy variables which we finally introduce into the return-volume relationship, allowing them to shift both the intercept and the slope.

8.4.1   Identifying the Policy Dummy Variables

We concluded in section 8.2 that returns are stationary and have little autocorrelation. Hence we assume that they can be adequately described by the simple model: $R_t = a_t + \mu$ where a_t will be referred to as the abnormal return or mean-corrected return at time t, R_t is the log return at time t and μ is the mean of return series. Tests of ARCH in returns (see Table 8.1) show strong evidence of low level ARCH in all return series. We therefore use the generalized ARCH (GARCH) model suggested by Bollerslev (1986) to analyse volatility in the return series. We begin with the GARCH (1,1) model to estimate return volatility as equation (8.8):

$$R_t = \mu + a_t$$
$$a_t = \sigma_t \, \epsilon_t \qquad \epsilon_t \sim \mathrm{iid}(0, 1)$$
$$\sigma^2_t = \omega_0 + \beta_i \, \sigma^2_{t-1} + \alpha_i \, a^2_{t-1} \qquad (8.8)$$

where σ^2_t is the conditional variance; the standard residual (ϵ_t) is a sequence of independent and identically distributed (iid) random variables with mean zero and variance 1, $\omega_0 > 0$, $\alpha_i \geq 0$, $\beta_i \geq 0$, and $(\alpha_i + \beta_i) < 1$. $R_t = \mu + a_t$ is the mean equation for R_t and the model for σ^2_t is the volatility equation for R_t.

Table 8.7 presents the results of parameter estimates and residual diagnostic tests for the GARCH (1,1) model. The constant terms in the conditional mean equations are very small and not statistically significant at any level. This is consistent with the summary statistics reported in Table 8.1. The coefficient estimates for the volatility equation are highly significant for all series, indicating the conditional variance σ^2_t is dependent on σ^2_{t-1} and a^2_{t-1}. Further, we note that the ARCH (1) test, Ljung-Box Q (7) and $Q^2(7)$ statistics are all insignificant even at the 10 per cent level, showing that the standard residuals for the conditional variance are free of ARCH effects and autocorrelation problems. Therefore, the specification of the mean and volatility equations is adequate and we do not explore higher-order GARCH models.

The abnormal returns (the residuals a_t) and the conditional standard deviations are plotted in Figures 8.2a to 8.2e. From these figures we can observe that the time series of stock returns for Shanghai A, Shenzhen A and ten individual stocks have volatility clustering and temporal dependence. That is, large changes tend to be followed by large changes, and small changes tend to be followed by small changes. By comparing Figures 8.2a, 8.2b, 8.2c, 8.2d and 8.2e, it can be noted that all return series tend to respond similarly to common news and economic factors, as three major volatility spikes can be observed: during January 1997-December 1997; during May 1999-April 2000 and during July 2001-June 2002. Shanghai A and Shenzhen A also show a similar pattern of volatility. For ten individual stocks, different

Table 8.7 Maximum likelihood estimates of the GARCH (1,1) model

	Shanghai A	Shenzhen A	Guangdong Electric	Heilongjiang Electric	Mengdian Thermal	Shandong Taishan	Shanghai Petrochemical	Shanxi Cooking	Shenergy Company	Shengli Oil Fields	Shenzhen Energy	Top Energy
$\mu(\%)$	-0.0109 (-0.2522)	-0.0215 (-0.5762)	-0.0129 (-0.2454)	0.0001 (0.0022)	0.0046 (0.0807)	0.0512 (0.9916)	-0.0867 (1.7593)	-0.0200 (-0.3591)	-0.0693 (-1.0872)	-0.0153 (-0.2826)	-0.0347 (-0.5976)	0.0312 (0.6057)
ω_0	0.00001 (3.3222)	0.00001 (1.7347)	0.00003 (3.7178)	0.00003 (2.0550)	0.00003 (3.0091)	0.00004 (2.7446)	0.00007 (4.7715)	0.00002 (2.5038)	0.00003 (2.3872)	0.00003 (2.8230)	0.00003 (3.2143)	0.00289 (3.1862)
α	0.2419 (4.3170)	0.1309 (2.5734)	0.1432 (4.5765)	0.0947 (3.5699)	0.1352 (4.0479)	0.1835 (5.1373)	0.2804 (4.6469)	0.0906 (3.8163)	0.1486 (4.5607)	0.1079 (4.1313)	0.1334 (4.7246)	0.0969 (3.7658)
β	0.7375 (15.810)	0.8590 (16.003)	0.8062 (22.949)	0.8502 (19.514)	0.8309 (24.405)	0.7649 (16.517)	0.6244 (10.604)	0.8782 (27.987)	0.8177 (22.016)	0.8533 (24.662)	0.8227 (24.432)	0.8622 (26.951)
J-B	153.94 [0.000]	1183.3 [0.000]	1070.3 [0.000]	337.71 [0.000]	661.89 [0.000]	1102.6 [0.000]	854.91 [0.000]	160.23 [0.000]	852.26 [0.000]	764.19 [0.000]	588.309 [0.000]	498.944 [0.000]
$Q(7)$	7.5419 [0.375]	11.185 [0.131]	3.0990 [0.876]	5.6204 [0.585]	9.0732 [0.247]	3.0885 [0.877]	4.7371 [0.692]	9.1041 [0.245]	6.0962 [0.529]	7.9204 [0.340]	5.8289 [0.560]	8.8865 [0.261]
$Q^2(7)$	4.4806 [0.723]	2.8840 [0.896]	3.1264 [0.873]	6.1534 [0.522]	9.7515 [0.203]	2.7699 [0.905]	8.9867 [0.254]	9.2862 [0.233]	6.7828 [0.452]	7.4199 [0.387]	4.9161 [0.767]	5.2390 [0.631]
Arch (1)	0.2436 [0.622]	0.8703 [0.351]	0.9099 [0.340]	0.8322 [0.362]	4.0716 [0.044]	0.0305 [0.861]	0.1667 [0.683]	5.4707 [0.020]	3.5796 [0.060]	1.5354 [0.216]	0.3352 [0.563]	2.5460 [0.111]

Notes: The effective estimation period is from January 1997 to December 31, 2002. J-B is the statistic for the Jarque-Bera normality test for the GARCH residuals. $Q(7)$ and $Q^2(7)$ are seventh-order Ljung-Box Q and Q-squared statistics for the GARCH residuals. ARCH(1) is the statistic for Engle's test for first-order ARCH in the GARCH model residuals. The figures in parentheses are t-statistics and the figures in square brackets are p-values.

sectors appear to have different volatility structures but those in the same sector have almost identical volatility spikes. These results suggest that the returns for each individual stock were affected not only by changes in general market regulations but also by sector-specific policy changes.

In fact, each of these spikes can be related to major changes in policies and a few important events. As summarized by Fan, Wu and Groenewold (2003), during 1997-2002 some important events and government policies had a significant impact on the Chinese stock market. These events include the Red Chips Craze which followed the handover of Hong Kong in 1997, the rally of 19 May in 1999 which followed the granting of permission for state-owned enterprises and insurance companies to enter the securities market and the introduction of taxes on interest earnings in saving accounts. In addition, WTO entry maintained bull markets in 2000. The opening of the B share market to domestic investors on 19 February 2001 diverted lots of funds into this surging market. The process of state share reduction drove the market toward decline in July 2001, while the suspension of the state share reduction scheme made market indices skyrocket.[2]

The individual stocks have also been affected by the reform of state-owned enterprises and energy policy changes. For example, from the plots for the electricity sector (Figure 8.2b), the last spikes for Guangdong Electric, Heilongjiang Electric and Mengdian Thermal are different from those of other sectors. This is because the Chinese government deregulated and liberalized the supply price for generators. Document No. 5 of the State Council on 11 April 2002 announced the government's intention to separate generation from transmission and to liberalize all types of electricity prices. From the plots for the oil sector (Figure 8.2c), the second volatility spike for Shandong Taishan, Shengli Oil Field and Shanghai Petrochemical is slightly different from others during September 1999-December 2000. As reform of the oil sector was proceeding during this period, the regulated crude oil price merged with international prices in September 1999, and the import tariff on crude oil was also removed in early 2000. Since then, the domestic price of crude oil has floated according to the world price. From the plots for the coal sector (Figure 8.2d), the second volatility spike for Shanxi Cooking and Top Energy is stronger and different from others during 1998. This spike reflected the forced closure of small mines. In December 1998, State Council announced in Document No. 43 the intention to close small mines. Since then, coal output for the whole country has been continuously declining. This has not only caused coal prices to rise but has also led to improvement in production management and performance of listed coal companies. Figure 8.2e shows the second volatility spike for Shenergy and Shenzhen Energy is different from others during 2000. The programmes "West Gas to East" and "West Power to East" started from early 2000 and the two programmes had a significant impact on Shenergy and Shenzhen Energy (Wu, 2003).

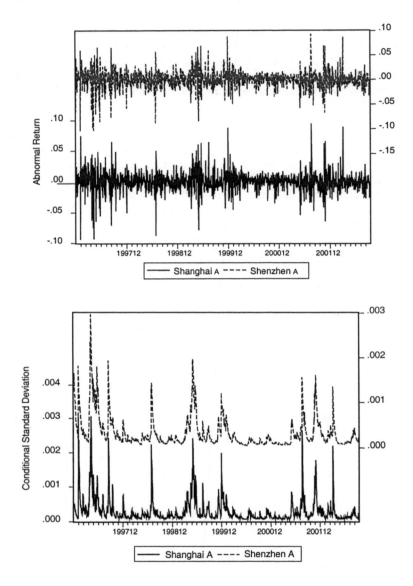

Figure 8.2a   The plots of abnormal return and conditional standard
deviation for Shanghai A and Shenzhen A

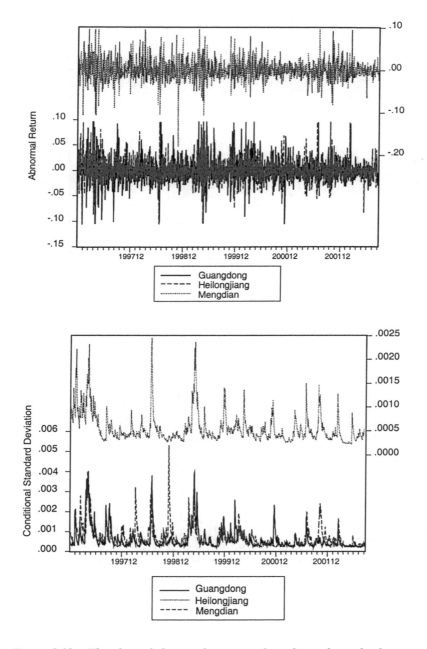

Figure 8.2b   The plots of abnormal return and conditional standard deviation for the electric sector

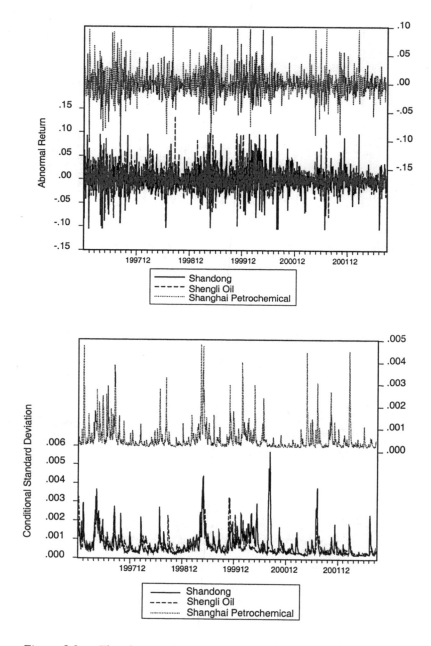

Figure 8.2c The plots of abnormal return and conditional standard deviation for the oil sector

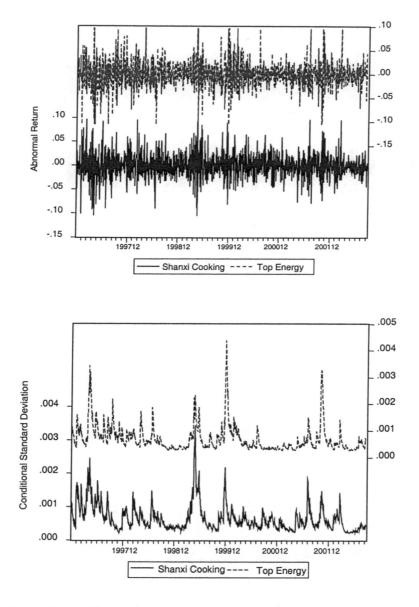

*Figure 8.2d   The plots of abnormal return and conditional standard
deviation for the coal sector*

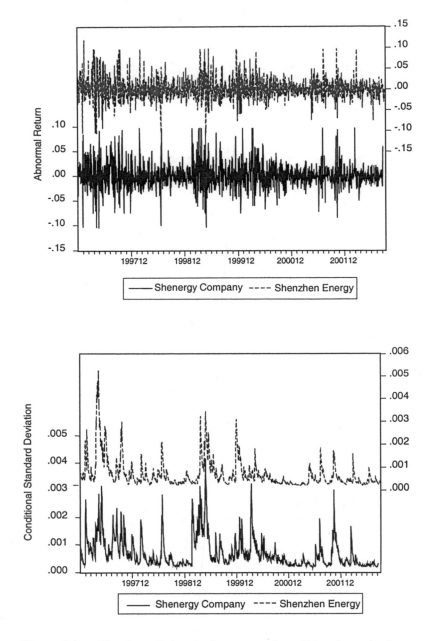

*Figure 8.2e   The plots of abnormal return and conditional standard
deviation for the composite service companies*

On the basis of the above analysis of the GARCH results and policy documents, we introduce one sector-specific dummy variable, D_0^i, for each of the four energy sub-sectors and five dummy variables D_1, D_2, D_3, D_4, and D_5 for the whole stock market as follows:

The oil and gas sector-specific dummy variable:
$$D_0^1 = \begin{cases} 1 : \text{between September 1, 1999 and December 31, 2000} \\ 0 : \text{otherwise;} \end{cases}$$

The electricity sector-specific dummy variable:
$$D_0^2 = \begin{cases} 1 : \text{between April 11, 2002 and December 31, 2002} \\ 0 : \text{otherwise;} \end{cases}$$

The coal sector-specific dummy variable:
$$D_0^3 = \begin{cases} 1 : \text{between January 1, 1999 and December 31, 2001} \\ 0 : \text{otherwise;} \end{cases}$$

The dummy variable specific to Shenergy and Shenzhen energy:
$$D_0^4 = \begin{cases} 1 : \text{between January 1, 2000 and December 31, 2000} \\ 0 : \text{otherwise;} \end{cases}$$

The five general stock market dummy variables:
$$D_1 = \begin{cases} 1 : \text{between January 1, 1997 and December 31, 1997} \\ 0 : \text{otherwise;} \end{cases}$$
$$D_2 = \begin{cases} 1 : \text{between January 1, 1998 and May 18, 1999} \\ 0 : \text{otherwise;} \end{cases}$$
$$D_3 = \begin{cases} 1 : \text{between May 19, 1999 and April 30, 2000} \\ 0 : \text{otherwise;} \end{cases}$$
$$D_4 = \begin{cases} 1 : \text{between May 1, 2000 and June 30, 2001} \\ 0 : \text{otherwise;} \end{cases}$$
$$D_5 = \begin{cases} 1 : \text{between July 1, 2001 and June 24, 2002} \\ 0 : \text{otherwise.} \end{cases}$$

8.4.2 Policy Effects on the Stock Return-Volume Relation

In order to examine the effects of sector-specific policies and market regulations on the relation between trading volume and stock return, we add the sectoral policy dummy variables D_0^1, D_0^2, D_0^3 and D_0^4 to the relevant regression of trading volume on stock returns and estimate these equations. We allow for both intercept and slope effects so that the simple regression for a stock in the ith sector becomes:

$$V_t = \alpha_0 + \eta_0^i \, D_0^i + \alpha_1 R_t + \gamma_0^i \, D_0^i \, R_t + \varepsilon_t \quad (i=1,\ldots 4) \tag{8.9}$$

Then we add the market regulations dummy variables D_1, D_2, D_3, D_4 and D_5 to the regression for each of the series as follows:

$$V_t = \alpha_0 + \sum_{i=1}^{5} \eta_i \, D_i + \alpha_1 R_t + \sum_{i=1}^{5} \gamma_i D_i \, R_t + \varepsilon_t \tag{8.10}$$

The estimation results are presented in Tables 8.8a and 8.8b. From Table 8.8a we can see that all but one (Mengdian Thermal) of the estimated coefficients η_0^i for the sector dummy variable are statistically significant at the 10 per cent level or lower level. In contrast, the estimated coefficients γ_0^i are almost all insignificant. Thus, sector-specific changes generally resulted in a temporary change in volume rather than a change in the way in which return affects volume. Of these, the coefficients for Guangdong Electric, Heilongjiang Electric and Mengdian Thermal are negative while the others are positive. The signs of the coefficients show the negative or positive effect of the sector policies. For the electricity sector, the liberalization of electricity price led to the decrease of electric companies' profit after April 2002. For the coal sector, the compulsory closure of small coal mines would cause the big companies' profits to rise. As expected, the signs of coefficient for Shanxi Cooking and Top Energy after December 1998 are positive. For the oil sector, the coefficients for Shandong Taishan, Shanghai Petrochemical and Shengli Oil Fields are positive because rising crude oil prices would increase the profits of these companies. For the composite service companies, the programmes "West Gas to East" and "West Power to East" would encourage the investor sentiment. As a result, the coefficients for Shenergy Company and Shenzhen Energy are positive.

For the dummy variables which capture the changes in general stock market regulations, we can observe from Table 8.8b that about half of the estimated coefficients η_i and γ_i are significant at the 10 per cent or lower level, although the intercept shifts are more often significant than the slope shifts. Of the five dummy variables, for the dummy variable D_1 three of the estimated coefficients η_1 and five of the coefficients γ_1 are statistically significant, implying that the listed companies issuing the Red-chip shares

Table 8.8a Regression results with sector dummy variables $V_t = \alpha_0 + n\,\alpha_1\,R_t + \eta_0^i\,D_0^i + \gamma_0^i\,D_0^i R_t + \varepsilon_t$

	Guangdong Electric	Heilongjiang Electric	Mengdian Thermal	Shandong Taishan	Shanghai Petrochemical	Shanxi Cooking	Shenery Company	Shenzhen Energy	Shengli Oil Field	Top Energy
α_0	0.0826	0.0566	-0.00051	-0.6448	-0.9303	-0.1408	-0.1867	-0.8323	-0.3708	-0.1040
	(0.2628)	(0.4984)	(-0.0349)	(-1.7716)	(-1.5682)	(-2.3073)	(-0.6453)	(-1.9956)	(-2.0578)	(-1.2744)
α_1	49.226	23.129	28.893	45.986	99.807	9.9306	56.483	76.998	29.434	10.165
	(4.5962)	(4.8076)	(4.9910)	(3.8055)	(4.3221)	(3.8290)	(5.0057)	(3.7446)	(4.0731)	(5.9501)
η_0	-0.9107	-0.5166	-36.845	2.6895	4.3723	0.2824	1.0757	4.7952	1.4575	0.2020
	(-2.2390)	(-3.5604)	(-0.1202)	(2.9084)	(2.3188)	(3.0648)	(1.7937)	(4.5697)	(2.7681)	(1.3415)
γ_0	4.2306	-8.2459	23.751	16.406	138.202	1.4696	-4.2264	24.966	41.187	5.8177
	(0.2192)	(-1.0078)	(1.1224)	(0.6976)	(1.3746)	(0.3484)	(-0.1852)	(0.6002)	(2.0959)	(1.9344)
F-statistic	0.0395	0.0343	0.4468	0.05315	0.06191	0.0366	0.0567	0.1181	0.0736	0.0333
	[0.000]	[0.000]	[0.000]	[0.000]	[0.000]	[0.000]	[0.000]	[0.000]	[0.000]	[0.000]
$\overline{R}^2$	0.0748	0.0656	0.0840	0.0985	0.1133	0.0695	0.1044	0.1403	0.0920	0.0637

Notes: t-statistics are in parentheses. p-values are in square brackets.

Table 8.8b Regression results with policy dummy variables $V_t = \alpha_0 + \alpha_1 R_t + \sum_{i=1}^{5} \eta_i D_i + \sum_{i=1}^{5} \gamma_i D_i R_t + \varepsilon_t$

	Shanghai A	Shenzhen A	Guangdong Electric	Heilongjiang Electric	Mengdian Thermal	Shandong Taishan	Shanghai Petrochemical	Shanxi Cooking	Shenergy Company	Shenzhen Energy	Shengli Oil Field	Top Energy
α_0	9.8962 (0.010)	90.292 (0.1346)	-0.9324 (-2.8065)	-0.5487 (-5.5626)	-0.3138 (-2.3859)	-0.0016 (-9.8566)	0.8416 (0.6265)	-0.2417 (-7.349)	-0.03078 (-0.0615)	-1.1038 (-1.876)	-0.3161 (-2.616)	0.1347 (0.8990)
α_1	217000 (1.9434)	117000 (1.7340)	18.129 (1.0867)	7.0106 (1.3794)	19.029 (1.7170)	-0.0089 (-0.6994)	211.99 (2.1935)	2.1557 (0.6682)	68.766 (1.9256)	6.5796 (0.1543)	-1225.9 (-0.171)	19.097 (1.3767)
η_1	408.66 (0.3916)	500.36 (0.6354)	1.8261 (1.4365)	0.4413 (1.0554)	0.1954 (0.6063)	0.0031 (2.6482)	1.9168 (0.9550)	0.33546 (2.0182)	0.8918 (1.4350)	3.2643 (2.1208)	0.5616 (0.9592)	0.0787 (0.3553)
η_2	-1057.6 (-1.0464)	-2124.0 (-2.9983)	-1.6859 (-4.2752)	0.0570 (0.2440)	-0.1866 (-0.9167)	-1.6949 (-5.1353)	-60.702 (-4.8449)	-0.2374 (4.0760)	-1.7803 (-3.2558)	-3.3340 (-5.428)	-1.0741 (-3.400)	-0.7228 (-4.4090)
η_3	511.59 (0.3921)	1990.7 (1.7148)	2.8799 (3.9737)	-0.7205 (-3.5316)	0.5166 (1.7876)	2.7505 (3.2051)	2.5163 (1.0289)	0.5740 (3.6895)	1.3803 (1.8197)	2.6616 (2.8592)	1.0523 (1.3057)	0.5263 (1.6744)
η_4	1158.6 (1.0989)	727.08 (0.9538)	2.3794 (5.0909)	1.4175 (6.5178)	0.9907 (3.2561)	4.6677 (5.2322)	2.0642 (0.9526)	0.6932 (6.6951)	0.4961 (0.8408)	3.7482 (4.0426)	1.3865 (3.1846)	0.0566 (0.2782)
η_5	-679.88 (-0.6286)	-871.39 (-1.1531)	0.37303 (1.0568)	0.4338 (3.4882)	0.2165 (0.9680)	0.8225 (2.0644)	-2.6922 (-2.0703)	0.0553 (1.0745)	-0.1463 (-0.2144)	0.4211 (0.7547)	-0.1823 (-0.819)	-0.5272 (-3.3330)
γ_1	-214000 (-1.9132)	-106000 (-1.5536)	51.687 (1.6791)	24.752 (1.9133)	8.8159 (0.6514)	74.282 (2.7959)	-126.448 (-1.2501)	9.3214 (1.5070)	-24.523 (-0.6384)	104.73 (1.8764)	151.76 (1.3199)	-0.9677 (-0.6837)

γ_2	-198000	-101000	3.3739	28.040	3.8953	52.773	-152.73	6.8005	-20.932	15.373	41.632	-10.429
	(-1.7635)	(1.4783)	(0.1906)	(1.8401)	(0.2521)	(2.5367)	(-1.5563)	(1.7990)	(-0.5425)	(0.3535)	(3.5626)	(-0.7294)
γ_3	-212000	-788000	31.102	6.9827	3.0841	70.705	-33.973	11.971	-17.544	56.372	54.035	-2.4346
	(-1.8798)	(-1.1207)	(1.3792)	(0.9227)	(0.2077)	(3.4188)	(-0.3162)	(1.9636)	(-0.4165)	(1.2079)	(3.1733)	(-0.1696)
γ_4	-206000	-115000	142.00	6.7084	53.872	37.628	64.267	8.1547	-5.8760	106.274	75.267	-2.7999
	(-1.8248)	(-1.656)	(0.6451)	(0.7778)	(1.8688)	(1.3867)	(0.32544)	(1.3932)	(-0.1410)	(1.4799)	(3.7692)	(-0.1789)
γ_5	-157000	-737000	15.813	5.1748	8.9289	60.790	-163.04	1.8224	19.664.2	42.786	35.397	-12.513
	(-1.4177)	(-1.1324)	(0.6288)	(0.7748)	(0.5138)	(2.4289)	(-2.0249)	(0.4033)	(0.3897)	(1.0927)	(1.6954)	(-0.872)
F	16.5093	0.03053	0.0369	0.0179	0.0188	0.0366	0.03318	23.8284	26.7543	37.4654	20.7187	0.0269
	[0.000]	[0.000]	[0.000]	[0.000]	[0.000]	[0.000]	[0.000]	[0.000]	[0.000]	[0.000]	[0.000]	[0.000]
$\overline{R}^2$	0.1057	0.1837	0.2169	0.1154	0.1205	0.2248	0.1984	0.1494	0.1656	0.2185	0.1315	0.1663

Note: t-statistics are in parentheses. *p*-values are in square brackets. F=F-statistic.

were affected by the handover of Hong Kong in 1997, generally with a temporary increase in volume and greater sensitivity of volume to return fluctuations. For dummy variable D_2, most of the estimated coefficients η_2 are negative and significant, reflecting a general fall in trading volume as a result of the market policies during 1998-May 1999 taken by the government to ease the overheating of the market following the Red Chips craze. For dummy variables D_3 and D_4, most of the estimated coefficients η_3 and η_4 are positive and significant, implying that the market-support measures during May 1999-July 2001 successfully pushed stock market volume upward. However, the dummy variable D_5 is almost always insignificant, indicating that in this sample period there was no effect of policy change or that government policies were too short-lived to have any effect on the stock market. In fact, the scheme of state share reduction was implemented and then suspended twice during July 2001 and June 2002, so that market credibility about the government's intention may well have been low.

Overall, the sector policy changes led to a shift of the V-shaped curve but less often had an effect on the slope of the regression of trading volume on return. However, the market regulations affected both the intercept and the slope of the V-shaped curve although the number of significant η_i (intercept dummies) is more than that of γ_i (slope dummies).

8.5   CONCLUSION

This chapter examines the relationship between trading volume and stock return at both aggregate and company levels in China. It also investigates the impact of regulatory changes in the stock market as a whole and in the energy sector.

We found that the contemporaneous relationship between detrended trading volume and stock return is asymmetrically positively V-shaped, with the trading volume response to a rising return being stronger than that to a falling return.

Second, we found that stock returns significantly cause trading volume but found little evidence supporting the causation of returns by trading volume except for Shanghai A and Shenzhen A. This is somewhat different from the findings of previous studies focusing on the earlier periods of Shanghai A and Shenzhen A.

Third, we found that the absolute value of returns is significantly caused by volume which, combined with our second finding, indicates that volume can significantly predict the magnitude but not the sign of future returns.

Fourth, by estimating a GARCH (1,1) model, we found that stock returns for Shanghai A, Shenzhen A and ten individual stocks are not temporally independent processes but tend to show volatility clustering. Moreover, high return volatility can be observed in the two A share markets and ten individual stocks. The volatility spikes for Shanghai A and Shenzhen A are very similar, while for the individual stocks those in different sectors show different volatility structures whereas those in the same sector are mostly similar in volatility spikes. We used these features of the data in conjunction with known policy shifts to identify structural changes in either the stock market as a whole or individual sectoral markets. Dummy variables were constructed to capture these shifts.

Fifth, by adding dummy variables related to policies to the stock return-volume regressions, we found that the estimated coefficients for the sectoral policy dummy variables are mostly significant for the intercept of the regression but not for the slope. For the electricity sub-sector we found that the deregulation of the supply price depressed activity in the stock market for the affected companies but all other policy changes increased volume – the deregulation of oil prices, the forced closure of small coal mines and general energy market integration.

Sixth, and in contrast, we found that the general stock market regulatory changes affected both intercepts and slopes. The Red Chips craze preceding the Hong Kong handover significantly increased share market activity and the subsequent measures to cool the market clearly had their intended effect while subsequent policy changes to stimulate the market in 1999-2001 were also effective. On the other hand, the market seems not to have found the government's constantly changing policy on state share reduction to have been credible since there was little discernible significant effect on trading volume.

NOTES

1. Tsay (2002) suggests that the performance of the Q test may be sensitive to lag length. We follow his suggestion and choose $m = 7 \approx \ln(T)$ (Tsay, 2002).
2. See Walter and Howie, (2001), and Fan, Wu and Groenewold, (2003).

9. Summary and conclusions

9.1 MAJOR FINDINGS

This book set out to examine the performance of the Chinese stock market in terms of efficiency, predictability and profitability. Its main aim was to test whether the changing regulatory environment has a significant impact on the performance of the Chinese stock market. While the Chinese economy is growing rapidly and becoming increasingly integrated with the rest of the world, its emerging stock market has underperformed by the standards of the developed world. The major problems of the Chinese stock market are illiquidity, a policy-based market, lack of long-term institutional investors, incomplete law and regulations, and excessive speculation. It appears that these problems are caused mainly by the dominance of SOEs, which comprise the majority of all listed firms in the Chinese stock market. In the last three years, the Chinese government has gone a long way to addressing such problems in its stock market, in particular, by selling a major holding of SOEs, attracting foreign institutional investors and deregulating the banking sector. The main question that we have addressed in this book is whether the Chinese stock market becomes more efficient as a result of the implementation of many financial reforms.

The first major finding is that there was evidence of departures from weak efficiency in the form of predictability of returns on the basis of their own past values as well as systematic day-of-the-week and holiday effects. Over the whole sample period, predictability was most marked for the B shares on both the exchanges and absent altogether in the index for the 30 leading stocks on the Shanghai exchange. These results suggest that much of the apparent predictability simply reflects thin trading so that there may be little if any unexploited profit in this predictability. We also found evidence that efficiency suffered when banks were excluded from the stock market in 1996 and efficiency improved when they were re-admitted in early 2000. We offered a tentative explanation in terms of liquidity given the traditionally dominant role played by the banks in the Chinese financial system – when the banks were excluded, liquidity suffered and information transmission was less efficient, and this process was reversed in 2000.

Secondly, the Chinese stock market is largely efficient if we use profitability as a criterion for efficiency. Using daily data and forecasting equations estimated over the entire sample period, we found that portfolios based on trading rules substantially outperform an equity buy-and-hold strategy. However, this finding is not robust to the choice of the beginning of the evaluation period and to the length of the period over which the forecasting equation is estimated. Furthermore, when we used recursive estimation to more nearly approximate the actual information likely to be available to a trader as well as taking into account transaction costs, we found that trading according to the forecasting rule actually lost money as small daily excess returns were more than completely eroded by transaction costs. This was generally not the case, however, when we used weekly or monthly data so that trading was restricted to occur at weekly or monthly intervals. With less frequent trades some rules returned a better end result than a buy-and-hold strategy.

Thirdly, we found a significant positive contemporaneous relationship between the absolute value of returns and turnover for all markets under study with further tests showing this to be an asymmetric V-shaped relationship. In addition, we found at the 1 per cent significance level that turnover Granger-causes returns in Hong Kong, while returns Granger-cause turnover for Shanghai A, B and Shenzhen B. The finding that turnover on the Hong Kong exchange Granger-causes returns is consistent with the consensus that trading volume leads market returns for the well-developed markets. Also, we found a one-way spillover effect running from Hong Kong to Chinese B share markets. We believe that recent relaxation of rules governing foreign ownership rights facilitates an increasing inflow of foreign investment into China which significantly strengthens the integration of the Chinese stock market into the world scene.

The fourth major finding concerns the inter-relationship between the stock markets in mainland China, Hong Kong and Taiwan. We found that the mainland Chinese market has been relatively isolated from the other two markets considered. This was borne out by the regression results but particularly by the dynamics – simulation analysis showed clearly that shocks to the mainland market were felt primarily in that market itself and that shocks in the other two markets had relatively little impact on the mainland Chinese market. However, we found some evidence that the inter-relationships strengthened during the course of the 1990s, particularly between the mainland market and Hong Kong. However, whether the modest growth in inter-relationships is due to the occurrence of the Asian crisis in 1997-98 or to the greater integration of the Chinese economy into the world economy will require more detailed and disaggregated structural modelling.

Lastly, we study the impact of general and sector-specific regulatory changes on the whole market and on individual energy shares. We concluded from the study that general stock market regulatory changes affect both intercepts and slopes of the relationship between trading volume and returns. The Red Chips craze preceding the Hong Kong handover significantly increased share market activity, and the subsequent measures to cool the market clearly had their intended effect while subsequent policy changes designed to stimulate the market in 1999-2001 were also effective. On the other hand, the market seems not to have found the government's constantly changing policy on state share reduction to have been credible since there was little discernible significant effect on trading volume. For sector-specific regulatory changes, we find that the deregulation of the supply price depressed activity in the stock market for the affected companies in the electricity sub-sector, but that all other policy changes increased volume – the deregulation of oil prices, the forced closure of small coal mines and general energy market integration.

9.2   PROSPECTS FOR THE CHINESE STOCK MARKET

The Chinese stock market has only emerged in the last decade in response to the growing demand for private investment funds from an increasingly market-oriented economy. It suffers from the usual symptoms of an emerging, immature market such as excessive speculation, pervasive manipulation, and isolation from the world market. Moreover, a unique problem facing the Chinese market is its overwhelming proportion of illiquid SOE shares. Our empirical findings confirm that the Chinese stock market, in many instances, violates the weak form of EMH on the basis of predictability and profitability. However, we also find that efficiency has improved in response to the general and sector-specific financial reforms. More importantly, the Chinese stock market is becoming more integrated with other markets in the region as a result of the relaxation of restrictions on foreign investment.

There is little doubt that the trend of further integration of different classes of shares in the Chinese stock market will continue. It started in late 2001 when individuals and legal persons in China were allowed to buy and sell B shares, which are denominated in US or Hong Kong dollars. Originally, the state feared that their control over foreign exchange would be compromised if local Chinese were allowed to trade in B shares. Currently, however, the People's Bank of China appears to be more concerned about releasing the appreciation pressure on Renminbi. In addition, the WTO stipulates that foreign securities firms can establish joint ventures (with foreign ownership less than 1/3) to engage in underwriting A shares, in underwriting and trading B and H shares, as well as government and corporate debt without a Chinese partner within three years of accession to the WTO. Recently implemented schemes such as the Qualified Foreign Institutional Investor (QFII) scheme, which allows a handful of foreign brokers into the A share market, and the Qualified Domestic Institutional Investor (QDII) scheme, which allows selected domestic fund managers access to securities abroad, will help further integrate A and B share markets and foreign markets.

At the moment, there are more than 100,000 SOEs in China. Most of these SOEs are unprofitable, mismanaged companies in which executive appointments are based on political considerations rather than performance and in which management accountability is largely absent. Consequently, these SOEs cannot compete with foreign firms in either domestic or global markets. With the implementation of WTO regulations, foreign firms are getting an increasing share of the Chinese domestic market, adding pressure on SOEs to compete. As a result, in the third plenum of the 16th Party Congress in 2003, President Hu Jintao announced the central government's intention to privatize all SOEs (except only 196 major firms) and delegated the State Owned Assets Supervision and Administration Commission (SASAC) to take charge of privatizing SOEs.

How the government resolves the issue of its holding of SOE shares will be a key factor in influencing the future development of the Chinese stock market. SASAC is currently looking at ways to sell down government holdings in SOEs below 50 per cent while yet maintaining a say in management. If SASAC is able to privatize SOEs such that the rights of shareholders are respected, executive appointments are based only on performance, and management is held accountable for their acts, we expect that the privatized SOEs will experience an improvement of profitability and efficiency as they become subject to the discipline of financial markets. The efficiency of the overall stock market will also be improved since illiquidity will be greatly reduced, insider manipulation kept in check and foreign institutional investment will increase. The decision to restructure SOEs is thus a welcome move in the right direction for enhancing China's financial development and economic growth in the long run.

No one knows for certain how long it will take for the restructuring of SOEs to take effect. Some experts estimate that it will take 10 years or more for privatized SOEs to reach management standards commonly found in developed markets. (*South China Morning Post*, 6 Nov 2003, A4). In its quest for improving corporate governance, SASAC faces a huge task of aligning interests of different government bodies at the state and provincial levels. The conflict among battling bureaucracies has made SASAC's role increasingly difficult. For example, how to deal with those chief executives of SOEs who are members of the Central Party Committee at the ministry level? How to deal with the relationship between SASAC and others, such as the economic planning group, the central bank and other financial institutions? How to deal with the rising power of local governments who do not automatically follow orders from Beijing? These are critical issues for SASAC and the Chinese leaders to grapple with. What is certain is that the development of the Chinese stock market and the financial sector in general will be jeopardized if these critical issues are not resolved properly in the near future.

Bibliography

Abdel-Khalik, A. R., Wong, K. A. and Wu, A. (1999), "The Information Environment of China's A and B Shares: Can We Make Sense of the Numbers?", *The International Journal of Accounting*, 34, 467-489.

Aggarwal, R., Leal, R. and Hernandez, L. (1993), "The Aftermarket Performance of Initial Public Offerings in Latin America", *Financial Management*, 22, 27-53.

Alexander, G. J., Eun, C. S. and Janakiramanan, S. (1987), "Asset Pricing and Dual Listing on Foreign Capital Markets: A Note", *Journal of Finance*, 42, 151-158.

Almanac of China's Finance and Banking (2002), Beijing: China Finance Association.

Ang, J. S. and Ma, Y. (1999), "Transparency in Chinese stocks: A Study of Earnings Forecasts by Professional Analysts", *Pacific-Basin Finance Journal*, 7, 129-155.

Arestis, P. and Demetriades, P. (1999), "Financial Liberalization: The Experience of Developing Countries", *Eastern Economic Journal*, 25, 441-457.

Arshanapalli, B., Doukas, J. and Lang, L. H. P. (1995), "Pre and Post-October 1987 Stock Market Linkages between U.S. and Asian Markets", *Pacific-Basin Finance Journal*, 3, 57-73.

Ayuso, J. and Blanco, R. (2001), "Has Financial Market Integration Increased During the Nineties?", *Journal of International Financial Markets, Institutions and Money*, 11, 265-287.

Bailey, W. (1994), "Risk and Return on China's New Stock Markets: Some Preliminary Evidence", *Pacific-Basin Finance Journal*, 2, 243-260.

Bailey, W., Stulz, R. M. and Yen, S. (1990), "Properties of Daily Stock Returns from the Pacific Basin Stock Markets: Evidence and Implications", in S. G. Rhee and R. P. Chang (eds), *Pacific-Basin Capital Market Research*, Elsevier Science Publishers, 155-171.

Ball, R. and Brown, P. (1968), "An Empirical Evaluation of Accounting Income Numbers", *Journal of Accounting Research*, 7, 159-178.

Barry, C. and Lockwood, L. J. (1995), "New Directions in Research on Emerging Capital Markets", *Financial Markets, Institutions and Instruments*, 4, 15-36.

Basci E., Suheyla, O. and Kursat, A. (1996), "A Note on Price-Volume Dynamics in an Emerging Stock Market", *Journal of Banking and Finance*, 20, 389-400.

Beck, T., Levine, R. and Loayza, N. (2000), "Finance and the Sources of Growth", *Journal of Financial Economics*, 58, 261-300.

Bergstrom, C. and Tang, E. (2001), "Price Differentials Between Different Classes of Stocks: An Empirical Study of Chinese Stock Markets", *Journal of Multinational Financial Management*, 11, 407-426.

Bessembinder, H. and Chan, K. (1995), "The Profitability of Technical Trading Rules in the Asian Stock Markets", *Pacific-Basin Finance Journal*, 3, 257-284.

Bhagat, S. and Bhatia, S. (1996), "Trading Volume and Price Variability: Evidence on Lead-Lag Relations from Granger-Causality Tests", *Working paper*, University of Colorado at Boulder.

Blackman, S. C., Holden, K. and Thomas, W. A (1994), "Long-Term Relationships between International Share Prices", *Applied Financial Economics*, 4, 297-304.

Blume, L., Easley, D. and O'Hara, M. (1994), "Market Statistics and Technical Analysis: The Role of Volume", *Journal of Finance*, 49, 153-181.

Bollerslev, T. (1986), "Generalized Autoregressive Conditional Heteroskedasticity", *Journal of Econometrics*, 31, 307-327.

Brock, W., Lakonishok, J. and LeBaron, B. (1992), "Simple Technical Trading Rules and the Stochastic Properties of Stock Returns", *Journal of Finance*, 47, 1731-1764.

Campbell, J. Y. (1991), "A Variance Decomposition for Stock Returns", *Economic Journal*, 101, 157-179.

Campbell, J. Y. and Perron, P. (1991), "Pitfalls and Opportunities: What Macroeconomists Should Know About Unit Roots", in O. J. Blanchard and S. Fischer (eds), *Macroeconomics Annual 1991*, Cambridge: MIT Press, 141-201.

Campbell, J. Y. and Shiller, R. J. (1989), "The Dividend-price Ratio and Expectations of Future Dividends and Discount Factor", *Review of Financial Studies*, 1, 195-228.

Cha, B. and Oh, S. (2000), "The Relationship between Developed Equity Markets and the Pacific Basin's Emerging Equity Markets", *International Review of Economics and Finance*, 9, 299-322.

Chakravarty, S., Sarkar, A. and Wu, L. F. (1998), "Information Asymmetry, Market Segmentation and the Pricing of Cross-Listed Shares: Theory and Evidence from Chinese A and B Shares", *Journal of International Financial Markets and Money*, 8, 325-355.

Chen, C. H. and Shih, H. T. (2002), *The Evolution of the Stock Market in China's Transitional Economy*, Cheltenham, UK and Northampton, MA, USA: Edward Elgar.

Chen, G., Firth, M. and Rui, O. M. (2001), "The Dynamic Relation Between Stock Returns, Trading Volume, and Volatility", *The Financial Review*, 38, 153-174.

Chen, G. M., Kwok, C. C. Y. and Rui, O. M. (2001), "The Day-of-the-Week Regularity in the Stock Markets of China", *Journal of Multinational Financial Management*, 11, 139-163.

Chen, G. M., Lee, B. S. and Rui, O. (2001), "Foreign Ownership Restrictions and Market Segmentation in China's Stock Markets", *The Journal of Financial Research*, 24(1), 133-155.

Cheung, Y. W. and Ng, L. K. (1996), "A Causality-in-Variance Test and its Application to Financial Market Prices", *Journal of Econometrics*, 72, 33-48.

China Securities Regulatory Commission (1992-98), *Zhengquan qihuo fagui huibian (The Collection of the Laws of Securities and Futures)*, Beijing: Falu chubanshe (The Law Publishing House).

Chow, G. C., Fan, Z. Z. and Hu, J. Y. (1999), "Shanghai Stock Prices as Determined by the Present-Value Model", *Journal of Comparative Economics*, 27, 553-561.

Chui, A. C. W. and Kwok, C. C. Y. (1998), "Cross-autocorrelation Between A Shares and B Shares in the Chinese Stock Market", *The Journal of Financial Research*, 21, 333-353.

Chung, H. and Lee, B. S. (1998), "Fundamental and Nonfundamental Components in Stock Prices of Pacific-Rim Countries", *Pacific-Basin Journal of Finance*, 6, 321-346.

Clare, A. D., Thomas, S. H. and Wickens, M. R. (1994), "Is the Gilt-Equity Yield Ratio Useful for Predicting UK Stock Returns?", *Economic Journal*, 104, 303-315.

Corhay, A., Tourani, R. A. and Urbain, J. P. (1993), "Common Stochastic Trends in European Stock Markets", *Economics Letters*, 42, 385-390.

Crouch, R. L. (1970a), "A Nonlinear Test of the Random Walk Hypothesis", *American Economic Review*, 60, 199-202.

Crouch, R. L. (1970b), "The Volume of Transactions and Price Changes on the New York Stock Exchange", *Financial Analysts Journal*, 26, 104-109.

Darrat, A. F. and Zhong, M. (2000), "On Testing the Random-Walk Hypothesis: A Model-Comparison Approach", *The Financial Review*, 35, 105-124.

Dickey, D. A. and Fuller, W. A. (1981), "The Likelihood Ratio Statistics for Autoregressive Time Series with a Unit Root", *Econometrica*, 49, 1057-1072.

Divecha, A. B., Drach, J. and Stefek, D. (1992), "Emerging Markets: A Quantitative Perspective", *Journal of Portfolio Management*, 19, 41-50.

Efron, B. and Tibshirani, R. (1993), *An Introduction to the Bootstrap*, New York: Chapman and Hall.

Engle, R. F. and Granger, C. W. J. (1987), "Cointegration and Error Correction: Representation, Estimation and Testing", *Econometrica*, 55, 251-276.

Epps, T. W. (1975), "Security Price Changes and Transaction Volumes: Theory and Evidence", *American Economic Review*, 65, 586-597.

Epps, T. W. (1977), "Security Price Changes and Transaction Volumes: Some Additional Evidence", *Journal of Financial and Quantitative Analysis*, 12, 141-146.

Epps, T. W. and Epps, M. L. (1976), "The Stochastic Dependence of Security Price Changes and Transaction Volumes: Implications for the Mixture-of-Distributions Hypothesis", *Econometrica*, 44, 305-321.

Errunza, V. R. (1994), "Emerging Markets: Some New Concepts", *Journal of Portfolio Management*, 20, 82-87.

Errunza, V. and Losq, E. (1985), "International Asset Pricing under Mild Segmentation: Theory and Test", *Journal of Finance*, 40, 105-124.

Eun, C. S and Janakiramanan, S. (1986), "A Model of International Asset Pricing with a Constraint on the Foreign Equity Ownership", *Journal of Finance*, 41, 897-914.

Eun, C. S and Shim, S. (1989), "International Transmission of Stock Market Movements", *Journal of Financial and Quantitative Analysis*, 24, 241-256.

Fama, E. F. (1970), "Efficient Capital Markets: A Review of Theory and Empirical Work", *Journal of Finance*, 25, 382-417.

Fama, E. F. (1991), "Efficient Capital Markets II", *Journal of Finance*, 46, 1575-1617.

Fama, E. F. and French, K. R. (1993), "Common Risk Factors in the Returns on Stocks and Bonds", *Journal of Financial Economics*, 33, 3-56.

Fan, X., Wu, Y. and Groenewold, N. (2003), "The Chinese Stock Market: Development and Prospects", *Discussion Paper* 03.04, Department of Economics, University of Western Australia.

Fernald, J. and Rogers, J. H. (2002), "Puzzles in the Chinese Stock Market", *Review of Economics and Statistics*, 84, 416-432.

Friedmann, R. and Sanddorf-Kohle, W. G. (2002), "Volatility Clustering and Nontrading Days in Chinese Stock Markets", *Journal of Economics and Business*, 54, 193-217.

Gallant, A. R., Rossi, P. E. and Tauchen, G. (1992), "Stock Prices and Volume", *Review of Financial Studies*, 5, 199-242.

Gao, S. Q. and Ye, S. (1991), *China Economic Systems Reform Yearbook 1990*, Beijing: China Reform Publishing House, 76-78.

Geweke, J. (1982), "Measurement of Linear Dependence and Feedback between Multiple Time Series", *Journal of the American Statistical Association*, 77, 304-313.

Glosten L. R., Jagannathan, R. and Runkle, D. E. (1993), "On the Relation between the Expected Value and the Volatility of the Nominal Excess Return on Stocks", *Journal of Finance*, 48, 1779-1802.

Godfrey, M. D., Granger, C. W. J. and Morgenstern, O. (1964), "The Random-Walk Hypothesis of Stock Market Behavior", *Kyklos*, 17, 1-30.

Granger, C. W. J. (1969), "Investigating Causal Relations by Econometric Models and Cross-Spectral Methods", *Econometrica*, 37, 424-438.

Granger, C. W. J. and Morgenstern, O. (1963), "Spectral Analysis of New York Stock Market Prices", *Kyklos*, 16, 1-27.

Gregory, A. W. and Hansen, B. E. (1996), "Residual Based Tests for Cointegration in Models with Regime Shifts", *Journal of Econometrics*, 70, 99-126.

Groenewold, N., Tang, S. H. K and Wu, Y. (2001), "An Exploration of the Efficiency of the Chinese Stock Market", *Discussion Paper 01*.13, Department of Economics, University of Western Australia.

Gunasekarage, A. and Power, D. M. (2001), "The Profitability of Moving Average Trading Rules in South Asian Stock Markets", *Emerging Markets Review*, 2, 17-33.

Harvey, C. R. (1995), "Predictable Risk and Returns in Emerging Markets", *Review of Financial Studies*, 8, 773-816.

Henry, P. B. (2000a), "Do Stock Market Liberalizations Cause Investment Booms?", *Journal of Financial Economics*, 58, 301-334.

Henry, P. B. (2000b), "Stock Market Liberalization, Economic Reform and Emerging Market Equity Prices", *Journal of Finance*, 55, 529-564.

Hess, P. J. and Lee, B. S. (1999), "Stock Returns and Inflation with Supply and Demand Disturbances", *The Review of Financial Studies*, 12, 1203-1218.

Hiemstra, C. and Jones, J. D. (1994), "Testing for Linear and Nonlinear Granger-Causality in the Stock Price-Volume Relation", *Journal of Finance*, 49, 1639-1664.

Hu, J. W. S., Chen, M. Y., Fok, R. C. W. and Huang, B. N. (1997), "Causality in Volatility and Volatility Spillover Effects Between US, Japan and Four Equity Markets in the South China Growth Triangular", *Journal of International Financial Markets, Institutions and Money*, 7, 351-367.

Huang, B. N., Yang, C. W. and Hu, J. W. S. (2000), "Causality and Cointegration of Stock Markets among the Unites States, Japan, and the South China Growth Triangle", *International Review of Financial Analysis*, 9(3), 281-297.

Hudson, R., Dempsey, M. and Keasey, K. (1996), "A Note on the Weak Form Efficiency of Capital Markets: The Application of Simple Technical Trading Rules to UK Stock Prices – 1935 to 1994", *Journal of Banking and Finance*, 20, 1121-1132.

Johansen, S. (1988), "Statistical Analysis of Cointegration Vectors", *Journal of Economic Dynamics and Control*, 12, 231-254.

Johansen, S. and Juselius, K. (1990), "Maximum Likelihood Estimation and Inference on Cointegration - with Applications to the Demand for Money", *Oxford Bulletin of Economics and Statistics*, 52, 169-210.

Johnson, R. and Soenen, L. (2002), "Asian Economic Integration and Stock Market Comovement", *Journal of Financial Research*, 25, 141-157.

Jun, S. G., Marathe, A. and Shawky, H. A. (2003), "Liquidity and Stock Returns in Emerging Equity Markets", *Emerging Markets Review*, 4, 1-24.

Kang, J., Liu, M. H. and Ni, S. X. (2002), "Contrarian and Momentum Strategies in the China Stock Market", *Pacific-Basin Finance Journal*, 10, 243-265.

Karpoff, J. M. (1987), "The Relation Between Price Changes and Trading Volume: A Survey", *Journal of Financial and Quantitative Analysis*, 22, 109-126.

Kawakatsu, H. and Morey, M. R. (1999), "Financial Liberalization and Stock Market Efficiency: An Empirical Examination of Nine Emerging Market Countries", *Journal of Multinational Financial Management*, 9, 353-371.

Kramer, C. (1999), "Noise Trading, Transaction Costs, and the Relationship of Stock Returns and Trading Volume", *International Review of Economics and Finance*, 8, 343-362.

Lan, Y. S. (1997), "The Stock Market in China: Problems and Prospects For Domestic and Foreign Investment", *Working Paper 1997-7*, Department. of Economics, University of Adelaide.

Lee, B. S. (1995), "The Response of Stock Prices to Permanent and Temporary Dividend Shocks", *Journal of Financial and Quantitative Analysis*, 30, 1-22.

Lee, B. S. (1998), "Permanent, Temporary and Non-Fundamental Components of Stock Prices", *Journal of Financial and Quantitative Analysis*, 33, 1-32.

Lee, C. F. and Rui, O. M. (2000), "Does Trading Volume Contain Information to Predict Stock Returns? Evidence from China's Stock Markets", *Review of Quantitative Finance and Accounting*, 14, 341-360.

LeRoy, S. F. (1989), "Efficient Capital Markets and Martingales", *Journal of Economic Literature*, 27, 1583-1621.

Levine, R. (1997), "Financial Development and Economic Growth: Views and Agenda", *Journal of Economic Literature*, 35, 688-726.

Levine, R. and Zervos, S. (1998), "Stock Markets, Banks, and Economic Growth", *American Economic Review*, 88, 537-558.

Levine, R., Loayza, N. and Beck, T. (2000), "Financial Intermediation and Growth: Causality and Causes", *Journal of Monetary Economics*, 46, 31-77.

Li, C. J. (1998), *The History and Development of China's Securities Markets*, Beijing: Zhongguo Wizi Chubanshe (China's Material Publishing Housing).

Li, H. G. (2002), "The State Shares Reduction: What is the Effect on All Kinds of Industry", Lihe Zhengquan Companies from the web page http://www.cninfo.com.cn.

Li, H. and Maddala, G. S. (1996), "Bootstrapping Time Series Models", *Econometric Reviews*, 15, 115-158.

Liu, H. R. (1992), *Zhongguo Zhengquan Shouce (China Securities Handbook)*, Shanghai: Shanghai People Publishing House.

Liu, X., Song, H. and Romilly, P. (1997), "Are Chinese Stock Markets Efficient? A Cointegration and Causality Analysis", *Applied Economics Letters*, 4, 511-515.

Lo, A. W. and MacKinlay, A. C. (1988), "Stock Market Prices Do Not Follow Random Walks: Evidence from a Simple Specification Test", *Review of Financial Studies*, 1, 41-66.

Lo, A. W. and MacKinlay, A. C. (1990), "When Are Contrarian Profits Due to Stock Market Overreaction?", *Review of Financial Studies*, 3, 175-250.

Long, D. M., Payne, J. D. and Feng, C. (1999), "Information Transmission in the Shanghai Equity Market", *The Journal of Financial Research*, 22, 29-45.

Ma, J. and Folkerts-Landau, D. (2001), "China's Financial Liberalization Agenda", *Research Report May 2001*, Global Markets Research, Deutsche Bank, Hong Kong.

Ma, X. H. (1996), "Capital Controls, Market Segmentation and Stock Prices: Evidence from the Chinese Stock Market", *Pacific-Basin Finance Journal*, 4, 219-239.

Masih, A. M. M. and Masih, R. (1999), "Are Asian Stock Market Fluctuations Due Mainly to Intra-Regional Contagion Effects? Evidence Based on Asian Emerging Stock Markets", *Pacific-Basin Finance Journal*, 7, 251-282.

Masih, R. and Masih, A. A. M. (2001), "Long and Short Term Dynamic Causal Transmission amongst International Stock Markets", *Journal of International Money and Finance*, 20, 563-587.

McMillan, J. (2003), "Market Design: the Policy Uses of Theory", Proceedings of 2003 Australian Meeting of the Econometric Society, Sydney.

Mok, H. M. K. and Hui, Y. V. (1998), "Underpricing and Aftermarket Performance of IPOs in Shanghai, China", *Pacific-Basin Finance Journal*, 6, 453-474.

Mookerjee, R. and Yu, Q. (1999a), "An Empirical Analysis of the Equity Markets in China", *Review of Financial Economics*, 8, 41-60.

Mookerjee, R. and Yu, Q. (1999b), "Seasonality in Returns on the Chinese Stock Markets: The Case of Shanghai and Shenzhen", *Global Finance Journal*, 10, 93-105.

Morgan, I. G. (1976), "Stock Price and Heteroscedasticity", *Journal of Business*, 49, 496-508.

Nieh, C. C. (2002), "The Effect of the Asian Financial Crisis on the Relationships among Open Macroeconomic Factors for Asian Countries", *Applied Economics*, 34, 491-502.

Pesaran, M. H. and Shin, Y. (1998), "Generalised Impulse Response Analysis in Linear Multivariate Models", *Economics Letters*, 58, 17-29.

Pesaran, M. H. and Timmermann, A. (1992), "A Simple Nonparametric Test of Predictive Performance", *Journal of Business and Economic Statistics*, 10, 461-465.

Pesaran, M. H. and Timmermann, A. (1995), "Predictability of Stock Returns: Robustness and Economic Significance", *Journal of Finance*, 50, 1201-1228.

Pesaran, M. H. and Timmermann, A. (2000), "A Recursive Modelling Approach to Predicting UK Stock Returns", *Economic Journal*, 110, 159-191.

Phillips, P. C. B. and Perron, P. (1988), "Testing for a Unit Root in Time Series Regression", *Biometrika*, 75, 335-346.

Poon, W. P. H. and Fung, H. G. (2000), "Red Chip or H Shares: Which China-Backed Securities Process Information the Fastest?", *Journal of Multinational Financial Management*, 10, 315-343.

Pretorius, E. (2002), "Economic Determinants of Emerging Stock Market Interdependence", *Emerging Markets Review*, 3, 84-105.

Ratner, M. and Leal, R. P. C. (1999), "Tests of Technical Trading Strategies in the Emerging Markets of Latin America and Asia", *Journal of Banking and Finance*, 23, 1887-1905.

Ratner, M. and Leal, R. P. C. (2001), "Stock Returns and Trading Volume: Evidence from the Emerging Markets of Latin America and Asia", *Journal of Emerging Markets*, 6, 5-22.

Rogalski, R J. (1978), "The Dependence of Prices and Volume", *Review of Economics and Statistics*, 6, 268-274.

Saatcioglu, K and Starks, L. T. (1998), "The Stock Price-Volume Relationship in Emerging Stock Markets: The Case of Latin America", *International Journal of Forecasting*, 14, 215-225.

Shanghai Stock Exchange Fact Book (2001), Shanghai: Shanghai Stock Exchange.

Sharpe, I. (1983), "New Information and Australian Equity Returns: A Multivariate Analysis", *Australian Journal of Management*, 8, 21-34.

Shenzhen Securities Information Company, http://www.cninfo.com.cn. Accessed December 2002.

Shenzhen Stock Exchange Fact Book (2001), Shenzhen: China Capital Publishing House.

Silvapulle, P. and Choi, J. S. (1999), "Testing for Linear and Nonlinear Granger Causality in the Stock Price-Volume Relation: Korean Evidence", *Quarterly Review of Economics and Finance*, 39, 59-76.

Sjöö, B. and Zhang, J. H. (2000), "Market Segmentation and Information Diffusion in China's Stock Markets", *Journal of Multinational Financial Management*, 10, 421-438.

Smirlock, M. and Starks, L. T. (1985), "A Further Examination of Stock Price Changes and Transaction Volume", *Journal of Financial Research*, 8, 217-225.

Smirlock, M. and Starks, L. T. (1988), "An Empirical Analysis of the Stock Price-Volume Relationship", *Journal of Banking and Finance*, 12, 31-41.

Song, F. M., Jiang, J. and Li, C. (2003), "Volatility in the Shenzhen Stock Markets", unpublished research report, Research Institute of Shenzhen Stock Exchange (http://www.cninfo.com.cn/finalpage/2003-02-19/10147383.pdf. Accessed June 2003).

Soydemir, G. (2000), "International Transmission Mechanism of Stock Market Movements: Evidence from Emerging Markets", *Journal of Forecasting*, 19, 149-176.

SSB (State Statistics Bureau), various issues, *Zhongguo Tongji Nianjian (China Statistical Yearbook)*, Beijing: Statistical Publishing House.

Su, D., (2003), *Chinese Stock Market (A Research Handbook)*, Singapore: World Scientific Printers Pty Ltd.

Su, D. and Fleisher, B. M. (1998), "Risk, Return and Regulation in Chinese Stock Markets", *Journal of Economics and Business*, 50, 239-256.

Su, D. W. and Fleisher, B. M. (1999), "Why Does Return Volatility Differ in Chinese Stock Markets?", *Pacific-Basin Finance Journal*, 7, 557-586.

Sun, Q. and Tong, W. H. S. (2000), "The Effect of Market Segmentation on Stock Prices: The China Syndrome", *Journal of Banking and Finance*, 24, 1875-1902.

Surry, M. (2000), "Fair Shares: China Adjusts Rules to Boost its Stock Markets", *Asian Business*, 36, 18-20.

SZSE (Shenzhen Securities Exchange), "Different Types of Shares in China's Stock Market", http://www.cninfo.com.cn.

SZSE (Shenzhen Securities Exchange), "Reasons for the Introduction of State Shares and Legal Person Shares", http://www.cninfo.com.cn.

Tsay, R. S. (2002), *Analysis of Financial Time Series*, New York: John Wiley & Sons, Inc.

Van der Hart, J., Slagter, E. and van Dijk, D. (2003), "Stock Selection Strategies in Emerging Markets", *Journal of Empirical Finance*, 10, 105-132.

Walter, C. E. and Howie, F. J. T. (2001), *"To Get Rich is Glorious!": China's Stock Markets in the 80s and 90s*, London: Palgrave Press.

Wang, J. (1994), "A Model of Competitive Stock Trading Volume", *Journal of Political Economy*, 102, 127-168.

Westerfield, R, (1977), "The Distribution of Common Stock Price Changes: An Application of Transactions Time and Subordinated Stochastic Models", *Journal of Financial and Quantitative Analysis*, 12, 743-765.

Wheelock, D. C. (1994), "On the Glass-Steagall Act", New Palgrave Dictionary Money and Finance, Vol. 2, London: Macmillan, 243-244.

World Development Report 2000, *Attacking Poverty*, Washington, D.C.: World Bank.

Wu, L. and Xu, L. (2002), "Impact of Market Stablization Measures on Stock Prices and Suggested Improvement", unpublished research report,

Research Institute of Shenzhen Stock Exchange (http://www.cninfo. com.cn/finalpage/2002-07-01/613018.PDF. Accessed June 2003).

Wu, Y. (2003), "Deregulation and Growth in China's Energy Sector: A Review of Recent Development", *Energy Policy*, 31, 1417-1425.

Xu, K. C. (2000), "The Microstructure of the Chinese Stock Market", *China Economic Review*, 11, 79-97.

Yeh, Y. H. and Lee, T. S. (2000), "The Interaction and Volatility Asymmetry of Unexpected Returns in the Greater China Stock Markets", *Global Finance Journal*, 11, 129-149.

Zivot, E. and Andrews, D. W. K. (1992), "Further Evidence on the Great Crash, the Oil-Price Shock, and the Unit-Root Hypothesis", *Journal of Business and Economic Statistics*, 10, 251-70.

Zou, G. D. (2002), "Testing for A and B Share Market Segmentation", unpublished research report, Research Institute of Shenzhen Stock Exchange (http://www.cninfo.com.cn/finalpage/2002-06-18/608588.pdf. Accessed June 2003).

Index

2526047
K MacDonald
West, stk